BRINGING THE THUNDER

BRINGING THE THUNDER

The Missions of a World War II
B-29 Pilot in the Pacific

Gordon Bennett Robertson, Jr.

STACKPOLE
BOOKS

Published by
STACKPOLE BOOKS
5067 Ritter Road
Mechanicsburg, PA 17055
www.stackpolebooks.com

Printed in the United States of America

10 9 8 7 6 5 4 3 2 1

FIRST EDITION

Library of Congress Cataloging-in-Publication Data

Robertson, Gordon Bennett.
  Bringing the thunder : the missions of a World War II B-29 pilot in the Pacific / Gordon Bennett Robertson, Jr. — 1st ed.
     p. cm. — (Stackpole military history series)
  Includes index.
  ISBN-13: 978-0-8117-3333-5
  ISBN-10: 0-8117-3333-5
  1. Robertson, Gordon Bennett. 2. World War, 1939–1945—Aerial operations, American. 3. World War, 1939–1945—Campaigns—Pacific Area. 4. World War, 1939–1945—Personal narratives, American. 5. United States. Army Air Forces—Officers—Biography. 6. Air pilots, Military—United States—Biography. 7. B-29 bomber. I. Title. II. Series.

D790.2.R63 2006
940.54'4973—dc22

2006011692

For my children, Bruce and Becky, and my
daughter-in-law, Sherry.

We few, we happy few, we band of brothers
For he that day that shed his blood with me
Shall be my brother
—William Shakespeare, *Henry V*, Act IV, Scene iii

This story is dedicated to those 29th Bomb Group flight
crew members who paid with their lives while fighting to
avenge the grievous, wrongful, criminal injustice of
Pearl Harbor and to preserve our way of life—
especially those of the 43rd Squadron,
who were my brothers and comrades in arms.

Table of Contents

Preface

World War II began on September 1, 1939, with Hitler's invasion of Poland. Hostilities raged until August 15, 1945, when actual fighting stopped, and ended on September 2, 1945, when the Japanese formally surrendered on the foredeck of the battleship *Missouri* in Tokyo Bay. The carnage involved every major nation in the world and accounted for the loss of approximately 53 million lives worldwide—over half of which were noncombatants. The U.S. forces exceeded sixteen million people in uniform serving their country with about two million, three hundred seventy-five thousand in the U.S. Army Air Corps. A relatively small number of these—perhaps about five percent—were aircrew members actually flying the airplanes, from pilots of single-place fighters to ten- or eleven-member crews of our heavy and very heavy bombardment aircraft.

After being trained as a fighter pilot and spending about one and a half years in the Training Command as an instructor, I found myself headed for the Pacific and the final showdown with Japan as the aircraft commander of a B-29 very heavy bomber.

My story is not intended to be anything more than the recollections of a B-29 line pilot engaged in the massive air offensive against the home islands of Japan in 1945. It is not an intellectual dissertation, it is not a political treatise—although there are political comments—and it certainly is not politically correct. Nor is it intended to be critical or defensive. It is simply a recounting of an experience.

The story has been a long time coming. Like most returned servicemen, I was busy through the '50s and '60s raising children and paying mortgages, and except for my continuing love of flying and interest in aviation, I didn't really think too much about my military exploits. But, from time to time, in answer to a question or because some incident reminded me, a story would come out, to the amusement (or to the amazement) of the listener. Then in the early 1980s, the founders of the 29th Bomb Group Association located me, and I attended my first reunion. This gave me an opportunity to relive 1945 with some of the people—including my surviving crewmembers—with whom I had shared it. Since then, friends, family, 29th Bomb Group Association members, and my crew members have suggested, even encouraged, that I write it all down. As one of them put it, "If you people who were there—who fought the battles—don't record it, it will forever be lost to our heirs and to history." And given that we all are now in our late seventies and early eighties, there's not much time left to get it on paper and prevent the revisionist writers from distorting the story.

I did relatively little research, as such, during the writing of the story. Others who have written about the same period and subject have done an excellent job of reporting the statistical aspects of military operations, and I did not feel it necessary or desirable to duplicate their work. As a matter of fact, I wanted to avoid too much research because I felt it would influence and distort the story which I wanted to tell as a personal recollection and accounting. My research therefore was principally intended to affirm and validate my memory rather than to discover new material.

I called a couple of my surviving crew members on occasion to check their memories against mine, I reread a diary which I kept for about the first three months when I was in the Marianas Islands, and I reread many letters which I wrote to my father and my wife during my overseas tour there. I also occasionally referred to my logbooks and, infrequently, to flight manuals of the time. There have been no ghostwriters; the words are all mine. The story is accurate to the degree that my memory can be accurate sixty years later. There very well may be some errors or misconceptions in the telling, the human mind being what it is, and if there are, I apologize, but I have done my best to keep the story as I saw it, as I lived it, and as I felt it. I have tried not to take poetic license with my recollections, but only to describe the thoughts, actions, responses, and perceptions of a young man engaged in a small portion of a period of history that may have been the most important of the twentieth century. I have had to put my head in reverse and immerse myself in the past in an attempt to recreate my mindset and attitudes of 1945.

If it helps succeeding generations to understand who we were, what we were, why we were what we were, and what we accomplished, then my narrative will have served its purpose, and I will be gratified.

In war, perhaps more intensely and frequently than in all the rest of life, there are humorous events—yes, even hilarious events—and then there are the frightening, the near-tragic, and the tragic events. This story has them all. So here goes . . . come fly with me.

Missions Flown by the Author, 1945

1.	March 9–10	Night	Tokyo
2.	March 16	Night	Kobe
3.	March 25	Night	Nagoya
4.	April 4	Night	Shizuoka
5.	April 12	Day	Koriyama
6.	April 13	Night	Tokyo
7.	April 15	Night	Kawasaki
8.	April 18	Day	Kanoya
9.	April 22	Day	Suzuka
10.	April 26	Day	Miyazaki
11.	May 3	Day	Tachiari
12.	May 10	Day	Otake
13.	May 14	Day	Nagoya
14.	May 17	Night	Nagoya
15.	May 24	Night	Tokyo
16.	May 26	Night	Tokyo
17.	June 5	Day	Kobe
18.	June 10	Day	Tachikawa
19.	June 15	Day	Osaka
20.	June 18	Night	Kagoshima
21.	June 19	Night	Shizuoka
22.	June 22	Day	Tamashima
23.	June 26	Day	Nagoya
24.	June 28	Night	Nobeoka
25.	July 1	Night	Shiminoseki
26.	July 3	Night	Tokushima/Temma
27.	July 6	Night	Kofu
28.	July 9	Night	Gifu
29.	July 19	Night	Okazaki
30.	July 24	Night	Handa
31.	July 26	Night	Omuta
32.	July 28	Night	Ogaki
33.	August 1	Night	Mito
34.	August 5	Night	Fukae
35.	August 14	Night	Kumagaya

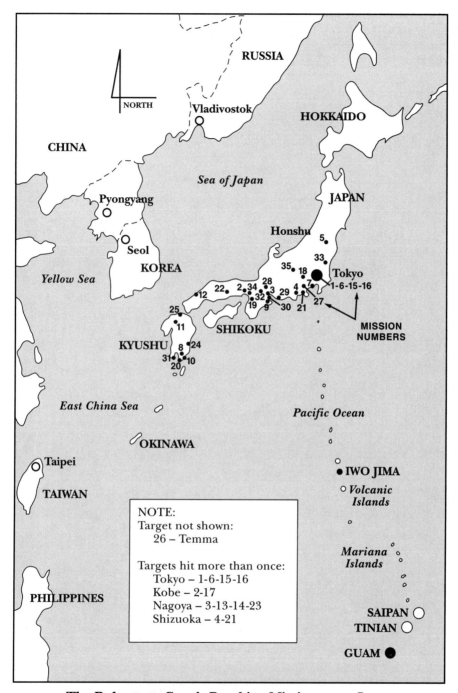

The Robertson Crew's Bombing Missions over Japan

CHAPTER 1

The Baptismal

We were young warriors, eager for the battle. It was early evening on March 9, 1945. We had been alerted the day before that we were scheduled to fly a mission to Japan, and now, following the flight-crew briefing at which the target had been identified as Tokyo, we were standing around the nose of our loaded ship prior to boarding, talking about the mission to come and the information divulged to us at the briefing. We also indulged in comments about what we were going to do to the Japs and how it should convince those who might be left in the morning to give up the fight. We joked good naturedly about "if we come back tomorrow," but there wasn't a man among us who really had any doubt about it—we *would* be back in the morning, and so would the others. Young men always believe in their own invincibility and immortality. We were cocky, almost to the point of having chips on our shoulders—not smart-alecky, but cocky in the sense of exuding confidence, invincibility, superiority, and dedication to our purpose. At long last, after all those months and years since Pearl Harbor, we stood on the threshold of retribution—to give back to the Japs, in their homeland, in spades, what they had dished out to us all over the Pacific. We had the airplane to do it, and we had the resolve to do it. This was to be the beginning of the end.

My mind, however, was somewhat preoccupied. At our briefing we were dumbfounded and wondered if Bomber Command had gone crazy: the tactics to be used on this mission were a complete departure from the design objectives of the airplane and, to us, tantamount to a suicide strike. Gen. Curtis LeMay, over the objections of some of his planners, had concluded that because of the difficulties of achieving the max-

1

2 BRINGING THE THUNDER

imum bombing effectiveness at high altitude in daylight because of reduced bomb loads, weather (including 250 mph jetstream winds), the strain on engines, high fuel burn, fighter opposition, and the lack of the element of surprise, he would send the B-29s to Japan with absolute maximum loads, at very low en route and bombing altitudes. He had also concluded, based on intelligence estimates in response to projected airplane and crew losses, that Japan had relatively few night fighters, so the strike force would not be subjected to the air-to-air opposition that it would if flown in daylight.

Thinking about all of this, I had many concerns: the take-off would be dangerous, exacting, and challenging; there was considerable weather en route; we would have neither guns nor ammunition (removed to save weight); Tokyo was the most heavily defended city in Japan; and we would fly the bomb run at only 230 miles per hour at only 5,600 feet altitude. We would be overloaded; our take-off weight was 138,000 pounds—13,000 pounds over the design limits of the airplane. This was to be a maximum-effort, low-level, night incendiary raid with over 300 Superforts participating. We were not scheduled to be in the initial attack force, so the fires would be burning merrily upon our arrival. (The consequences of this would be evident later.) The mission objective was to kill and dehouse as many Japs as possible in order to deprive them of a labor force, destroy their in-home cottage manufacturing industry, and break their will to continue their resistance. The type of mass destruction we planned to rain on them would, we hoped, motivate the Japanese people to overthrow their military leaders and force the emperor to seek peace. What rational people wouldn't?

Our en route procedure would be that each ship would take off sixty seconds behind the ship ahead of it, fly a timed leg on the runway heading, then make a procedure turn onto the course for Japan. This meant that there would be three ships on the runway at a time: one just lifting off, one in the middle of the runway gaining speed, and one just beginning to roll. It was thought unlikely that a crash would occur except at lift-off, and if that occurred, the ship at the halfway point on the runway would be expected to lift off over the crash and the third ship would do the same or brake and abort the takeoff.

The first ship would climb to 400 feet and level off, on course. The second ship would climb to 600 feet and level off, on course. The third ship would level off at 800 feet on course, and so on up to 1,200 feet, at which point the stack would start over again at 400 feet. This would result in a series of "stair-step" formations comprised of five B-29s, each one minute apart in time and 200 feet apart in altitude, all on course to Tokyo. Our cruising altitude for this mission was 400 feet. We were on the bottom of the stack.

The low en route altitude was meant to accomplish several things: first, to conserve fuel—it takes a lot of gas to haul a heavily loaded airplane to high altitude; second, to avoid detection by radar or by any Japanese ships that might be in the Pacific near our course; and third, to avoid weather and jet-stream winds which we would encounter at higher altitudes. The objective was to have the aircraft stream across the target in approximately the same formation as when they started; however, as a practical matter, this would be difficult to achieve. There would be timing errors of seconds—perhaps only fractions of seconds—beginning with the actual lift-off of each aircraft; the time when the procedure turn was begun; the time to complete the turn and climb to the assigned altitude (which was slightly different for each aircraft), all of which would skewer the proposed plan somewhat. There were also other factors: the slightly different performance of each aircraft in both climb and airspeed, the slightly different effect of weather on various aircraft in the stream, and the slightly different fuel consumption rates of various aircraft. These small differences, minor at first, when multiplied by 7 or 7.5 hours flying time to the target, would become quite significant at the objective. Therefore, at the target, single B-29s would be overflying the target area on whatever course and at whatever altitude their individual instruments put them. In other words, there obviously would be some degree of variation from the flight plan so each pilot would "fly it as he saw it" as he arrived at the target. However, this was not a precision bombing mission where everyone would be expected to pinpoint his drop, but a general target area to be saturated, so the plan was expected to work. The low bombing altitude had two objectives: to ensure saturation of the target and, it was hoped, to put us at the extreme range of the smaller anti-aircraft guns but too low for the big anti-aircraft batteries to track us.

A glance at my watch, synchronized at the briefing with all other pilots' watches, told me that it was time to board. My crew had already pulled the props through—two men to a blade for sixteen blades—until all four engines had been purged of any oil in the bottom cylinders, and we scrambled up the nose wheelwell ladder into the forward compartment as the gunners and the radar officer boarded the waist compartment through its door. We settled into our positions, donned headsets, turned on the intercom and other equipment, picked up checklists and started the on-board preflight routine. The exterior preflight inspections and checks of the airplane had already been performed by the ground crew and armorers together with the appropriate members of the flight crew, and a final inspection by the pilot prior to boarding. Each crewmember had certain things to do befitting his station and specialty and, following his individual checklist, proceeded to prepare himself and his equipment for flight. The bombardier, after seating himself and adjusting his seatbelt and harness, determined that all the switches on his panel were in the "off" position, checked his fuse panel for active and spare fuses, synchronized his clock with that of the navigator and pilot, set his altimeter, recorded the outside air temperature in his log, and checked the dovetail alignment of his bombsight, the locking pins and secure position of the cannon plugs, and many other aspects of the functioning of the bombsight and its servo motors.

The pilot and copilot likewise seated themselves, adjusting their belts, and began their preflight procedures, with the copilot reading the checklist and the pilot responding both verbally and physically by performing the act called for in the sequence of the checklist. The emergency ignition switch was turned on;

the control surfaces and the throttles were unlocked; the parking brake was set; the emergency landing gear release, emergency bomb release, and emergency cabin air pressure release handles on the control panel were properly set; throttles were advanced to "full" and retarded again to ensure that they were free functioning; the central fire control gunner in his astrodome observed the function and travel of the control surfaces as the pilot moved the control column and rudder pedals through their arcs, reporting to the pilot on the intercom on the performance of each; flaps were extended to their full down position and retracted again as the side blister scanners reported their proper functioning to the pilot on the intercom; aileron, elevator and rudder tabs were set in the neutral position; main system hydraulic pressure was checked; the clocks were synchronized; the altimeter was set; the autopilot master switch was thrown to the "off" position and all autopilot control knobs turned to the "pointers up" position; the turbocharger knob was set to the off position; all the gyros were caged until after engine start; the propeller limit switches were depressed until the lights on the panel flashed; and various other checks following which the pilot would announce on the intercom "stand by to start engines." During the time the pilot and copilot were completing their checklist, every other crew member had been accomplishing similar routines at his station—the engineer, navigator, radio and radar operators, and each of the gunners/scanners. The tail gunner had the least to do at this juncture, so immediately after boarding the rear compartment, he started the auxiliary power unit and reported to the pilot over the intercom: "Putt-putt on line." This unit, a small gasoline engine powering a generator, when operating, gave us electrical power on the ground.

The engineer, having completed his preflight checklist, which was concerned almost entirely with the engines, acknowledged my "stand by" announcement as I determined that at least two of my ground crew members were standing by with fire extinguishers in front of number one engine, watching me. I would then hold up one finger of one hand, make a

circular motion with a finger of the other hand, and command, "Start one." The flight engineer would then turn the
boost pumps on, set the throttle and mixture control for the
number one engine, and hit the starter switch while at the
same time intermittently operating the primer as I watched
that huge sixteen and one-half foot prop start to turn. After
three or four blades, the engineer turned on the magneto
switch, and the engine sprang to life. Big radial engines have
their own peculiar starting characteristics and sounds: they
cough and backfire and belch huge clouds of blue smoke, and
then as they explode into life, the slipstream blows the smoke
behind the airplane and the engine settles into its distinctive
rumble. The engineer immediately set the mixture control to
"auto lean" and set the throttle for an 800 RPM idle as he prepared to start the next engine. The ground crew then moved
to number two engine and the signals and commands were
repeated. Then numbers three and four were started in the
same manner, after which the ground crew chief took a position directly in front of the nose where he and I could see each
other. He stood with his arms and hands about half-out-
stretched with his thumbs pointing outward. This stance
informed me that the wheel chocks had been removed, and as
far as he was concerned, I was ready to taxi. My copilot continued our checklist to completion; I called for 25 degrees of flaps
and closed the bomb bay doors. As my crew chief backed aside
giving me a "good luck" wave, I edged forward to take my place
in the line of B-29s, tails slowly bobbing as the procession of
ponderous, winged, elephantine shapes made their way to the
head of the runway for takeoff.

As I turned and lined up in takeoff position on the runway,
I could see the two preceding aircraft right where they were
supposed to be: one halfway down the runway and one lifting
off. I called for mixture, full rich, and cowl flaps closed to 7.5
degrees. I stood on the brakes and opened the throttles,
revving the engines to full power, the plane shaking and rock-
ing from the restraint as wisps and streams of vapor came off
the prop tips in the moist tropical air. Then, with a signal from

the tower, I released the brakes and we began to roll. I danced on the rudder pedals feeling for control, and I soon had it as my copilot began calling out the airspeed: "70 . . . 80 . . . 95 . . . 110 . . . 135." I could feel the lift beginning to build under the wings and the rumble of the wheels on the runway lessen somewhat as the landing gear struts extended. I held slight backpressure on the control column and began to finesse the elevator trim tab ever so slightly. Under these load conditions, I didn't want to pull the airplane off at a given airspeed or point on the runway, and I didn't want to risk stalling it off by getting the nosewheel too high. I wanted to fly it off, so as I felt the lift giving me control, I kept the airplane just on the verge of flying until it did—smoothly, but laboriously and slowly into the air. I tapped the brakes to stop the spinning of the wheels, and, as soon as I was positive that I was out of ground effect, I called for wheels up, and my copilot retracted the gear. I flew on about 20 or 25 feet above the terrain to the cliff at the end of the island where I could dive 200 or 300 feet down to the water and pick up airspeed. As I did this, I called for flaps up and my copilot milked them up two or three degrees at a time until they were fully retracted. I had achieved close to cruise speed at this point and, after reducing power, called for head temperatures. My engineer responded, "All in the green," as I banked into the procedure turn and started the climb to my assigned altitude of 400 feet, on course to the target. We were now committed to whatever fate had in store for us.

I trimmed the ship for level flight, turned on the autopilot, and settled in, more or less, for the seven-hour flight to the target. I instructed the aft crew members to shut down the "putt-putt" and busied myself with all the inflight activity typical of piloting a large aircraft: monitoring the engines, in this case with the assistance of the flight engineer; adjusting mixture controls to ensure conservative fuel consumption without raising cylinder head temperatures; monitoring throttle settings to practice efficient cruise control; keeping the props synchronized; listening to the engines for any slight change in their steady sound; observing the engines for oil leaks or a change in the blue flame of the exhaust; watching for ice build-up on the wings, sometimes with the help of a spotlight; and monitoring the whole instrument panel with a sweep of the eyes every minute or so. I was particularly alert and attuned to every nuance of sound and vibration of the airplane as a result, perhaps, of anxiety, apprehension, and adrenaline.

In the first hour or so of the flight, it was not quite dark. There were fleecy cumulus clouds in the sky, the last streaks of the setting sun were fading, and stars were visible above. Sometime later, daylight was gone and darkness had enveloped us. The bombardier had already gone back to the bomb bays to arm the clusters of incendiary bombs we were carrying as the navigator climbed into the astrodome to take one last shot with his sextant before the stars disappeared. We were about abreast of Iwo Jima when the weather closed in around us. I switched off the autopilot as I always flew the airplane manually when on instruments. There was light to mild turbulence from time to time, but nothing really severe. There was, however, considerable electrical activity with great flashes of lightning illuminating the ethereal white mass around us so that we appeared to be flying in an opaque atmosphere all by ourselves. At times the airplane was covered by St. Elmo's fire, a static electrical discharge that made the whole ship glow like a huge neon sign. There were no B-29s visible to us when we entered the storm, but the possibility and fear of collision with other ships were constantly in the back of my mind. About an hour later, the navigator came on the intercom advising me that, according to the flight plan, we were at the point where the climb to our approach altitude should begin. I increased the engines to climb power and started an ascent to 5,600 feet, still concerned about who else might be there in the soup with me.

Through these hours of flight, I was busy flying the airplane with only an occasional comment on the intercom to my engineer or my copilot or receiving one from the navigator such as "correct two degrees right," so my thoughts and fears or concerns about the target had not saturated my mind as it may have for some other crew members on this, our first mission to Japan.

I leveled off at our assigned altitude, and we broke out of the clouds fifty to seventy-five miles off the coast of Japan, and even from that distance we could see the target ablaze, bright as a sunset. We put on our flak vests and helmets and prepared for the bomb run. We had not seen another B-29 since we turned on course off the end of Guam, but as we proceeded into the target area, several were visible, more or less on the same course as we were. The target area was so wide that I was able to look it over and select a way in. There was a dark area down the middle that was not burning, so I approached it. At that moment, Rich Ranker, one of my gunners, with some tension and apprehension in his voice, suddenly warned me on the intercom of a B-29 directly above us with his bomb bay doors open. I immediately slid out from under him.

The fires on each side were burning fiercely—a veritable inferno fanned by seventy-five mile an hour winds created by the firestorm itself. There was a B-29 on each side of me bracketed by a half dozen or more searchlights; I thought I might escape the searchlights by going in between the unfortunate ones already caught, and I did—until just after "bombs away," when the cockpit was suddenly illuminated brighter than daylight with the blinding white lights of batteries of searchlights. They had found us. If it were not for the huge fires below, I would not have been quite sure which way was up and which way was down. The lights seemed to be coming from every direction—below, behind, from the side, and straight out in front of us—and I had never experienced such brightness. At our briefing we had been told not to look outside the cockpit. It had even been suggested that the pilot lower his seat and fly on instruments on the approach and bomb run, but how could a twenty-five-year-old pilot pumped full of adrenaline on his first mission be expected not to look around?

Seconds after the lights hit us, the flak started exploding around us. We could hear it raining against the fuselage, and I immediately began evasive action like a broken field runner. My copilot had a couple of ack-ack batteries spotted, and he would watch them fire, then he'd yell at me and I'd roll to the left or right and then straighten out for a second or two when we would see the puffs of ack-ack exploding off our wingtip; then I'd roll further or back the other way. I was balls-out on the throttles indicating 290 miles an hour in my dash across the target in a desperate attempt to prevent the anti-aircraft batteries from tracking us. This went on for what seemed an eternity but actually was only a fairly brief fifteen minutes or so: turn, straighten out, turn again, roll out, turn, climb, dive, and then it happened—we plunged into the roiling maelstrom of smoke and thermals for a slamming that I feared might destroy the airplane. The first giant updraft shot us up so violently and with such force that the blood drained from my head—approaching blackout—and for a moment or two I couldn't lift my feet off the floor or lift my arms to control the airplane. Some pilots later reported gaining as much as 5,000 feet in altitude in this first thermal. Other crews flying through the firestorm reported seeing flying debris—burning door and window frames, for example—shooting up past their airplanes. Others reported the overwhelming stench of burning flesh. We, however, didn't experience these two phenomenon. I worried about the negative "Gs" on the wings. I had no idea, of course, what force we were actually sustaining, nor did I know what the negative "G" load limits were for the aircraft. I knew of instances where aircraft had been torn apart in thunderstorms, and this was worse than any thunderstorm I had ever been in. However, the ship was hanging together, and we were flying. Fortunately, we were now comparatively light, having dropped our bomb load and burned half or more of our fuel.

The next one, of course, was a downdraft that pressed us against our seat belts and bounced everything that was loose against the ceiling, followed by up, then down again—*hard*. We were being bumped and tossed around like a cork on water in a hurricane when a huge thermal flipped us over. We were not completely inverted, but the wings were well past the vertical; we were still rolling, and going down. Rich, the same gunner who had warned me earlier of the B-29 above us, concerned about the traffic over the target, looked up again through the CFC astrodome and saw nothing but raging fire. Then, as dirt, cigarette butts, oxygen masks, and other debris started floating past his face, he looked down through his blister and saw nothing but clouds and smoke reflecting the fire. We were upside down. Inverted flight at around 5,000 feet in a four-engine, sixty-ton airplane was not exactly an approved maneuver. The airspeed was building up rapidly as we rolled further on our back, but the altimeter was not unwinding, which confused me briefly. It took only a second to remember that an altimeter is just an aneroid barometer and lags way behind the change in atmospheric pressure in a dive. For a brief second, I thought that, perhaps when we were flying through the flak, some damage had been sustained that affected the instruments and therefore I should not believe them, so I shouted to my copilot to ignore them. I thought, "Jesus, maybe this is it!" "The hell it is!" I rapidly answered myself. I came to my senses and was instantly aware that all four engines were producing power, and the airplane was still flying, albeit erratically. Years and thousands of hours in the air dictated a "seat-of-the-pants" response, and I flew the airplane through a "split-S" maneuver to recover from our inverted position. The airspeed exceeded 400 mph, and I burned the speed off in a climb designed to put all the sky between us and the ground that I could. Leveling off, but still in the target area, I called for the radar officer to "give me a heading out of here," thinking he would be monitoring his scope and know exactly where I was, but before he could respond, the navigator came back instantly with "fly one-seven-zero." He had apparently been following my wild flight with his gyrocompass and therefore was on top of all my course changes—or maybe not: since we both knew the reciprocal heading from Guam to Tokyo, he may have instantly fired it at me from memory. I don't know why I had to ask for it except that I might have been a little excited—outward appearances notwithstanding.

I called for a crew check, and each man, in turn, responded with an "all O.K." Even though we had no guns or ammunition on board, I cautioned the gunners to watch for night fighters as I throttled back and headed out to sea. I conferred with my flight engineer about our fuel burn and concluded that with careful cruise control, we had enough to get home. After a while—maybe fifty miles off the coast without seeing any other airplanes, either fighters or B-29s—we began to relax and unwind and engage in some chatter about what had happened, with the glow of a burning Tokyo still visible behind us. I dove 400 or 500 feet to get the ship "on the step," throttled way back to only 1650 or 1700 RPM, and "coasted" all the way back to Guam in a very slight descent—the rate-of-climb instrument needle resting just below the zero mark. It was now necessary to fly back through the storm we had encountered enroute to Japan, so once again I settled down to manually fly the airplane on instruments. My logbook shows that on this mission I flew a total of five hours of instrument flight.

As we escaped the storm and were back in clear weather a couple of hours north of Guam, I began to feel the strain of twenty-four hours without sleep and thirteen hours in the cockpit, but as we approached the Marianas, I felt somewhat rejuvenated at the prospect of being back at the base. Despite what we had been through, which had sobered us somewhat, we were on our way home, uninjured and undamaged. It was good to be flying in clear daylight again, and I felt reassured that despite what we had been through, the ship had functioned and performed admirably, as had the crew. I felt proud of them and wouldn't have traded them for any other outfit on the field. Reflecting, I thought that, except for the wild ride over the target and getting shot at, the mission had gone pretty much as planned, although I still had serious concerns about a weakness of the mission plan: that of exposing every ship to the possibility, either en route or in the target area, of a midair collision or the possibility of dropping bombs on another B-29. However, we had seen no B-29s go down, and we had not experienced a near miss ourselves. Nevertheless, the concern lingered in my mind. I could not decide whether or not I had been frightened, simply because I had not known what to expect. Once I was confronted with what should have scared the bejabbers out of me, I was too busy flying the airplane to think about it.

As we neared Guam, two or three other B-29s were visible, and as my copilot and I completed our landing checklist, I fell into position behind them for the final approach. We touched down and rolled out after fifteen hours and forty-seven minutes in the air. As I started the turnoff to the taxiway, I acknowledged the chaplain waving at us, checking each ship back to its home base. I turned into our hardstand and shut down the engines. "Little John" Miller, my crew chief; "Big John" Miller, his assistant; Luigi; and others of the ground crew were there to greet us. We climbed down to terra firma, and the euphoria of having made it—having done it, having succeeded, having survived—began to sweep over me. I felt somewhat triumphant and a little like a hero. Everyone was eager to hear just what had happened and we smiled as we told them how all Tokyo was burning. Even to us, once back at our home base in broad daylight, the night's escapade didn't seem so bad. It was a little like a nightmare that was already a part of the past and no longer bothered you. I had a short conversation with John about the performance and mechanics of the airplane, and then I made a visual inspection expecting to find a lot of holes in the wings and fuselage, but to my surprise there were none—lots of little dents and scratches made by bits and pieces of shrapnel, but no holes. I also looked for popped rivets, expecting many as a result of my "split-S" and 400-plus mile-an-hour dive over Tokyo, but found none—a great testimonial to the integrity of Boeing airplanes.

The six-by-six truck was waiting for us, and we scrambled aboard to be taken to the debriefing hut where we were plied with donuts and coffee by a couple Red Cross girls and a couple shots of whiskey by the debriefing officers. A look around the room saw pilots talking excitedly with their hands simulating flight as pilots are wont to do and others matter-of-factly telling their stories. There were some smiles, but mostly tired, somber faces as each crew member was interrogated about what he saw and did.

We left the debriefing hut for our quarters, a Quonset hut housing the officers of three flight crews. As we stumbled into the hut looking forward to some rest and sleep, we were shocked and astounded and stopped in our tracks. All the personal effects of the other two crews had been removed; only our stuff remained. Musser and Johnson had failed to return. But how did they know so soon? Was there a radio transmission? Did some other B-29 crew see them go down? Was there a midair collision? Did they make it out of the target area and crash at sea? Did they run out of gas? Could they have bailed out and been captured? Could they have ditched and perhaps still be picked up? We prayed and hoped for that all day, but we didn't ever find out what actually happened—they simply were gone. These were boys with whom we had talked and joked and lived only hours before, and now they were . . . gone.

As the day wore on and reconnaissance photos came in and intelligence reports arrived, this mission was quickly recognized as the most destructive air raid in the history of warfare. Almost sixteen square miles of Tokyo were reduced to ash and rubble; by the Japanese government's own count, over 83,000 people were killed, over 100,000 injured, and 1.5 million made homeless. Approximately 300 B-29s participated, out of which fourteen airplanes and crews were lost—slightly less than 5 percent of the strike force. The loss for the 29th Bomb Group was approximately 10 percent.

When the flight crew reports were analyzed, it looked like my fears about the mission had become reality for some crews: there were reports of midair collisions of B-29s. Perhaps statistically from a planning perspective, the losses were "acceptable" in light of the "success" of the mission, but the loss from our Quonset hut affected me and my crew quite profoundly.

In addition to the effect that the two crew losses from our hut had on us, there was another somewhat personal misfortune involved. Dorothy Reger, wife of Bob Reger, copilot on Musser's lost crew, had become very good friends with my wife during our training at Pratt. They were both California girls, about the same age, and had found much in common in their backgrounds. When we left Kansas in our new airplane, the girls drove home to California in my old Ford. Dorothy was pregnant with their first child when we left, and I dreaded having to comfort her in her time of loss.

The realization of all that had happened slowly crept over us, and we didn't feel so nonchalant anymore. We no longer smiled when we thought of what we had been through, and we didn't feel much like heroes. We wondered what brought us back and not others. Training? Pilot skill? Or just luck and faith? We were inclined toward the latter. We were bewildered and a little lost as some realization of what the ugly business of war was all about came over us: You would have to coax an overloaded airplane off the ground while sweating out an engine failure, fire, explosion, or runaway prop on takeoff, any of which would probably be fatal; then endure the stress of a seven- or eight-hour flight to the target, much or all of it on instruments in storms. Then you had to fight the Jap and take all that he threw at you, and maybe he would get you, or at least hurt or damage you enough so that it would be difficult to get home, or maybe you couldn't get home and would have to ditch. And your friends died . . .

Welcome to war.

CHAPTER 2

The Road to Tokyo

I t all started many years before, when, as a boy, I was already in love with airplanes and flying. I knew all the World War I fighters—the SE-5, the Spad, the DH-4, the Sopwith Camel, the Nieuport, the Fokker, and the Albatross, as well as the engines that powered them—the Liberty V-12, the Hispano Suiza V-8, the Gnome, the LeRhone, and others. I built models of them and hung them by thread in my basement workshop and my room at home. In the 1920s one of the most common barnstorming airplanes touring the country was the old Curtiss Jenny, powered by the OX-5 engine. These did not see combat service in Europe, but they were fairly common in the postwar period, and I saw them on more than one occasion, usually operating out of some farmer's pasture, when I was a small boy. Then aviation's most epochal event of the 1920s captivated the country and a small boy: Lindbergh's solo flight across the Atlantic to Paris, after which he was lionized throughout the western world, and the potential possibilities of both civilian and military aviation became apparent to everyone.

My first experience riding in an airplane came in 1931 when I was visiting a friend in Pierre, South Dakota, during spring vacation. My transportation back to Omaha via surface transport required my leaving on Saturday, but my friend's father offered to have me flown home in his airplane on Sunday, enabling me to stay one more day if my father would consent to the change in plan. My father readily consented by telephone, so on Sunday I climbed into the front cockpit of a bright red, two-place, open-cockpit biplane, and we took off. I no longer remember, but it may have been a Travelair, a popular aircraft of the time. I was fascinated—the world laid out below like a three dimensional map through stereopticon glasses: hills, valleys, streams, rivers, roads and highways, railroad tracks, farms with their patchwork of fields and woodlots, and small towns with their railroad stations, church steeples, small main streets, hotels, and houses scattered neatly about. It all formed a mosaic that made perfect sense, and whether you knew the country or not, finding your way was easier than when traveling on the ground.

We weren't long into the flight when, despite my fascination with flying, I began to feel queasy—blustery Nebraska and South Dakota spring weather doing its bit to make a bumpy ride—and I suddenly puked all over the side of that pretty red airplane. It was the first and only time I have ever been airsick. (As an adult I have been seasick, but never again airsick.) I don't think the pilot was too happy about it, but at least it was better than puking in the cockpit. We stopped somewhere en route to refuel, and I remember people coming over and looking at the side of the plane and then at me. They didn't say anything to me, but their expressions conveyed, at least in my imagination, things like "dumb kid" or some such. I think the fellow helping the pilot refuel said something like "kid puked, huh?" as if it wasn't patently obvious. I was terribly embarrassed, but I didn't know what to do or say, so I just sat there and said nothing. When we arrived in Omaha that afternoon, I was still pretty green around the gills and a little wobbly, but despite all that, I vowed to myself that someday I, too, would fly airplanes. I was hooked.

Although still barely out of its infancy, aviation made considerable progress in the late '20s and early '30s and received much publicity from the newspapers and broadcast media. Sport aviation became quite popular, and pylon races as well as cross-country races were held all over the Midwest. Two of the most famous races were the Bendix Trophy Race and the Thompson Trophy Race, although there also was the Schneider Trophy Race and the National Air Races. These were covered in detail by the press. Famous aviators of the period who participated in these events were Jimmy Doolittle, Roscoe

Turner, Clyde Pangborn, Jimmy Wedell, Steve Wittman, Jimmy Haizlip, Lee Gehlbach, and others.

Jimmy Doolittle and Roscoe Turner were probably the best known. Doolittle already had a significant reputation as the army's and perhaps the country's top pilot. He instructed cadets in Texas in 1918 and 1919 and then, in 1922, set an east-to-west, coast-to-coast record of twenty-two hours and thirty-four minutes in an Army DH-4 averaging a speed of 101 miles per hour. Then, in 1925, he won the Schneider Trophy Race for seaplanes; then in Chile, he flew his Hawk over the Andes Mountains—history's first such flight. In May 1927, he performed aviation's first outside loop and in 1929 he completed the first blind take-off and landing. He resigned his Army commission in 1930 and went to work for Royal Dutch Shell, and while with Shell, he won the 1931 Bendix Trophy Race and the Thompson Trophy in 1932. In the Thompson, he set a new landplane speed record of 296 miles per hour.

Roscoe Turner's career also began in the Army where he learned to parachute from a balloon in 1917, but he reached the European front just as the Armistice was signed, so he was discharged in 1919. After learning to fly in 1921, his reputation began to grow as a stuntman and pilot barnstorming the U.S. in Curtiss Jennys, doing acrobatic airshows and flying as a stuntman for the movies. He was a daring, accomplished pilot, but perhaps first and foremost a superb showman. He affected a powder blue pseudo-military uniform complete with a black visored cap, a Sam Browne belt, and black boots. He sported a waxed handlebar mustache and had a lion cub named "Gilmore" as a mascot who flew with him on occasion as his "copilot." The aviation community looked upon Turner as a "dude" trying to gain notoriety by publicity stunts instead of serious aviation accomplishments. However, Turner proved them wrong as he began to break speed records starting with the Los Angeles–New York route in 1929 and he continued to break his own record over the next several years. He won the Thompson Trophy Race in 1934, 1938, and 1939—the only person to win three times. In 1933 he won the Bendix transcontinental race, and in 1934 he and Clyde Pangborn placed third flying a Boeing 247 in the MacRobertson England-to-Australia race.

Another intrepid air adventurer of the early and middle '30s was Wiley Post, a self-educated and unassuming Oklahoman who, despite the loss of his left eye in an oil field accident, went on to become, with his Lockheed Vega the *Winnie Mae*, the second most celebrated team in aviation after Charles Lindbergh and the *Spirit of St. Louis.* Post won the Los Angeles-to-Chicago Air Derby in 1930 and went on to fly twice around the world in the next three years in the *Winnie Mae.* Then, in August 1935, flying a Lockheed Orion on floats on an Alaska charter by Will Rogers, he crashed after lifting off from a small lake near Point Barrow, killing himself and the popular American humorist.

One of the most famous pylon racing airplanes of the time was the unorthodox GeeBee—a short, fat airplane (because the fuselage retained the shape and size of the huge radial engine all the way back to the tail) with clipped wings, landing gear fairings, and wheel pants. The cockpit was also unorthodox as it abutted the vertical stabilizer. It was unstable and difficult to fly, but it dominated many of the races in which it was entered.

Airplanes for the growing airline industry were being developed to replace the old Ford Trimotors and Curtiss Wright Condors. I remember when the first United Airlines Boeing 247 came through Omaha in 1933—it had made it from Denver nonstop in less than three hours! (Denver was 600 miles away, a twelve- or fourteen-hour drive in a car.) The Boeing 247 eventually lost out to the Douglas DC-2 for worldwide acceptance by the airlines, but that 247 flight established the viability of commercial aviation for me.

General aviation airplanes were also advancing with the Piper Cub J-series, the Aeroncas, Taylorcrafts, and others filling the small economic training category and with the executive and small transport craft coming from such famous airman/designers as Benny Howard with his DGA ("damn good airplane") series, Clyde Cessna and his "Airmaster," Walter Beech with his outstanding Staggerwing and D-18 series, and, of course, Stinson's Gullwing and Reliant, as well as the Waco, Fairchild, Spartan, and Lockheed aircraft. Each of these was a considerable improvement over its predecessors and was "state-of-the-art" for its time. Other famous 1930s aircraft included the Boeing Monomail, the Pitcairn Super Mailwing, the Northrop Alpha, the DH-86, and various foreign craft including several Fokkers (German), Farmans (French), Piaggios (Italian), and Savoia-Marchettis (Italian), but these were not manufactured in large numbers and were seldom, if ever, seen in the Midwest.

In 1933, I attended the World's Fair in Chicago, and one of the impressive sights there (besides fan dancer Sally Rand) was the Italian armada of twenty-three Savoia-Marchetti Flying Boats, which had flown in formation from the Orbetello seaplane base north of Rome, via Amsterdam, Ireland, and Iceland, to a Lake Michigan mooring at the foot of what is now known as Balbo Drive in Chicago. The ships were of a very unusual and unorthodox design incorporating two hulls attached by the wing somewhat like the configuration of a catamaran. Twin engines were mounted in a push-pull arrangement on a superstructure on top of the wing directly over the cockpit. The empennage was attached to the hulls by a skeletonized boom arrangement. The fleet was led by Italo Balbo and, for 1933, was a significant accomplishment.

1937 and 1938 saw the last two major around-the-world attempts: the first being Amelia Earhart in a Lockheed Electra ending when she was lost in the Pacific trying to make Howland Island; and the second in 1938 being Howard Hughes flying a Lockheed 14 transport plane. This flight broke most of the existing records, being completed in three days nineteen hours seventeen minutes with no unscheduled stops, and never a deviation from their prescribed course. The flight originated in New York, and proceeded to Paris, Moscow, two stops in Siberia, Alaska, Minneapolis, and back to New York. Hughes's flight ended the around-the-world derby started by the U.S. Army World Flight in 1924.

Military aviation was also showing progress in the development of its aircraft. I remember when the Boeing P-26 became operational in 1934 (in those days the "P" stood for "pursuit"). It was a single engine, single place, low wing monoplane, and it looked like it would be a joy to fly. It looked fast even sitting on the ground—and it was. It was powered by a 600-horsepower radial engine that gave it a cruising speed of 200 mph and a service ceiling of over 28,000 feet. It was the first all metal monoplane, but the last open cockpit, fixed landing gear fighter in the Air Corps' arsenal.

Aside from the record-setting accomplishments and speed runs, there were other events affecting aviation in the middle '30s. One of the most publicized, ill-planned, and tragic was Franklin Roosevelt's 1934 politically motivated cancellation of the airline mail contracts and subsequent ordering of the Army Air Corps to fly the mail. Roosevelt perceived that there had been collusion in the awarding of the mail contracts. This perception was due in part to a report generated by the postmaster general in the Hoover administration following a meeting with airline executives in which duplication of routing, not collusion, was the discussion. However, Roosevelt was determined to punish the airlines. It was an unfortunate decision. He took this action without a hearing or trial, thereby subjecting the Air Corps to a blood bath. Charles Lindbergh sent Roosevelt a much publicized telegram which was highly critical of his decree, and Eddie Rickenbacker was so incensed that a speech in which he had planned to criticize the mandate was denied air time by NBC after receipt of orders from Washington. Both of these preeminent members of the aviation community and the airline industry were concerned not only about the gross injustice of the situation on the airline side, but also about the lives of the Air Corps pilots that would be lost. Rickenbacker categorized it as "legalized murder." The prophesy of these two men proved to be all too true: within two months, thirteen Air Corps pilots had been killed.

Neither the Army's equipment nor their pilots were qualified or adapted to fly the mail. In those days Army pilots averaged only about 180 hours of flying time per year, and there were only three Army pilots with as much as 5,000 hours. They probably spent 99 percent of their meager air time flying in clear weather, practicing military manuevers. They were not instrument qualified. Contrasted to airline pilots who flew day and night in good weather and bad, they were woefully inadequate. So was their equipment, which lacked the instrumentation and radios that the airlines had. Some of the pathetic but remarkable survival stories were those of pilots who had crashed in blinding snowstorms or thunderstorms while trying to visually follow a canyon, or a highway, or a railroad track while flying only feet above ground level in an open-cockpit, single-engine airplane. Something had to be done, so the mail contracts were reinstated and the Army program cancelled. Roosevelt then decreed that no airline president who held office before the cancellation of the mail contract could continue in office after the reinstatement. This was grossly unfair and besmirched the names and reputations of the executives involved. Thereafter, United Airlines sued the government. It took seven years for the case to wind its way through the courts, but the adjudication was in favor of United and against the government. However, by then World War II had started, and people were no longer interested. They took little notice of the decision. The whole episode had been extremely costly for a political escapade.

By 1939, the aircraft/airline industries had matured into an era of dependability, safety, and endurance not formerly known. The venerable Douglas DC-3 had supplanted the DC-2, and more than 1,000 of them were flying worldwide for all the major airlines. Many of the airlines that are familiar to us today were flying routes that still form the nucleus of their service areas. In Europe these included Royal Dutch Airlines (KLM), Swissair, Finnair, and Lufthansa; in the United States, American Airlines, TWA, United Airlines, Northwest Airlines, Pan-American World Airways, and Eastern Airlines. Navigation and communication equipment both in the aircraft and on the ground also showed considerable advancement and contributed to the efficiency of the airline and general aviation operations.

The military establishment was motivated to improve their inventory of aircraft and gradually new types evolved. Combat

planes were continually improving in speed and range as well
as armament. Many of the airplanes which would become the
mainstay of the World War II Allied Air Forces were conceived
and designed in the late '30s. Prototypes built included America's foremost heavy bomber, the B-17, which first flew in 1937
after two years of development as the Model 299 and the YB-
17. America's most ominously beautiful fighter, the P-38, first
flew in 1939 as the prototype XP-38.

I kept abreast of all this through the periodicals of the time
such as the old *Popular Aviation* (predecessor to today's *Flying*
magazine) and everything else I could get my hands on. I also
had become acquainted with two FBO's at the local airport:
Marion Nelson and Steve Krantz, both of whom—together
with a couple of their instructor employees—gave me flying
lessons in 1941 and 1942. In addition to their informal "now
and then" ground school, I began taking correspondence
courses from an aeronautical school in Theory of Flight, Navigation, Basic Meteorology, and related subjects. Nelson and
Krantz would also, on occasion, let me fly with them as a non-
paying passenger on one-way charter flights. If the charter passenger was only one person, as was many times the case, I
could go along riding in the back seat until the customer was
delivered, and then on the return flight, I could occupy the
right seat and get some instruction and some time at the controls. It was not time I could log, and it was mostly straight and
level, but it was experience nevertheless and invaluable exposure to flying and navigation. The aircraft used for this service
were the four- or five-place ships of the era—the Howard, the
Waco Cabin Plane, the Stinson Gullwing and, occasionally, if I
was really lucky, the Beechcraft Staggerwing.

The trainers that I took lessons in were the ubiquitous Piper
J-3 Cub, the Taylorcraft, the Aeronca (Airknocker), the Stinson
105, and the Luscombe Silvaire. I got all the basics and a little
cross-country before I entered the Army Air Corps. When I was
building time locally, I used to chase migrating ducks and
geese. In the J-3 Cub, we were pretty evenly matched for speed,
and I had quite a chase until the birds learned that they could

turn and climb faster than I could, and then they were gone. Cross-country flying in those days in the training airplanes mentioned was strictly pilotage and dead reckoning—time/distance/heading problems and flying in reference to the ground. In the small training planes, we had no radios and no navigational aids. We flew strict, pre-determined patterns around the airport and kept our heads on swivels. On final approach for landing, we watched the tower for a red or green light. Red obviously meant "go around—do not land," and green meant "cleared to land." If there was no tower, you just visually cleared yourself—while spacing yourself and adhering to the requirements of the pattern and approach—and landed. This system, except for airline and general aviation traffic, still works today and is in use at many small uncontrolled airports and airstrips outside the major metropolitan areas and larger cities.

Instrumentation in the small airplanes consisted of a tachometer and oil temperature and pressure gauges. The fuel gauge was nothing more than a wire protruding through a hole in the center of the gas cap, the bottom end of which was attached to a float in the tank. There were neither electrical nor vacuum systems. For flight instruments we had a magnetic compass, an altimeter, a rate-of-climb indicator, a turn-and-bank indicator, and an airspeed indicator. The basic drill was to coordinate "needle, ball, and airspeed" throughout the maneuvering of the aircraft. However, the real objective was to learn to fly the airplane without reference to the flight instruments, to do it by feel—"seat of the pants" it was called—to be able to sense an incipient stall without reference to the airspeed indicator, to be able to coordinate a turn without skidding or gaining or losing altitude and with no reference to the needle and ball, to fly straight and level by reference to the ground and the horizon and not the rate of climb indicator, to be able to sense updrafts and downdrafts and crosswinds and their consequences without reference to the instruments—in short, a sensory awareness of the position and progress of the craft through its medium as you made it do what you wanted it to do and go where you wanted it to go. For example, when solo flying the tandem seat trainers such as the J-3 Cub, you flew from the back seat with the front seat empty. The nose blotted out forward visibility in anything but straight and level flight or a descent. Therefore, when making three-point landings, the position and direction of the airplane was perceived by looking out the side of the airplane after the flare was started rather than looking over the nose. Elemental as all this may have been, it was, nonetheless, flying.

Most of the young men who were trying to get into the flying game worked at getting a private license followed by an instructor's rating, which would enable them to keep flying and get paid a little bit for it as they built time toward being able to qualify for application to the airlines for a copilot's slot which required a minimum of 200 hours and a commercial license. This was not reasonable or logical for me since I'd still have to work at something else to support myself and attend college while slowly gaining flying time. It appeared that it would take years for me to meet the minimum.

The other path to a flying career, of course, was the military—the best flying education you could get. War clouds were gathering. Europe was already embroiled, and despite the strong isolationist attitude in the U.S., it appeared that we would be involved sooner or later in one way or another. In the meantime, enlistment in the RCAF looked appealing. I investigated it, but there were some problems. The biggest one was the possibility of losing U.S. citizenship by enlisting in the armed forces of another country. So I procrastinated; being a soldier-of-fortune was not my objective. As it turned out, the people who did enlist and subsequently went to England to fight did not lose their U.S. citizenship. They were eventually absorbed into American units in England after we got into it.

In 1940, the U.S. Army Air Corps did not have a program for which I could qualify, and I did not have the grades to get into West Point, so I continued to plug away at getting a minimum of two years of college in order to get an appointment as an aviation cadet in the U.S. Army Air Corps. As the golden age of aviation was drawing to a close, anticipating military training sometime in the future, I continued to fly sporadically as my limited resources permitted.

I loved to explore the countryside by air, and I loved everything about flying: the exhilaration, the pure fun of it, the challenge, the freedom, the absence of restraints or boundaries other than the mechanical limitations of the airplane, and the sense of control and destiny. The sky seemed to be my element. I felt comfortable and "at home" when I was aloft. Like people who have an affinity for water and are natural sailors, I seemed to have an affinity for the air and was captivated by the prospect of being able to fly all the time. I desperately wanted to get the training that would enable me to do that.

In the fall of 1941, I was anxiously anticipating entrance into the Air Corps in early 1942 since I would have the college credits needed to qualify at semester's end in January. Then Pearl Harbor was attacked, war on Japan was declared, and the country was galvanized into action. I remember being with my father in a group of men on or soon after December 7, 1941. They were discussing the attack when my father said, "Well, it won't take long to end this—there are too many of us who know how to . . ." and he swung his arms up as though mounting a shotgun and drawing down on a cock pheasant streaking over the top of the corn or a canvasback barreling through a pass out in the sandhills. For my friends and me, our moral and patriotic obligations were obvious, and we responded immediately by enlisting. Besides, here was the opportunity to fly, and if we were going to fight a war, we wanted to do it in airplanes.

After Christmas vacation, I went to the dean of men at school, explaining that I had enlisted in the Air Corps and was subject to call at any moment. I requested my grades without taking final exams. A patriotic state of mind prevailed, and my request was granted. There were several of us who had enlisted together, and the farewell parties soon started. But, alas, the Army had no place to immediately send us. The farewell parties became less frequent. We were alerted a couple of times, and that started the parties again, but it was June before training facilities had been established or expanded enough to start funneling eager cadets into them. We finally received our orders, and the Seventh Corps Area Army Recruiting Service gathered a couple of Pullman cars full of boys from Minnesota, Iowa, and Nebraska and shipped us off on the Union Pacific to the Pre-Flight Army Classification Center at Santa Ana, California.

CHAPTER 3

Training

Although Santa Ana Army Air Base had no airplanes, it served the purpose of initiating us into military life. We lost our hair and our civilian clothes and embarked on a program of close-order drill, physical training to get us in shape, and a fairly extensive ground school. Courses included refresher classes in math and algebra and physics and other things related to flying and navigation. The one thing that most readily comes to my mind now, however, was learning Morse Code. It drove us nuts—we were da-da-dit-ditting in our sleep. We would need to know it not so much to communicate with each other, but to be able to use radio navigational aids when we started flying. All the low-frequency radio ranges as well as position markers and station IDs were broadcast in Morse Code so it was imperative that we understand it.

Close-order drill was easy for me since I had been a member of an independent cadet regiment while in high school (after my graduation it was converted to an ROTC unit). In that regiment, we wore uniforms very similar to those worn by West Point or VMI cadets, and we practiced with antique rifles of a type I no longer remember. I particularly liked the routine of the "crack squad," which performed at parades and certain school functions.

There were also various tests, both physical and mental, including psychomotor evaluations administered at Santa Ana, presumably to aid in the selection process for future training, but I had enlisted in the Aviation Cadet Program to become a fighter pilot, and the thought never crossed my mind that I would ever be anything else.

After about six weeks, we were given a weekend pass, so we headed for Los Angeles. One of my friends who had enlisted

with me had an aunt in Pasadena, and she welcomed us to her
home, which became our headquarters on weekend passes as
long as we were in southern California.

The preflight process at Santa Ana ended after about three
months, and we received our orders to Primary Flying Schools.
I was assigned to the Mira Loma Flight Academy at Oxnard,
California. Others in Class 43-D went to Ontario, Hemet, and
Santa Maria, California. Mira Loma Flight Academy was one of
three civilian contract schools operated by one Maj. C. C. Mose-
ley. While commanded by the Army, the housing, mess, instructor staff, and the ground school personnel were civilians.

We followed a rather intense schedule of ground school for
half the day and flew during the other half. The ground school
courses included Theory of Flight, Navigation, Meteorology,
Engines, Aircraft Identification, and others. We were divided
into four "flights"—A, B, C, and D—with about fifty-five cadets
in each. There were eight instructors assigned to each "flight,"
so each one had about seven student pilots. We flew everyday,
with flights varying from thirty or forty minutes in the beginning to as much as two and a half hours or more. My logbook
shows a number of flights of over three hours and one of four
hours. This was quite a load for the instructors until their
charges started to solo. After that, an instructor flew with each
cadet on only about every third flight or so, and those rides
were to review previous lessons, evaluate the cadet's progress,
and teach some new aerial maneuver that would be practiced
by the cadet on subsequent solo flights.

We flew the classic Stearman open-cockpit biplanes. Our
model was the PT-17 with a 225-horsepower Lycoming engine.
These airplanes were designed by Lloyd Stearman, and many
were manufactured by Stearman Aircraft, Inc., along with preceding designs going back to the inception of the company in
1926. In 1938, Stearman Aircraft became a division of Boeing
Aircraft Company, and the Primary Trainers (PTs) were

renamed the "Boeing Kaydet," but we knew them as Stear-mans. The name prevailed for the PT-13, PT-17, and PT-18 and still does today. Incidentally, the only difference between the three models was the make of engine installed. There were Lycoming, Continental, and Jacobs engines used, all of about the same horsepower.

The airplane was built "hell for stout" with a welded steel-tubing fuselage. It was an exceptional performer with respon-sive controls, a rapid roll rate, and no bad habits that I can remember. We loved them. It had a tall narrow gear that required pilots to be on top of its behavior on the ground. While some cadets ground-looped them, if you maintained good rudder control and didn't use brakes excessively, there was no problem keeping them on their wheels.

The Stearman had no electrical system, so starting it meant hand propping it or using an inertia system whereby a line mechanic would insert a crank into the mechanism on the side of the fuselage behind the engine and crank the flywheel up to a speed that, when engaged, would turn the engine over sev-eral times. Woe unto the cadet who mismanaged the throttle and magneto switch and let the engine die, thus requiring the mechanic to crank it again.

It also lacked radios and an intercom system. The means of communication between cockpits was a primitive affair called a "Gosport." The instructor yelled into a funnel attached to a tube that ran back to the rear cockpit and was attached to the earpockets in the student's helmet. The student could not respond to the instructor except by nodding or shaking his head. If an exasperated or angry instructor really wanted to punish a cadet, he held the funnel out in the airstream, and the air pressure build-up in the cadet's ear really got his attention . . . *right away.*

While the Stearman could be flown from either cockpit, our arrangement was instructor in the front cockpit and stu-dent in the rear cockpit, with solo flights flown from the rear cockpit only. There were no flight instruments in the rear cock-pit except a magnetic compass and an altimeter, so the cadet had to learn to fly the airplane by "feel" with reference only to the ground and the horizon—just as we had learned to fly the Cubs and Aeroncas at home. In the Stearman however, we had an additional means of determining performance and airspeed: the wind in the rigging between the wings. It didn't take long to interpret and evaluate airspeed by listening to the wires throughout all the maneuvers of the aircraft. The whole idea here was to learn to fly; learning about instruments and radios and navigational aids would come later after flying the airplane was second nature and auto-responsive.

I took my first flight on October 3, 1942. It lasted about thirty minutes and was a demonstration flight by the instructor with me following through on the controls. Then one day, I was flying with an instructor in the local area doing airwork— pylon eights, crossroad eights, climbing turns, double needle-width 720-degree turns, stalls, spins, and other good stuff— when he retarded the throttle to idle. There was a mirror mounted on the underside of the upper wing in which instructor and student could see each other. I dropped the nose a little to maintain flying speed and looked up at the mirror. He was just sitting there looking at me, saying nothing, so I eased the throttle back on and resumed level flight. He immediately retarded it again, and I repeated my routine of dropping the nose and looking in the mirror. He was really glaring at me this time but still said nothing, so after two or three seconds, I started advancing the throttle again when he grabbed it, held it back, and screamed into the Gosport tube: "Forced landing! Forced landing!" I was thinking, "Well, why the hell didn't you say so—I'm not a mind reader." I looked around below me, picked out a bean field, and set up my plan. I maintained a gliding speed well above stalling, came across the upwind end of the field, turned on a fairly close-in downwind leg, and, monitoring my altitude, turned on a curving, descending base leg into the final approach. I was purposely a little high, and when I had the field made, I sideslipped to lose some altitude, lined up as I crossed the fence and prepared to land. I thought to myself, "Jesus, he's really going to let me land here!" But about ten feet above the ground, he yelled, "I've got it!" He took the controls and opened the throttle. We climbed out of there, heading back to the airbase. I thought, "Well, I guess he didn't like something I did because he isn't letting me fly."

We proceeded on back to the field, and when we were on the final, he suddenly kicked the airplane into a skid, pulled the nose up, and screamed, "You've got it!" I was surprised, but I immediately dropped the nose, gave it a little throttle, lined up with the runway again, chopped the throttle, flared, and landed. Again, he was on the controls yelling, "I've got it!" I was confused, wondering about all his screaming and not knowing what I was doing wrong. He "essed" over to a taxiway parallel to the runway, stopped, and got out of the airplane with his chute. He stood by the rear cockpit, almost nose-to-nose with me, and again started screaming: "How many hours do you have?"

I responded, "Today makes about seven and a half."

"That's not what I meant. How many hours do you have?"

"Oh, well, before I enlisted I went out to our local airport and took a couple of lessons just to see if I liked flying."

He glared at me for a few seconds, probably contemplating my veracity, and then, still screaming, said, "Take off and fly the pattern, and come back here and park the airplane."

I did as I was told. I took off, flew the pattern, landed, and parked the airplane; all the while with an ear-to-ear pig-eating-shit grin on my face that wouldn't come off even after I had parked the airplane. I didn't fly with him after that, so he may have been a pre-solo check pilot—I don't know. When I had said goodbye to my friends at the airport at home, they wished me luck and advised me not to say anything about my flying experience to the Air Corps—"the military has its own ways." So I'd kept still, and, even in this incident, didn't come completely clean.

There was a lot of screaming at cadets in those days. Some of it was the nature of instructors and others who, by tradition, treated the neophytes and plebes with disgust and disdain and made them pay their dues dearly. The other reason though was that the flying schools, whether civilian contract or pure military were under a lot of pressure to provide the pilots that were needed for the war effort. It was therefore imperative that they eliminate quickly those who couldn't make it or who couldn't take the pressure-physically or psychologically. They didn't have time to do otherwise. I don't recall exact figures, but it seems to me that our washout rate was about 30 or 35 percent at the primary flight school level. It was the "boot camp" of indoctrination into flying.

I soloed on my eleventh flight after just under eight hours in the first two weeks of training. After a few more solo flights, I met Bill Janss, who became my instructor for the rest of Primary Flight School. We liked each other and remained friends for the rest of our lives until his death in 1996. We always had a joke between us about which of us taught the other to fly—Bill said I taught him, but of course, he taught me. I remember once, when I was having trouble coming out of snap rolls with the wings level—I seemed to always be a little too soon or a little too late—Bill and I went out and did nothing but snap rolls for two hours until I could almost do it right. We learned most aerobatic maneuvers—loops, chandelles, Immelmans, slow rolls, snap rolls and barrel rolls, lazy eights, the falling leaf, "split S," slips, wingovers, and, of course, stalls and spins. I tried a few hammerhead stalls once, but after sliding back on my tail once, and whipping over into a spin once, I gave it up.

Primary training lasted just over two months, and we each accumulated between sixty and sixty-five hours of flying time. Then it was on to Basic where we were introduced to an all-metal, low-wing, enclosed-cockpit airplane with a 450-horse-power Pratt and Whitney engine driving a controllable pitch propeller. It was affectionately (or sometimes derisively) but universally called the "Vultee Vibrator." It had a full panel in both cockpits, radios, and an intercom system. Here the positions were reversed—the cadet flew from the front cockpit solo or dual, and the instructor occupied the rear seat. I was assigned to Minter Field just north of Bakersfield, California. This was not a contract school—all the personnel were U.S. Army Air Corps, including all of the instructors.

After checking out in the airplane, including aerobatics, we settled in for a somewhat different phase of training. We started formation flying, night flying, radio procedures, reading maps and charts, cross country flying (first using only charts and landmarks and later with radio and navaids), and the introduction to instrument flying. We also began learning military flying techniques like coming down the runway about 500 feet above pattern altitude in formation and then peeling off individually at precise intervals and diving into the downwind leg. Pretty. Instead of the standard 45-degree approach to the downwind leg at pattern altitude, we learned to make 360-degree overhead approaches from about 1,500 or 2,000 feet, sometimes from a formation, planning the circle so we ended up at the runway threshold at about fifty feet over the fence. We also practiced formation takeoffs and short field takeoffs and landings. We had three auxiliary fields, so we could practice all this without creating a traffic nightmare at the home base.

About halfway through our training, a "Tule" ground fog settled in the southern end of the San Joaquin valley, and we couldn't fly. There was considerable concern about being able to graduate the class on time, so the whole operation was moved to Bishop, California, to finish training. There were more cadets than airplanes, so an instructor and a cadet were assigned to each BT-13 for the trip, and the rest of the personnel went by ground transportation. My squadron commander, Capt. "Willie" Cumpston selected me to fly with him, and off we went—across the Tehachapi Mountains to Mojave and Trona and up the Owens Valley to Bishop. This was the longest cross-country flight I had ever made—four hours and thirty minutes. Because there were no navaids at that time on the eastern slope of the Sierra Nevada, it was strictly by landmarks.

We were the only ones at Bishop, so the field atmosphere was more relaxed and less military oriented than a typical Army air base. We went skiing at Mammoth Mountain in our time off—the first experience for most of us. Captain Willie broke his leg, but it didn't slow him down much—he just went on flying with a cast on one leg.

There were also more substantive benefits at Bishop. At Oxnard and Bakersfield, there was rarely any wind beyond a light breeze, but at Bishop there was plenty, and there were usually lenticular clouds in the sky indicating very strong upper atmosphere winds. We got invaluable experience in crosswind takeoffs and landings and mountain flying because of the turbulent air and major downdrafts on the leeside of the Sierra. Trying to fly formation in some of that turbulence really sharpened our reflexes and piloting skills. We lost one cadet in that flying atmosphere. He apparently flew up a box canyon and didn't turn around before the ground rose up and the sides closed in; he was past the decision point and hit the side of the canyon. This was a situation where I thought a hammerhead stall might have gotten him out of it, but I don't know—I wasn't there. With a heavy flying schedule, we each got our minimum time in—my logbook shows seventy-four hours and forty minutes—and we returned to Bakersfield for graduation.

The assignment to Advanced Flying School saw the class broken up, with some going to Twin-Engine Advanced and others going to Single-Engine Advanced. The selection was presumably made by a cadet's flying instructor and squadron commander based on their evaluation of a cadet's propensity and proclivity for bombers or fighters, his flying skills, and his overall grades. But who really knew? The Army's decisions were almost always a mystery to those who were affected. Anyway, I was assigned to Yuma Army Air Base, Yuma, Arizona. This was a Single-Engine Advanced School where I would fly the North American AT-6 and become a fighter pilot—exactly what I had wanted since enlisting.

The first sight of AT-6s on the line started a love affair that never ended. Here was an airplane that had to be one of the finest ever designed for its time and purpose. It had a superb airframe by North American, retractable gear, an exceptionally reliable high-performance Pratt and Whitney engine of 650 horsepower and a Hamilton-Standard controllable pitch propeller—a collection of features that together couldn't be surpassed and that resulted in a pilot's airplane of outstanding flight capability and performance. The U.S. Navy used them to train their future carrier pilots, and theirs were designated SNJs; the Canadians trained their fighter pilots in them and designated them NA-66 Harvards. Thailand, China, and New Zealand all used them, as well as twenty-six other nations. For many small countries around the world in the late 1930s and early 1940s, the AT-6—with three or four .30-caliber machine guns mounted on it—constituted their front line fighter. We couldn't wait to get all that power in our hands. (One of the people on the administrative staff at Yuma was Capt. Barry M. Goldwater, who later came to national prominence as the 1964 Republican candidate for President of the United States. He was Director of Ground Training in 1943.)

There is a quotation attributed to Ernest Hemingway that expresses a sentiment probably common to many pilots as they progress in their flying careers. "You love a lot of things if you live around them. But there isn't any woman, and there isn't any horse, not any before nor any after, that is as lovely as a great airplane. And the men who love them are faithful to them even though they may leave them for others. Man has one virginity to lose in fighters, and if it is a lovely airplane he loses it to, there is where his heart will forever be."

I don't know whether the AT-6 qualifies as my first love, but it was close. My career took a different course, and although I ached to get into the P-51, it was not to be. Had I transitioned into a P-51, it certainly would have been that "lovely airplane." I do, however, think the sentiment has always applied to my attitude about flying in general—any flying, just being in the air. Maybe in that sense I lost my virginity to that Travelair in 1931 even though I was only a passenger, or maybe to that first J-3 Cub. It was not just the aircraft itself so much as what it did

for me, where it got me, where it put me, and how. My love for
flying has never diminished.

At Yuma, we continued the routine of the Primary and
Basic Schools—with part of the day devoted to ground school
and part to flying—but in Advanced there was more emphasis
on flying, and the course consisted of more hours in the air
than the previous schools, and that suited me just fine. There
also was an emphasis in ground school on several courses that
we had only touched on in Primary and Basic, one being
Aircraft Identification. We got so we could recognize all the
German, Japanese, or Allied aircraft just from a quick glance at
a silhouette or a frontal view. This would be very important
once we got into combat. I seem also to remember that the
physical training was tougher. I can recall getting back to
the barracks out of breath and exhausted, but at that age we
recovered quickly.

Flying, though, was our principal activity. The weather in
southern Arizona in the winter brought clear skies and mild
temperatures, so we flew every day. After the BT-13, checkout
in the AT-6 came pretty naturally. At this point in our training,
we were expected to know how to fly, so the adaptation to a
new airplane could be accomplished rather quickly. Therefore,
training emphasized the progression to combat tactics.

The checkout included all the systems of the new airplane,
its performance parameters, lots of takeoffs and landings, and
all the basic aerobatics. Landing the AT-6 was duck soup if you
nailed the approach speed correctly. It would settle nicely into
a three-point rendezvous with mother earth, but if you didn't, it
could get a little complicated. Once we had achieved proficiency in the essentials, our curriculum stressed formation
flying, both ground and aerial gunnery, low-level target acquisition and strafing, aerial combat (dogfighting), navigation, day
and night cross-country flying, more instrument flying than
we'd had up to then, and night operations without lights.

We flew a lot of formation—the artistry of military flying—
including various echelons, single-file stacks, and simple three-
plane vee elements. This not only developed flying proficiency

but would help in combat to concentrate armament and fire-power in offensive situations and to protect ourselves in defensive situations. We also practiced a lot of low-level formation—fifty feet above ground level, plus or minus depending on obstacles and terrain. There were times when a ground-level view across the desert revealed nothing but chaparral when suddenly five or six airplanes would appear to be climbing right out of the ground. That would be a single-file (follow-the-leader) formation flying down in the All-American Canal when a bridge forced them into the air.

We learned a tactic to find our way if lost: fly until you intercept a railroad track, then follow the track until you came to a town, then circle the town at low altitude, picking out obstacles like radio towers and church steeples, and railroad semaphore signal towers, then drop down to about ten or twenty feet off the deck, fly up the track and read the railroad station sign, then climb up to about 500 feet and find the town on the map. Then you knew where you were. However, we used this procedure as an excuse to buzz and terrorize every little town and hamlet in southern Arizona. Or maybe just a railroad water stop or a cattle water tank. The cows really took off. It was fun for us, and no resident ever reported us or complained. There was a war on, after all.

As a matter of fact, we did quite a bit of "buzzing" as a legitimate training exercise, the purpose of which was learning to fly low as a means of avoiding radar detection and searching for targets of opportunity to strafe. We learned to do it safely, or at least with a knowledge of all the hazards that might be encountered. I once took a ride in the bombardier's seat in an A-20 out over the Mojave Desert on the same kind of flight, except the A-20 was an attack bomber rather than a fighter, but the purpose of the mission was the same. Watching the ground go by under you at 25 feet and 250 miles per hour was quite a thrill.

Map and aeronautical chart reading also became important for navigation planning and execution and for learning to interrelate the surveying of the landscape and interpreting what you were looking at below. I have flown all over the country under visual flight rules (VFR) with just my observations and the chart on my knee. I maintained a desired course by flying toward a selected prominent landmark on the horizon, picking subsequent landmarks when that one was achieved, noting all the geographical features along the way, and cross-referencing map to ground and ground to map, all the while noting and recording time segments—just like the scouts of 100 or 150 years ago navigated on the ground by noting a certain tree, stream, rock outcropping, promontory, or other geographical feature. We had better maps and charts, and our view from the air was unlimited and all encompassing, but we were doing essentially the same thing. Most pilots whom I knew became efficient at this with practice. If they didn't, they got lost.

Dogfighting was a serious aerial ballet for both the victor and the vanquished. We usually approached each other head-on, and at the moment of passing, wingtip to wingtip, we would each roll into a steep bank toward the other, and the fight was on to get on the other's tail and get him in the gun sights. We had to be careful not to exceed the limits of the airplane in our zeal; the airspeed redline for the AT-6 was 251 miles per hour, and the positive "G" load limit was nine "Gs." There was a "G" meter located up under the panel where it could not be seen by the pilot, but it was checked by the ground crew after every flight to be sure the limits had not been exceeded. I got to be pretty good at this, in part because of a little trick I taught myself which worked whether I was pursuing or being pursued. It was simply to chop the throttle momentarily and pull the stick back sharply so the nose would swing up through the target at the moment of firing. If I was being pursued, the tactic also worked by putting me farther inside the arc of my pursuer, and sometimes he would go screaming by underneath me when I would roll hard into him and then I would be on his tail. We also played "hunt and stalk," and the advantage here was almost always altitude—being on top. After takeoff, I'd sneak off somewhere on the deck away from the traffic and the practice areas, climb to eight or ten thousand feet and go hunting for AT-6s below.

When I sighted one, I'd roll on my back and dive on him. If he saw me coming, he'd start evasive action, and the dogfight was on. If he didn't see me, then he was a dead duck. These hunts taught us an invaluable lesson: when flying, you never had your head "in the cockpit"—your head was on a swivel, and your eyes constantly scanned the sky around you—above, below, ahead, behind, and to the sides. In combat, this could save our lives. Of course, all the dogfighting was done with gun cameras, not live ammunition.

About halfway through our training at Yuma, we were visited for about ten days by a group of RAF (Royal Air Force) pilots on a PR (public relations) and R&R (rest and relaxation) mission. They were "lend-lease" in reverse. They were Eton and Oxford men, spoke the King's English, and were, above all, gentlemen and superb pilots. They had flown Spitfires and Hurricanes all through the Battle of Britain in 1940 and 1941. While temporarily assigned to Yuma, they flew with us, opposed us in dogfights, and taught us many things they had learned in fighting the Germans. They were "hail fellows, well met," and I both admired and respected them—for what they had been through, for their abilities, and for teaching us what they did.

Their leader was a handsome, dapper little Scotsman with a clipped blond mustache whose name was McDonough or Donaldson or McDonald—I'm close, but can't quite remember—with the rank of wing commander. As part of his deal with the two governments and the Army Air Corps, his entourage was always accompanied by three or four giggling, squealing, bubbly, jumping young Hollywood starlets to add gaiety and spice to his mission (and his pleasure). You know the type—effervescent, like Alka Seltzer, only better. "Brevity" of dress both top and bottom was, of course, the order of the day for them—weather permitting, short shorts and brief halters.

The P-51D had just become operational, and there were not many of them around. Of course, the Scotsman had one—America's fastest and most versatile fighter. He would fly cross-country in it with a passenger (one of the other pilots, I would think) without parachutes. He never flew more than about fifty feet off the ground anyway, so who needed a parachute? The passenger would sit on the bottom with his butt in the bucket usually filled by a parachute, and the wing commander would sit on his lap, working the throttle and the stick while the fellow on the bottom worked the rudder pedals, and off they would go, hell bent for election. Anyway, the purpose of this little descriptive preamble is to segue into his morale-building and instructive exhibitions for all who were privileged to see him perform.

Everybody on the base, including the brass and visiting VIPs (even the mess hall cooks would come out to see this guy), would turn out and gather along the taxiway in front of the tower as the commander fired up and headed for the approach end of the runway. He didn't "ess"—he just made a beeline for his run-up spot. We heard the distinctive bark and whine of the big Merlin's exhaust as he turned all the horses loose and streaked toward us. When abreast of the crowd, I swear, he didn't levitate an inch; he just retracted the gear, and then, with a shallow nose up, he executed an eight-point roll on takeoff—the wingtips barely clearing the ground. As we watched in awe, he gained some altitude off the end of the field and swung around downwind so he could dive for the speed he wanted and went into a routine of continuous loops and rolls: vertical rolls, Cuban eights, speed runs on the deck, and I have forgotten what else. Then his finale: straight as an arrow down the runway on the deck, then, in front of the crowd, up into a tight loop, scribing a perfect circle and probably not exceeding 600 feet at the top. Two-thirds of the way up, the gear came out and, at the top of the loop, with the plane on its back, were fully extended. In the first quarter of the downside of the loop, the flaps deployed and he shut off the engine. He completed the loop with a dead-stick landing, and as the airplane decelerated, he threw the canopy back, climbed out of the cockpit and ran off the wingtip without a backward glance. The 51 rolled to a stop 100 or 150 feet away, and the crowd started surging toward him with the screaming starlets in the lead. They threw their arms around him and clung to him as he approached the crowd and acknowledged the applause and accolades directed at him. We could hardly believe what we had just witnessed, and we wondered whether we could ever achieve such superior command of an airplane.

Years later, after the war, on several occasions I saw Bob Hoover, the renowned and legendary North American test and exhibition pilot do a very similar routine in both the P-51 and the Shrike. As a matter of fact, Bob's execution was so perfect and the aerodynamic forces were so well in synchronization at exactly one "G" that a glass of water which he placed on the cowl remained there without spilling a drop. I have heard that sometimes he actually poured water in the glass while upside down in the roll and the water flowed up into the glass. I talked to Bob once after one of his shows about the finale of the loop and dead-stick landing, and he said, "That's just very efficient use of the kinetic energy remaining in the airplane." Talk about understatement! But he was right. However, the Yuma exhibition was the first time I had ever seen such a performance.

Gunnery school was instituted in the last few weeks of our training, and I was in the top percentile of my class in both ground and aerial gunnery. I received a grade of 100 percent in the course, and the number of hits in the targets earned an "expert" rating for me. I attributed my success in part to the fact that, since the age of eight or nine, I had been hunting ducks and pheasants and therefore understood lead and range. For all of us, but particularly for those cadets without such experience, there was a skeet range on the base, and its use was compulsory. I also taught myself to shoot in very short bursts—not to spray bullets all over the sky—and, on ground targets, to reduce power in the dive on the target to minimize the effect of torque on the trajectory of the bullets. This, too, was a lot of fun—the combination of flying and marksmanship was exhilarating, and we came back from each gunnery session talking about our hits. We also qualified with the U.S. Government Model 1911 .45-caliber auto pistol, and the Thompson .45-caliber-submachine gun (the "Tommy gun").

We did enough night flying to make us comfortable and competent, including several night cross-country flights. At the home field, we made takeoffs and flew the pattern in single file, then landed in the dark without lights of any kind except runway boundary lights—no landing lights on the airplanes were used, and no navigation lights except the white light on the tail so that we would not overtake another AT-6. There were some combat stations in the war zones where this would be pretty much standard operating procedure.

Instrument flying became important in Advanced. By graduation I had sixteen hours of hooded instrument time in the AT-6 and about eleven hours in the Link Trainer, a simulator that enabled us to fly the radio ranges and make procedure letdowns and approaches to airfields all while bolted to the floor in a miniature airplane with a full-sized cockpit and all the navaids.

As completion of the Aviation Cadet Pilot Training Program approached, I was reaching a pinnacle of confidence, self-reliance, resolve, and self-assurance. As Beryl Markham said in her classic *West with the Night*, "I saw how man can be master of a craft, and how a craft can be master of an element." We were masters of our element and of the craft with which we conquered that element. I perceived the airplane as an extension of my being, as though my nerves extended to the wingtips and the control surfaces. I wasn't just driving and manipulating a machine according to an instruction manual; I was in harmony with the subtleties and forces of the aerodynamics of flight; I was "flying" as much as any bird ever did. With my brain and eyes, I brought an aluminum and fabric structure to vibrant life, doing in some ways things a bird never thought of. Mine was not a mundane trip through the air like flying as a passenger on an airliner; mine was a thrilling exploration of the atmosphere and everything on the earth below— to climb, to dive, to turn and roll, to follow this ridge, to dip into that valley, to follow that dirt road or that stream.

Our heads were held high as we stood at attention on the parade ground in officer's pinks and white gloves, and our chests swelled with pride as we listened to the band playing martial music and the Air Corps song at our graduation ceremony. We had an enthusiastic, shared sense of common purpose; we had high morale; we had esprit de corps; we stood tall; we were the "Top Guns" of our day; we were hot; we were the best; we were invincible; we owned the sky; and we had the world by the tail. At last we were to be officially admitted to the elite brotherhood of pilots and to receive the coveted wings of a U.S. Army Air Corps pilot, as well as—perhaps not as important as the wings—second lieutenant's bars. Money came with the bars, too: our pay increased from $75 per month to $245 per month. I wondered what I would do with all that lucre.

I had invited a girl whom I had met and dated a few times while we were stationed in southern California to come to Yuma for our graduation. Her parents consented as long as she traveled with a close friend, who could be a chaperone as well as a blind date for Don Purdy, one of my classmates. After the ceremony, we squired them around the base, showed them an AT-6, and took them to the officers' club, to which we were now admitted—all to the envious stares of most of our classmates: "Hey, those guys have girls!" We later took them to Yuma's only visitor attraction, the old territorial prison just north of town, and then to dinner someplace in greater downtown Yuma. While neither the girls nor their parents had said anything to Don or me, we understood the parameters of their entrusting their daughters to us, so when we took them back to their hotel, we took them in our arms and kissed them goodnight. Then it was back to the air base for us. Different times. Different morals. Principles. Responsibility. Respect.

We lay awake that night, probably thinking about the girls but mostly about what our next assignment would be, where we would go, and what we would fly.

CHAPTER 4

First Assignment

The next few days were spent in frustrated anxiety. First, orders came through for transfer of the class to Florida for transition to P-38s and then, presumably, on to the ETO (European Theater of Operations), but five of us were not on the list. So we stewed about it: Why not? Something better in store for us? But what could have been better than P-38s? (Only P-51s!) Were we to stay at Yuma as instructors? We were told at one point that we were being held for other assignments because we were the top of the class, but we didn't buy that because we knew others in the class whose grades were as good as ours. That line sounded like some kind of a bone they were throwing at us to keep us quiet, but we weren't in a conciliatory frame of mind.

A few more days went by during which we assuaged our frustration by flying every chance we got, wringing out the AT-6 and, one day, an AT-9 that arrived at the field. A couple of us just sort of commandeered it. (Remember, we were officers now.) We sat side-by-side instead of in tandem. We had no twin-engine experience or check out, but what could be so difficult? It was an airplane, wasn't it? It had two engines, which were started one at a time, but once they were running, the only difference was that you had two throttles in your hand. We had no experience with asymmetrical thrust—with us it was thrust or no thrust, and it was longitudinal—but we didn't expect to lose an engine, and if we did, we'd handle it. Maybe not by the book, but we'd handle it. So we flew it.

I was also involved in checking out in one of the P-40s on the field. The first step was to fly the AT-6 from the rear cockpit (with a check pilot in front since solo flight from the rear was prohibited) to get used to all that nose out in front of you and the resulting change in perspective and visibility. The second step was to study the operating manual for the airplane and become familiar with its systems. The third step was to sit in the cockpit for hours if necessary, practicing the placement of your hands on every control and switch until you memorized it and could pass a blindfold test. There would be no instructor with you the first time you flew this airplane, so you'd better know what you were doing.

I was involved in this when orders for the five of us came through. We were to report to Victorville Army Air Base at Victorville, California. We immediately asked, "What do they have at Victorville?" Someone said they had dive bombers. The groaning response from all of us: "Dive bombers? We're fighter pilots! Not dive bomber pilots!" But when in the Army, you go where the Army sends you.

When we arrived at Victorville, we found a training command facility engaged in training bombardiers, bomb approach pilots, and navigators (or to be more accurate, navigator/bombardiers) in the AT-11. This airplane was developed from the twin-engine Beechcraft D-18 by installing small vertical bomb bays on each side of the fuselage behind the cockpit and redesigning the nose for the Sperry or Norden bombsight and a seat for the bombardier. It carried ten hundred-pound bombs. It was powered by bulletproof Pratt and Whitney radials of 450 horsepower each and was a nice flying airplane. Its distinguishing visual feature was the empennage—twin vertical stabilizers and rudders a la the Lockheed Lodestars and other Lockheed transports. You entered it through a door instead of climbing up on a wing and throwing your leg into the cockpit. However, it more or less represented, for us, the end of the pursuit type of flying around the countryside. Like any airplane, it would do a beautiful barrel roll, but the other stuff was pretty much prohibited beyond steep climbing turns and dives. We flew a lot of low-level missions, so our low-level backgrounds were appropriate, but the training routine dictated mostly precision straight and level flying.

We had a few dry lakebeds in the area—Harper's Dry Lake, Rogers Dry Lake, and Muroc Dry Lake (the last two are now known as Edwards Air Force Base)—which we used as auxiliary fields. About the second or third day that I was there, I went out to one of the dry lakes with an AT-11 check-out pilot and transitioned to twin engine in about two hours: takeoffs and landings, stalls (both dirty and clean—we didn't spin this airplane), and engine-out procedures at lift-off and then in normal flight. In the last engine-out exercise, the checkout pilot shut off the ignition and fuel to the "dead engine," completely shutting it down. He said he had never done that before, but I had a lot of dry lakebed ahead of me to maneuver and land. We had controllable pitch props, but we could not feather them, so on a "dead" engine, the prop continued to windmill and create drag. But it was all manageable, and I considered the twin-engine capability and rating as one more step in my flying accomplishments and education.

There were other systems to learn about in this airplane besides flying it. One of the most important was the operation of the AP-1 Autopilot, which was new to me since we didn't have autopilots in the single-engine airplanes. This device would maintain course and altitude as well as enable the pilot to make precision controlled turns and changes in attitude, but its most important function resulted from its being interconnected and slaved to the bombsight. This meant that corrective input by the bombardier as he sighted his target would result in course and heading changes by the airplane. In other words, when the bombardier moved his crosshairs to correct course or drift in relation to the target on the ground, the corrections were accomplished immediately by the airplane through the autopilot.

Our bombing range was scattered over the Lucerne Valley east of the airbase, and we flew prescribed patterns from one target to another as two or more cadets took turns on the bombsight while the pilot and/or the bombardier instructor (if one was on board) spotted the hits. The targets were circular markings on the ground with a simple wood pyramid—"the shack"—in the center for an aiming point. We flew missions at altitudes of 500 to 11,000 feet both day and night. On the night missions flown at 11,000 feet, we used oxygen from the ground up. 11,000 feet wasn't really all that high, but it was believed that our mental alertness and visual acuity would be enhanced by breathing oxygen. We wore the standard green rubber masks that covered our mouths and noses. The supply was a "demand" system. When you inhaled, a check valve at the top of the bottle opened and let the oxygen flow; exhaling closed the valve and your breath escaped through a vent in the mask. The cadets had to maintain a certain average CE (circular error) in order to stay in the course and graduate. The bombs we used were hundred-pound smoke bombs, which made spotting the impact easy.

Like the pilot's schools, there was a certain "washout" rate for those cadets who couldn't hack the course for one reason or another. I remember one kid who flunked out because he couldn't keep his cookies down. He'd put his helmet down beside the bombsight and start the aiming process, then lean over and flash his hash in his helmet, and then go back to sighting through the bombsight eyepiece, but in a few minutes he was barfing in his helmet again. Several times, I put him in the copilot's seat and let him follow me through on the controls and get a different perspective on the land below, and he was okay then. His problem may have been the disorienting feeling brought on by viewing the earth sliding by through the magnified aperture of the sight. Much as he wanted to be a bombardier, we had to wash him out.

A couple of years later, in the offensive against Japan, we had a B-29 bombardier who flew a lot of missions but had the opposite problem from my washed-out cadet. He reportedly never went over the target in the bombardier's seat—he went over strapped to the on-board toilet in the rear of the B-29, and the pilot dropped the bombs while he dropped something else.

We also taught the cadets pilotage and dead-reckoning navigation. On the crews of many of the small bombers, the individual crew designation was for the combined position: navigator/bombardier. One man functioned in both capacities. So this required cross-country flights to enable them to practice navigation skills. Occasionally a mission was scheduled to combine both objectives—navigate to the target and bomb it, just like combat. As reported in Dusty Worthen's book *Against All Odds*, one cadet in his class got carried away in his enthusiasm and determination. He navigated to San Bernardino, found his target, completed a classic approach and bomb run, and bombed the railroad marshaling yards. I don't know why they had bombs on board; it was only to be a simulated run. No one on the ground was hurt, and the damage was slight, but there was plenty of ass-chewing about that one.

On another occasion, a similar mission was scheduled to be flown at night over Los Angeles. From Victorville we popped over Mt. San Antonio (Mt. Baldy) in the San Gabriel range at 11,000 feet and suddenly saw the spectacular panorama of lights of the whole Los Angeles basin. We were fascinated with the view—none of us had ever seen anything like it before. The West Coast Defense Command had been alerted, and they treated our invasion like a real air raid except that they didn't shoot at us. I don't know whether they alerted the populace or set off the air raid sirens, but they did have all the searchlights going. However, they treated the occasion like a Hollywood movie premier, and the lights danced around the sky criss-crossing each other and going on and off. A light would hit us for two or three seconds and then flick on to something else—nothing like the intensity and concentration I would experience over Japan a couple of years later. We made a wide swing over the basin, then back across the mountains to Pearblossom, Littlerock, and the airbase.

I also was involved in training bomb-approach pilots. I would have thought that this technique would have been taught in twin-engine advanced flying school, but it wasn't. I taught pilots how to fly the bomb run from the initial point to the target, how to set up the autopilot, and how to coordinate with the bombardier. After a while I could bomb pretty well myself without the bombsight. I could hold my toe up in the nose and use it for a sight and hit fairly close. Of course, I was flying the same range everyday, day in and day out, and the practice gave me the knowledge of the trajectory of the bomb, and as a pilot, I could see and correct drift accurately without optical aids. This only worked at the lower altitudes, I couldn't do it very well from 11,000 feet.

We flew all the time—about a hundred hours a month. There were days when I was on the line for twelve or fourteen hours, flying 1.5–2 hour missions the whole time. I complained in some of my letters of being tired out—they were working us too hard—there was too much pressure—but there was a war on.

One day, I took off with a couple of cadets on board for a cross-country navigation mission to Kingman, Arizona, just as a major winter storm was moving into southern California. I was one of only two or three airplanes to get off. I was running ahead of the storm with a tailwind, but it was catching up. By the time we reached Kingman, the return flight was looking very iffy, but I wanted to get back; staying overnight in Kingman didn't appeal to me at all. I flew back into the weather and kept descending to stay under the clouds. I told the cadets to put away their computers and plotters and brought them up front with me. I put one in the nose and one in the copilot's seat and told them that I would show them another way to navigate. It was called "flying the iron compass." I picked up the railroad track, dropped down to about fifty or seventy-five feet, and followed it west. I had the cadets watch for traffic since forward visibility wasn't that good—water was streaming up the windshield in heavy sheets, but side and oblique visibility wasn't so bad. I met a Marine pilot in a Corsair doing the same thing that I was but in the opposite direction. Fortunately, we were each "driving on the right side of the road." I knew the country like the back of my hand, and so I continued my course until I reached the Mojave River, turned south in the riverbed, and, when I passed the smokestacks of the cement plant on the bank, called the Victorville Tower. A surprised tower operator answered with "Where are you? The field is closed!" I told him that I was in the riverbed and to watch the east end of the field for me in five minutes. At the appropriate spot, I climbed out of the riverbed, popped over the bluff, lowered the gear, and landed. The cadets were impressed. I don't know what the tower operator thought.

When I had a couple of cadets on board who had done a good job on the targets and who obviously enjoyed what they were doing, I rewarded them with the question, "You guys want to buzz one of the dude ranches on the way home?" I never got a "Well, ah, uh, do you think we should?" or anything like that. It was always "Sure!" "You bet!" "Lets go!" There was a particular ranch located about in the middle of the valley that I liked to buzz. Many of the married bombardier instructors lived there and commuted to the field every day. Their wives, who had nothing else to do, were usually in their bathing suits around the pool getting a tan, so I had a good audience. I had worked out a plan for this ranch that always seemed to take them by surprise. It was just like selecting a ground target for strafing. The valley was sparsely settled and those few residents were accustomed to seeing and hearing AT-11s in the air more or less constantly and didn't pay too much attention to them as long as everything seemed normal. I would follow the ridge of the mountains bordering the south side of the valley until I was about abreast of the ranch and then I'd throttle back and begin a dive that maintained a constant descent and followed the sloping terrain down the mountainside toward the ranch. With the reduced power, they didn't ever appear to hear me coming, and because I was not silhouetted against the sky, they didn't see me either. In the dive, with the throttles back, I'd advance the prop controls, and then, just before my arrival, I'd pour the coal to it, making the props wind up into a high-pitched screaming whine just as, almost over the pool, I rolled into a vertical ninety-degree turn and then rolled out, bringing the girls to their feet. I then climbed up, heading for the field. When we got back, we heard about a couple of women on the phone to the base, shrieking, "Your crazy hot-rod pilots are going to kill our husbands!" But the way I executed the buzz job, nobody on the ground—at least around the pool and quarters—could see a number on the airplane. All they could see was "U.S. ARMY" across the wing. I was discreet about the frequency of buzzing this particular ranch, so I never heard anything about it from my superiors at the airbase.

In the twelve months that I was based at Victorville, we only had one crash, and it had nothing to do with buzzing or any other unauthorized flying maneuver. It was a case of pilot error and a lack of attention to flying technique. They were flying a low-level (500 feet) bombing mission and caught a wingtip on the ridge of a low hill located to the left of the target. They cartwheeled across the desert, breaking the airplane in pieces and killing everyone on board. I don't remember whether a board of inquiry was convened, but I wanted to know what had happened. The weather had been clear and calm. There was no evidence of airframe failure (until it hit the ground), engine failure, or mechanical malfunction, so it had to have been human error. I was familiar with the target, so I went out and flew the course just as that pilot must have done. I had the bomb bay doors open and flew the approach in the standard pattern, and then, at the point when the bomb would have dropped, I threw my right arm over the seatback, and strained to look straight down through the open bomb bay door, watching for the target to slide by underneath so I could spot the hit. You can try this in your car—put your left hand on the steering wheel, your left foot on the clutch pedal (or brake), throw your right arm over the seatback, and look straight down at the floor in the back seat. What happens? Your left arm will extend tending to turn the wheel left, and your left leg will extend, tending to depress the pedal. That's exactly what happened when the pilot attempted to spot the hit and he rolled into a left turn without realizing it. At 500 feet, it takes only a few seconds to descend to the ground, and in this case it was less than 500 feet because the ridge was 150 or 200 feet high. I was positive I had discovered what had happened and how it had happened, but not why. Why didn't the pilot perceive that the ground he was looking at was moving sideways instead of straight back under him? I had spotted targets thousands of times, and I would have noticed this immediately and quickly glanced forward. And why didn't somebody else on board yell at him? Those things remained a mystery.

The first time I ever lost an engine in an airplane was in the AT-11. It wasn't that bulletproof Pratt and Whitney out on the right wing, though, but the mechanical linkage between the cockpit and the engine nacelle. I had been flying at 11,000 feet with the mixture leaned out for the thinner air, and the control lever became jammed as I descended, starving the engine for fuel. I did everything by the book—flew the pattern on one engine and landed without incident. It was my first emergency—just what we practiced for—but I decided that I wouldn't do it that way again: I would make a straight-in approach. Later in my career, I lost engines many times in B-29s and always made a straight-in approach to land.

On another occasion, I was droning along peacefully on a clear winter afternoon, the sun through the windshield bathing me in its warmth and making me just a little bit drowsy. My eyelids were at about half-mast when suddenly both engines quit. I came bolt upright in my seat and immediately understood and appreciated the expression "the silence was deafening." It was. My responses were deliberate and automatic. I dropped the nose to maintain flying speed, switched the fuel selector valve to another tank, and hit the wobble pump handle, operating it back and forth. It took a few seconds for the engines to resume their reassuring sound as they were again supplied with fuel. There were some wide eyes visible on board, but I didn't say anything to anyone and let them think that this was normal, just a part of the flying experience. However, that little shot of adrenaline kept me awake for the rest of the flight.

I gained a reputation on the field for competency. One of my superior officers in operations said one day in my presence and the presence of several others, "If you have a tough flying assignment, give it to Robbie—he can fly better by the seat of his pants than most people can by instruments." His metaphorical statement was a little off the mark—the last thing you want to be doing is flying by the seat of your pants when you are on instruments. That leads to graveyard spirals. However, he meant his remark as a compliment and recommendation.

All armies, since the beginning of time, have had to contend with the problems of soldier education and control to prevent the ranks from being decimated by disease or sickness and, in particular, by that insidious ailment resulting usually from a little intentional immoral debauchery or just the libidinous urges of young men. Military organizations have always been essentially male endeavors, isolated from ordinary social contacts except at those infrequent times when passes and leaves of absence let them loose on the rest of the populace.

In the World War II army, the education part of the problem was addressed by mandatory attendance imposed on all personnel to view VD movies at the base theater depicting the most gruesome, grotesque, grisly examples of untreated venereal disease imaginable. Close up, in technicolor. Both male and female. Treatment also was depicted that, until the discovery of penicillin, was so excruciatingly painful for men that, it was hoped, it would make a soldier so allergic to women as to alienate them completely—at least for the duration of his leave. In addition to that, there were instructions to the soldiers on preventive steps to be taken after exposure and a list of off-base first-aid stations where they could get preventive treatment.

The control part of the problem was to declare certain towns, or parts thereof, off limits to military personnel. MPs patrolled such areas and arrested any soldiers found in the vicinity. Further control was exercised by providing the soldiers on pass with an approved list of houses of prostitution whose inmates were medically supervised and where patrons could get preventive treatment upon leaving. However, even all these measures did not stop the incidence of the "social diseases," so the final element of control was a brief genitalia specific monthly physical examination—usually on, or just before, payday. If a soldier was found to be infected, his pay was withheld and the time it took to cure him (called "bad time") was added on to his enlistment period and an entry made in his medical records about the reason.

In the spring of 1943, the first contingent of WAACs (Women's Auxiliary Army Corps) arrived for duty at our airbase. They filled clerical jobs at headquarters and administrative jobs in other departments around the field. They were accepted but viewed as something of an anomaly or curiosity, and as pilots, aircraft ground echelon, or cadets, we had little direct contact with them as we went about our duties. They were viewed by some as not having the highest morals. One day not too long after their arrival, a bunch of us were on the athletic field for about an hour of calisthenics, and we were winding up the physical training period with a fast, hard game of volleyball. One of the guys said, "Hey, look," and we all drifted over to the edge of the court. There was a whole platoon of WAACs dressed in hats, raincoats, and shoes being marched past the athletic field toward the base hospital. We knew they were naked under the raincoats and so the hoots and catcalls started: "Eee-yow! Ya-hooo! We know where you're go-o-o-o-ing! You'll be s-o-r-r-y-y!" They started blushing, but not a head turned our way. We went back to our game as they proceeded to the hospital where the hats and raincoats were removed and they were paraded for a venereal disease examination. For the boys it was called a shortarm inspection, and for the girls it was called a tunnel inspection.

Victorville was only about a hundred miles from L.A., so most weekends, if we weren't flying, were spent there. I once characterized Victorville Army Air Base as the "Army's utopia—nothing to do but go flying and go courting." Who could ask for anything more? And that's what we did. I had a 1936 Ford Phaeton, and it traveled to L.A. most Saturday afternoons and returned Sunday evenings with two or three passengers in various states of exhaustion and debilitation.

When my mother was young, she attended college in New England and roomed with another young woman with whom she taught school after their graduation. Both ultimately married, my mother and father eventually settling in Omaha, Nebraska, and her friend and her husband ultimately settling in Glendale, California. Each woman had three children—in my family two girls and a boy, and in their family two boys and a girl. The women maintained their friendship over the years until my mothers' death in 1938. I knew of the other family only through my mother's comments and the Christmas package they sent every year with a gift for each of us.

When Uncle Sam sent me to California, I, of course, was duty bound to look up this family that I had known of all my life but had never met. I did this, and by the time I was more

or less permanently based at Victorville, their home had
become my weekend headquarters, and I began dating their
daughter. We toured everything in southern California, from
Mount Wilson to Laguna Beach. One of our favorite Saturday
night hangouts was the old Bar of Music on Melrose Avenue
where we sipped scotch whiskey and listened to the twin grand
pianos render Rachmaninoff, Ravel, and Tchaikovsky. The
courtship blossomed into love, and early in 1944, we were married. I had decided that marriage was appropriate not just
because I was in love, but because I had become convinced
that I was never going to go to war, that I would spend the
duration in the Training Command.

However, within five or six weeks, I received orders for
four-engine transition school at Roswell. I might have suspected something because, during the last two or three months
at Victorville, I was scheduled for a lot of instrument flying. But
I didn't. I just considered that a matter of maintaining proficiency in my instrument flying capabilities. There was also one
other tip-off, but I didn't relate it either. With several other
pilots, I was placed on temporary duty and sent to a medical
flying laboratory at Santa Ana, California. We were given an
extensive physical examination and then put in a hyperbaric
pressure chamber. The pressure was reduced until it equaled
the density of air at 40,000 feet, then slowly increased to the
density at sea level. Our vital signs were again checked. I
couldn't see that I had been affected at all. I breathed oxygen
at the higher altitudes, but I did not suffer the "bends" or any
other impairment during the test or afterwards. Then it was
back to regular duty at Victorville.

Unknown to me (as was most Army planning), the XX
Bomber Command was canvassing the Training Command roster of pilots, looking for high time-experienced people for the
B-29 program—America's newest, biggest, fastest bomber. At
that time, I didn't know that I had been selected for the B-29
program; I had never even heard of a B-29. All I knew was that
I was going to four-engine school, another notch up in my
training and experience.

Despite Army instructions to the contrary—"do not take
dependents with you"—we drove to the new assignment at

Roswell, New Mexico, and found a cozy little unit in a motor court. I say cozy because the bed took up most of the room. There was a toilet and a shower in the space of a closet and a sink that doubled as a wash basin on the wall opposite the bed. A two-burner hot plate was on a nightstand. We could just roll over in bed and turn it on to start the coffee perking. But we were together, and who cared about the quarters? It was only temporary. In the evenings when I was not flying, we would take long walks in the desert behind the motor court. We found all sorts of desert flora and fauna including a big desert tortoise that we brought back to our room one evening. That was a mistake—during the night he peed here and there, and we woke up in the morning to a terrible stench. Out went the tortoise, and my wife washed the floor as I went off to the field.

I enjoyed the desert. At each of my assignments—Bishop, Yuma, Victorville, and Roswell—the weather was dry and hot, which seemed to agree with me, and there was rarely any weather that grounded us. At each station we flew virtually everyday. At Victorville, in the summer, the airplanes would get so hot that you couldn't touch them. We would get in them very gingerly and make quick run-ups and takeoffs to get up to altitudes where it was cool.

The curriculum at Roswell was much like the other transition schools: learning the systems of the new airplane and flying it. Compared to the AT-11, the B-17 was huge—its wingspan was just under 104 feet, and it was 80 feet long. It was not difficult to fly, and it was an exceptionally stable platform for instrument flying which was a major part of our training, as was cross-country flying. Formation flying was also practiced, and this turned out to be a labor-intensive exercise. The big airplane was not as responsive as the airplanes I had previously flown in formation, and so there was a lot more horsing the controls around to stay where you were supposed to be. But, of course, B-17 formations were not as tight either. The course lasted just two months, and I logged about 125 hours. It was just a lot of work and went routinely except for a couple of incidents that are worth recalling.

In those days I was mostly bone and gristle and weighed in at about 125 pounds sopping wet, twice dipped. As in all multi-

engine airplanes, we practiced engine-out emergency procedures. In-flight engine losses in a four-engine airplane were not
a big deal—you determined which engine had malfunctioned,
then you feathered the prop and shut the engine down,
retrimmed the airplane for level flight, and continued the mission. Amazingly, there have been some hairy incidents and perhaps some accidents caused by people who feathered the
wrong engine—a good engine. Anyway, those exercises became
routine. It was practicing engine-out procedures on takeoff
that sometimes became a little exciting. If it was an inboard
engine that failed, there was little effect on the track down the
runway. You feathered it to neutralize the drag, and kept going
with the other three wide open. You might use a little more
runway, but you got airborne. Loss of an outboard engine was
something else. The procedure in this situation was to deter-
mine which engine had failed (this really was a no-brainer,
because the resulting asymmetrical thrust swerved the airplane
to one side or the other), chop the other outboard engine
momentarily so you could reestablish the track down the runway, feather the dead engine, then get on the rudder and feed
the good outboard back to full power to become airborne. All
this had to be accomplished quickly and precisely or else you
would run out of concrete. In practice, of course, we didn't
actually feather the "dead" engine—it remained at idle, contributing to drag until airborne (when the point of the procedure was proved), and was then powered up.

Well, one day I was taking off under full power with the tail
up, and I was committed to fly when the instructor chopped
the throttle on the number four (outboard) engine. I immediately chopped the throttle on the opposite outboard engine,
stood on the rudder pedal, and fed the throttle back up; but
the track on the runway was still edging to one side when I
yelled, "Get on that rudder!" I needed a little help from the
copilot's seat. Just after lift-off, he advanced the throttle on
number four, and we climbed out as I neutralized the rudder.
Though wiry, I was tough and strong, but I wondered if 125
pounds was enough beef to control a B-17 on takeoff with an

outboard engine out. However, I ultimately mastered the technique and went on to complete the course.

The other incident was a navigational training flight to Denver, where we remained overnight. Everybody on the flight got properly swacked, so when we boarded the airplane the next morning, oxygen masks were donned immediately to cure the hangovers. I took off, and somewhere down around Colorado Springs, I bored into a big cumulus cell that I expected to fly through in a matter of minutes, but, to my surprise, I got on an elevator that was pushing me up at about 2,000 feet per minute. I had the throttles back almost to idle and the airplane in a nose down attitude, but to no avail. We blew out of the top of that thing at about 28,000 feet. The moral of the story is that if we had not been polluted the night before, inducing us to put on the masks and breath pure oxygen from the ground up, we'd have died of anoxia in the ascent. Well, maybe not quite, but it makes a good story. It did teach me about the power and velocity of updrafts and downdrafts in thunderstorms, though.

In August 1944 I was sent to the reassignment center at Lincoln, Nebraska, and after a leave of absence, which we spent visiting my father in Omaha, I was ordered to report to Pratt Army Air Base in Pratt, Kansas.

CHAPTER 5

The Big Bird

Our arrival at Pratt, in the rain, on August 24, 1944, was inauspicious. We arrived a day or two before I had to report to the field. I was thinking we would find a hotel while we hunted for an apartment. My orders to this new post had contained the usual admonition: "Dependents should not accompany military personnel; housing conditions are critical." Most of us had ignored this warning and took our wives with us.

Our first stop was at the Roberts Hotel in Pratt at about 4:30 in the afternoon. The lobby was jammed, and the clerk just laughed when I asked for accommodations. I walked back out to the car somewhat dismayed and just a little bit mad, but I wasn't really worried yet—there were three other hotels in town. The next two were just as full as the Roberts, but finally, at the fourth, the Briggs Hotel, the man said he had just one room left. I grabbed it, of course, and went back out to the car to tell my wife the good news. By this time we felt fortunate just to have a roof over our heads.

That hotel was really something. It dated to the 1870s, including its fixtures and furniture. The lobby was open to the roof where there was a huge skylight. The rooms were arranged around this atrium on each floor. There was no elevator; a single wooden staircase ascended from the lobby to the third floor with a landing halfway for the second floor. Every step to the top groaned under our weight.

Our room had a skylight above and a transom over the door to admit light. The ceiling was all of fourteen feet high, and there was one little forty-watt bulb there. Our closet was nothing more than a few nails pounded in the wall. We did have a semi-private bath, though, sharing it with the next room instead of the whole floor. However, there were no locks on the doors, and so to assure privacy, the management supplied us with a long pole which, when you entered the bathroom, you jammed between the two doors so neither could be opened from the outside. Depending on which fixture you were using, it was necessary to duck back and forth under the pole; but it was manageable, albeit humorous. That privacy provision was the subject of a lot of comment afterwards.

The next day, we started apartment hunting but found that to rent one of the available apartments in town required employment in an activity considered essential to the war effort—which did not include flying airplanes for the Air Corps! I guess the logic of that rule was that pilots could live in the BOQ on the airbase. So my wife went out to the field and got a job as a clerk-typist. We then qualified for a furnished apartment. It was huge compared to our one-room motor court; the kitchen was bigger than the whole unit in Roswell. We settled in quickly since everything we owned was in the car. The next day, I reported to Col. Carl R. Storrie, commanding officer of the 29th Bomb Group.

Colonel Storrie assigned me to the 43rd Squadron commanded by Lt. Col. Joseph G. Perry. Colonel Perry was a West Point graduate and had taken his Army flight training in grade; this was his first assignment as CO of a combat outfit. Our operations officer joined us a short time later. He was Maj. Harry L. Evans, a thoroughly likable officer who soon gained the respect and admiration of all the pilots, if not all members of the flight crews. Our executive officer was Capt. Alexander Yearly. He, too, was competent and likable and later became the group intelligence officer. Thus with our squadron organization well underway, we were eager to get to the business of training for combat.

At the time of my reporting in at Pratt, there were only B-17s on the field, no B-29s. The first time I flew a B-29 was about ten days after my arrival when a couple of civilian Boeing pilots brought one over from the factory at Wichita. Two or three of us went out with them, and each of us made a couple of takeoffs and landings. From a pilot's standpoint, the big bird flew beautifully and effortlessly, even nicer than the B-17. I was impressed and pleased with its performance and handling for such a big airplane. It was more responsive than I expected it to be. However, it was the first tricycle-geared airplane I had ever flown, so the landing technique had to change. In the B-17s and AT-11s, we usually made wheel landings and brought the tail down as we decelerated. This technique resulted in less stress on the airframe. In the B-29 this procedure was more or less reversed—we landed a little nose high and brought the nose down as the airplane decelerated. There were a number of advantages to the tricycle gear. For example, the airplane sat level on the ground, greatly improving visibility and simplifying taxiing. It also enabled us to use the brakes more aggressively when necessary without the danger of nosing over. Of course, we had to be careful not to land nosewheel first—it was not designed to take that kind of abuse.

After our takeoff and landing checkout, the Boeing pilots said, "OK, now you guys know as much as we do, so take us back to Wichita." It's somewhat of an exaggeration and over-simplification, but we returned to Pratt and, in effect, started the whole B-29 training process ourselves with that first air-plane. One of the other pilots on that first B-29 flight described the experience as being like "sitting in your bay win-dow and flying your house."

We had Boeing and Air Force manuals on how to fly the B-29, but there were no instructors with B-29 backgrounds and experience like the veteran B-17 pilots who had instructed us in that airplane. The B-29 was too new, and it was still a devel-opmental project long after we started flying it. While I studied the airplane's systems and manuals carefully and thoroughly, I really was self-taught when it came to flying it. Of course, I had been picked for the B-29 program along with many other pilots for my experience and, presumably, flying competence and expertise.

I instinctively liked the airplane very much. It was a sleek, beautiful craft with many innovations in its design. It was aerodynamically very clean: its bullet shaped fuselage had no projections into the slipstream except the turrets and the gunner/scanner blisters. The whole nose of the airplane was a "greenhouse" affording a panoramic perceptibility unequaled in any large aircraft. Visibility was unlimited in every direction except straight up. Butt-jointed skin and flush riveting added to its slipperiness. It had a completely new, long, thin, low-drag, high-performance, high-speed wing design with a newly conceived spar construction. Massive Fowler-type flaps enabled it to sustain lift at the low speeds necessary for landing. The area of the flaps alone was greater than the whole wing on a P-51, and the wing loading was twice that of the B-17. The gear was completely enclosed when retracted and in clean configuration (flaps and gear up and cowl flaps closed or nearly so), it was very fast. The specifications were impressive, both for its size and for its time. Depending on fuel load, bomb load, and altitude: top speed, 365 miles per hour at 25,000 feet; cruise speed at maximum weight, 230 to 260 miles per hour; landing speed, 90 to 120 miles per hour; service ceiling, 32,000 feet; range, 5,400 to 5,800 miles; empty weight, 70,000 to 72,000 pounds; maximum gross weight, 125,000 pounds; maximum bomb load, 20,000 pounds; maximum fuel load (with auxiliary bomb bay tanks), 10,000 gallons. In practice the fuel and bomb loads varied widely depending on the type of ordnance, distance to be flown, and altitude to be achieved. When it is considered that the B-17, our foremost heavy bomber, flew at 155 to 170 miles per hour and had a range of 2,000 miles with a 5,000-pound bomb load, the capacities and capabilities of the B-29 were remarkable.

It was also the most complex and technologically advanced aircraft of its time. It had a cabin supercharger that pressurized crew areas and the connecting tunnel, eliminating the necessity of wearing oxygen masks and heavy sheepskin-lined clothing except in an emergency. The system would maintain a cabin altitude and temperature of 8,000 feet even though the airplane might be flying at 30,000 feet. This pressurization system also meant the end of standard gun turrets wherein the gunner manually hung on to the guns and fired out an open window.

Instead, a new sophisticated computer programmed remote central fire control system was installed which corrected for range, altitude, temperature, and airspeed. It enabled any gunner—except the tail gunner—to take over more than one of the .50-caliber turrets at one time. The gunners sat in clear blisters containing only the gunsight which controlled the remote turrets by means of palm switches under their hands. They were relieved of the jar and shock of recoil and the noise of guns firing, which made it easier to track their targets. The four turrets—two upper and two lower—contained ten .50-caliber machine guns and the tail gunner had two more firing to the rear. I considered this tremendous firepower and decided that this was the airplane to fly into combat. A single B-29 had firepower and system accuracy far superior to any of its predecessors. A formation of B-29s could throw so much lead that a fighter would never be able to penetrate the curtain.

The B-29 had other less dramatic—but no less important— systems that were major advances for combat aircraft. For example, it had a fuel-management system that enabled the pilot and flight engineer to practice precise cruise control with efficient monitoring of fuel consumption. Other airplanes had fuel gauges on each tank to show the amount of fuel in that tank, but they were almost totally unreliable. The B-29 had fuel-flow meters to keep track of fuel consumption. This was a very reliable means of determining how much fuel was being used and therefore how much remained on board at all times. It also gave an accurate record of the fuel consumption of each engine.

The cockpit was exceptionally spacious with an armchair seat for each of the pilots, and this was the first bomber to have three crew members on the flight deck—pilot, copilot, and flight engineer. The flight engineer sat back-to-back with the copilot and faced a large panel with all the engine instruments, starting switches, primers, fuel flow and transfer controls, mixture controls, and other instruments measuring different vital functions of the airplane. This arrangement left the pilot's panel for flight instruments and relieved the pilots of much of the routine burden of monitoring mechanical systems. They could then concentrate on flying the airplane.

Our group was in the initial stages of organization. This was not a school for transition to a new airplane, but a "to-be-formed" combat unit assembling crews for training and deployment to the Pacific Theater of Operations. We expected to be in the Pacific by January 1945. Pratt was one of four or five Midwestern bases engaged in this endeavor. Bombardiers, navigators, flight engineers, copilots, radio operators, and gunners were arriving on the airbase daily from their various schools and training facilities. 29th Bomb Group Headquarters began the assignment of each of them to a numbered crew already headed by a pilot.

Perhaps here is the place to mention the new crew designations imposed by the Air Force: the pilot of a B-29 was henceforth to be called an "airplane commander" and the former copilot was to be called the "pilot." I considered this to be some sort of military bureaucratic obfuscation and a denigration of everything implicit in the venerable and revered term "pilot." It was like changing the designated name "janitor" to "maintenance engineer." It might have sounded loftier, but it didn't change the duties or functions of the job, and it demeaned the term "engineer," a job requiring considerable study. The responsibility for the operation of the airplane and the conduct and safety of others on board was still the pilot's alone. "Pilot," when used in conjunction with an aircraft, was synonymous with "captain" when used in conjunction with a vessel at sea. And like that captain, the pilot was the final authority. And since when was a copilot a pilot? He was skilled but didn't have equal responsibility, or equal training, or equal experience, or equal judgmental capacity. He was there to assist by doing what the pilot ordered him to do when the pilot ordered him to do it, and to learn all he could from the pilot. I don't say this with any rancor or ill will toward copilots—in my day that's just the way it was. Copilots only came into being as airplanes became multi-engined and more complicated to operate. They shared the flight deck, but they were not pilots of B-29s or any other large aircraft.

An airplane commander could have been somebody behind a desk somewhere commanding a bunch of airplanes in flight, much like an infantry commander who directs the battle from a tent behind the lines using reports received from the front. The guys flying the B-29s were *pilots*. Maybe a better designation would have been "pilot and aircrew commander"—but that would have been redundant.

But enough about all this. It was just that I had worked hard to become a pilot and I was proud to be one. I didn't want my occupational identity diluted just for the sake of expediency. Years later, I heard that there was a proposal at about this time to promote all B-29 pilots, but it would have upset the rank quota, so they gave us the new title instead. For us, the old terms "pilot" and "copilot" prevailed as common usage, although all official Army documents—such as awards and orders—used the new title of aircraft commander or AC. I reiterate, I hold no rancor toward copilots, and obviously, many pilots and captains once served their time as copilots. In my individual case, I liked my copilot very much, and he performed his duties well, but I did not consider him my equal in the cockpit. How could I? He was just out of flying school!

Crews were rapidly being formed, and as assignments were being made to me, I considered and evaluated each man based on his training and my "gut feelings" about him. I asked that several replacements be made. There was one gunner who, in my opinion, had an attitude problem and would never be accepted by the other crew members. I didn't want him on my team, so he was replaced along with a couple of others. The original bombardier was also replaced but for reasons that I no longer remember. The same with the original flight engineer. I finally ended up with nine men who worked well together and stayed together throughout our training and overseas tour.

My copilot was Leroy B. "Bud" Preuth from Cincinnati, Ohio, a flight officer and recent flying school graduate. The bombardier was Alfred "Al" Rothman from Cincinnati, Ohio, a pawnbroker before getting involved with Uncle Sam. My navigator was Fred D. "Freddie" Schneider from Bartlesville,

Oklahoma, and among his claims to fame was that he was a star pitcher on a St. Louis Cardinals farm team. My flight engineer was Don A. "Pic" Piccirillo from East Orange, New Jersey. My radio operator was James M. "Jim" Kingston from Wayne, Nebraska. The four gunners were Merle C. Sampley from Pasadena, California; Richard R. "Rich" Ranker from Narrowsburg, New York; Chester J. "Chet" Retlewski from Bay City, Michigan; and Harold I. "Hal" Seelig from Hartford City, Indiana. Years later, Jim Kingston told me that the first time the whole crew got together on the flight line, he seriously thought the Army had made a mistake. Al and Fred were six-foot 180 pounders, and then there I was at five feet eight and 125 pounds. Jim thought, "This little guy is going to fly that big airplane?"

With the crews pretty well formed, we embarked on an intense program of bombing practice, gunnery practice, and long cross-country flights to perfect navigation and fuel-management and cruise-control skills. Because of the scarcity of B-29s, all but one of our first seven missions as a crew were flown in a B-17. By about the first week of October 1944, there were enough B-29s on the field so that only an occasional training mission was flown in a B-17, and our experience and confidence in the B-29 was becoming an established reality. We were on a twenty-four-hour-a-day, six-day-a-week schedule. The one day per week that we had off was not necessarily the same day every week. Most of the time, we were on a rotating eight- or nine-hour schedule, reporting to the flight line at 8:00 A.M. the first day, 12:00 noon the second day, and 4:00 P.M. the third day. Then the routine started over again. One of the three days was devoted to ground school. We studied engineering, communications, radar, combat techniques, navigation, meteorology, gunnery, and various other subjects. It was a grueling schedule and really messed up our sleep patterns. However, it accommodated night missions and gave us a taste of the erratic agenda and conditions we might encounter at our combat stations.

As we gained experience with the B-29, we came to understand and appreciate the fine airplane it was, but we also learned its weaknesses and problems. Nearly all were associated with the Wright R-3350 engines. The Wright "Whirlwind" and "Cyclone" engines had proved to be exceptionally reliable over more than two decades and had powered many thousands of airplanes, including Lindbergh's *Spirit of St. Louis* and most Boeing airplanes over the years as well as those of many other manufacturers. Wright R-1820 nine cylinder engines powered the nearly 13,000 B-17s built just before and during World War II; their performance and dependability were legendary. It was logical therefore for the Boeing Company to specify the Wright engine for the B-29. A further reason was that the R-3350 was the only air-cooled radial engine under development that had the large displacement necessary to provide the power required by the B-29 but still met the size and weight limitations specified by Boeing.

However, the only R-3350 engines that had been delivered to the Air Force prior to being ordered for the B-29 program were seven for use in the Douglas XB-19. The engine program had been on low priority but was suddenly put on fast track for the requirements of the B-29 schedule. Normally, five years were required to bring an engine design to reliable service status, but the R-3350 had only two years. In the rush to meet design and development criteria and actually manufacture and deliver the thousands of engines needed, many problems were encountered both on the test stand and in use on the airplanes being flown that might have been avoided or eliminated if there had been more time. But, there was not more time. The twin defeats of U.S. Forces at Pearl Harbor and in the Philippines in early 1942 jolted the country into the realization and acute awareness that the oceans no longer constituted geographic barriers to invasion. Further, it would be up to us to defeat Japan by ourselves since our allies were fully committed to the war in Europe. Not only that, but our feelings about Japan were somewhat different. While the Axis Powers had declared war on the U.S. and were attacking our transports in the North Atlantic, Japan had physically attacked *our* country, and to us, that meant *we* had to defeat them. With Japan in control of the Pacific, development and production of a long range bomber able to bomb their homeland was urgently required. The B-29 program was therefore absolutely imperative.

As pilots, we became very concerned about the problems with the engines. I sought information and development history in order to understand what I would be up against and how to deal with in-flight emergencies. I learned of the crash in Seattle of an XB-29 prototype on February 18, 1943—about eighteen months before I started flying the airplane. The cause was originally thought to be an in-flight engine fire which burned a wing off but later was determined to have been a fire in the leading edge of the wing. This fire was caused by test instrument tubing running from the cockpit to the outboard engine which, when ignited, burned like punk. The tubing had come in contact with the exhaust system, igniting it, and in turn, the combustion ignited fuel in a drainage scupper inside the wing causing an explosion that blew the leading edge off the wing and resulted in the fire that caused the crash. This crash killed Boeing's chief test pilot, Eddie Allen, and all thirteen others on board. The remedy was to move the fuel filler neck behind the spar eliminating the cause of this mishap. I wouldn't have to worry about this particular fire hazard happening to me, but there were myriad other problems which would bedevil us all during the operational period of the aircraft.

The Wright factories were fighting such basic problems as the ability to acquire manufacturing materials—including mica for spark plugs and a particular type of sand used by the foundries to cast the engine cylinders—as well as serious malfunctions of the completed engines. These breakdowns included such difficult problems as reduction gearing and nose-section problems, which resulted in runaway props at takeoff RPMs; both carburetor and ignition malfunctions and severe cylinder cooling problems which affected the airplane's ability to reach high altitude.

Among our other difficulties, one of which related directly to the cooling problem, were exhaust valves that broke or burned off in the combustion chamber (we called this failure in flight "swallowing a valve"), which happened more often than I like to remember. Hydraulic lock after shutdown, induction system and exhaust system fires, and push-rod oil leakage were some of the other malfunctions that worried us. The fires were definitely life-threatening, but some of the other things were just annoyances. For example, we handled the hydraulic lock problem by pulling the props through on each engine by hand before start-up. This didn't stop the oil getting by the piston rings and collecting in the bottom cylinders, but it prevented any damage when we cranked the engines. Oil leaks were common and more or less constant—there were puddles of oil under each engine on every hardstand on the line.

Many of the problems were remedied in late 1943 and early 1944, before I started flying the airplane, but the engines were still prone to fire, runaway props, swallowing valves, hydraulic lock, and ignition failures. Toward the very end of the war, the engine was equipped with fuel injection rather than a carburetor, and the cylinders were forged rather than cast, resulting in a great improvement in cooling. New valves had hollow stems filled with sodium, considerably alleviating the "swallowed valve" problem. All of this was the natural result of evolution and the many thousands and thousands of hours of experience accumulated by the flight crews flying the missions against the Japanese and the dedicated maintenance and ground crew personnel working on the 3350s. The engine eventually became a very reliable and successful powerplant and was used in the Super Connie, the DC-7, and other programs. Today, highly modified, it powers the fastest prop plane in history, the Grumman built "Rare Bear." It has been clocked at 528 mph using approximately 5,000 horsepower; it flies in the unlimited class of racers.

To the best of my knowledge, at least at the time, the R-3350 was the only engine to go into production which was comprised of two engines joined back-to-back at the crankcase. The cylinders were staggered between each other. The cooling problem was obvious—the airflow through the engine nacelle clearly would be less effective in cooling the rear bank of cylinders unless cowling, baffling, and cowl flap design could overcome this deficiency. On a different aircraft this might have been accomplished, but the B-29 nacelles were tight—the frontal area for air intake was only 1,164 square inches. That was less than the B-17 had at 1,417 square inches to cool only one row of cylinders. The B-29 nacelle airflow had to cool twice as much engine. If that wasn't enough, the B-29 had twin exhaust-driven turbosuperchargers in that nacelle to add to the heat. One might think that increasing the ram air over the engine by opening the cowl flaps more would help. But that was a self-defeating procedure. As cowl flaps were deployed, there was more drag created, which had a decaying effect on airspeed, which in turn required more throttle, which then created more heat. It was a "damned if you do, damned if you don't" situation. In the spring of 1944, a crew started a takeoff run with the cowl flaps full open in an attempt to keep the engines cool. This was in a light airplane—bomb bays empty and probably less than a full fuel load. Witnesses became alerted to a troubled aircraft. It used nearly all of a 1.5-mile runway and then staggered into the air wallowing like a sick whale; unable to gain more than 50 feet in altitude, it slid to one side to let a barn go by. Those listening and watching expected to see the dreaded black cloud of smoke, but in a few minutes, it came back over the field flying normally. The lesson? A B-29 cannot take off with full open cowl flaps.

Overheating was really the number one problem in the B-29 program. An overheated engine was ruined—even if it lasted the duration of the flight until touchdown. In an overheated engine, all the gaskets were cooked, the push rod housings were carbonized, and bearings melted—the engine literally would melt internally. Of the first contingent of B-29s deployed to India in April 1944, in a period of only two days, five crashed near Karachi with overheated engines. Two of the airplanes were completely demolished, and five crew members were lost.

My first experience with this problem resulted in an aborted training mission and a lesson in R-3350 operation. Early in our practice bombing missions, we used hundred-pound smoke bombs to mark the hits, just as I had done in the AT-11s at Victorville. However, we couldn't hit anything. The bombing accuracy was wildly erratic. The problem was perceived to be the wild buffeting of wind in the huge bomb bays of the B-29. At that time it was our practice to fly the whole bomb run with the bomb bay doors open, both to stabilize the airplane in that configuration and to avoid the long time interval involved in cranking the electrically operated doors open and closed. The turbulence in the bomb bays affected the trajectory of the small hundred-pound bombs at the instant of release. Instead of falling horizontally out of the bays and nosing down in a normal pattern, they tumbled all over the place with no predictable accuracy.

On this particular day, I was flying the bomb run at only 180 mph in an attempt to reduce or eliminate the buffeting when I swallowed a valve in the number one engine. I immediately feathered the prop and shut the engine down, all the while watching for any sign of smoke or fire. The sequence of events at the time of this engine malfunction presented the real hazard of fire and possible destruction of the aircraft. The stem of the exhaust valve would burn through, and the valve head would pop off, rattling around in the combustion chamber. If it broke a hole in the top of the piston, that would force fuel into the crankcase where it would ignite immediately. The crankcase and blower sections were made of magnesium, and if they ignited there was no way to put the fire out. The fire would rage against the wing spar, and in thirty or forty seconds, the wing would fold. That would be the end of the airplane and crew, particularly if this happened at high altitude. At high altitude there was not enough time to dive to an elevation where it was safe to bail out before the wing would collapse.

Not every swallowed valve resulted in a fire, and to the best of my knowledge, no one in the 29th Bomb Group ever experienced a fire after swallowing a valve. At any rate, I obviously did not have a fire on this occasion, and I proceeded back to the airbase with number one feathered. Many months later, my crew told me that the landing following this aborted mission was the best one I ever made in a B-29. They never felt the wheels kiss the concrete. Maybe they were apprehensive because this was the first engine failure in an airplane that they knew little about; indeed, they may have never experienced an "engine out" situation before and may have been afraid.

The next day, the commanding officer of the 29th Bomb Group, Col. Carl R. Storrie, called me to his headquarters office to critique the flight. Maj. Harry L. Evans, our operations officer was there, as were, I believe, Capt. William "Marc" Marchesi and someone from the engineering section. We discussed the whole flight from beginning to end with emphasis on cooling problems. I had kept the cylinder head temperatures within the recommended permissible range on each engine, but the conclusion after the discussion was that we would no longer "slow fly" the bomb runs—we would fly them at normal cruising airspeeds. The replacement airplanes we later received in the Marianas came equipped with pneumatically operated bomb bay doors that took only two seconds to pop open just before the bombs were released and popped shut again after the last bomb cleared the airplane. These doors eliminated the problem I was trying to solve.

On October 8, 1944, we lost the Cannon crew and three passengers in an unusual and spectacular crash near Dallas. They were flying the number three position in a three-plane formation at about 21,000 feet when the ship in the number two position aborted the mission with a mechanical problem. Their pressurization system had malfunctioned and they were low on oxygen. They therefore left the formation to return to base. Cannon thereafter elected to cross over into the number two position just vacated. As the Cannon aircraft passed behind and under the lead ship, it hit the prop wash of the leader causing it to bounce and rock in flight. Almost immediately and very abruptly, as it was coming up into the number two position, it pitched into a vertical nose-down position. As it dove toward the ground, it started to spin to the right, and then, at about 4,000 feet above the ground, it became inverted. The spin continued all the way to the ground when it crashed, still inverted, into a warehouse and machine shop on the West Dallas Field of the Texas Oil Company.

Following the accident, a board of inquiry was convened which included some Boeing engineers and the witnesses were interrogated. Ultimately, an official report was issued, but it was not, to my knowledge, circulated among the other pilots in the group so that we could benefit from the findings. I don't know whether this was intentional or just an oversight, but I felt it should have been the subject of a critique for the pilots of the group. I was always interested in accidents and crashes and severe mechanical malfunctions experienced by others because, in each, there was a lesson for the rest of us. For years afterwards, I always wondered if they had had a fire at altitude, given all the engine problems we were experiencing at the time. It has only been recently that I have been able to talk to the witnesses and read a copy of the official report on the mishap.

This report assigns responsibility for the crash to airframe failure of the "right and left horizontal stabilizer tips" as recovery from the effects of the prop wash was being attempted "throwing the aircraft into a dive, followed by an inverted flat spin." The basis for this conclusion was, at least in part, the fact that the stabilizer tips as well as sixteen feet of the left wing and parts of both left and right ailerons were found "within an area of three to five miles from the crash (site)." The report further stated that "possible contributing cause of Pilot Error of Technique [sic]" and recommended that "pilots have a minimum of 200 hours First Pilot time in four engine aircraft before being assigned as Airplane Commander of a B-29."

I cannot believe any of this. I have flown through prop wash dozens of times—perhaps more than one hundred times, both intentionally and unintentionally—and while it causes a "bump" or "burble" in the flight of the airplane, it was never sufficiently destabilizing to lose control or break the ship. In my opinion, the breakup of the aircraft was the result of the initial dive and subsequent spin, not the prop wash.

The two witnesses to this event were gunners on the lead ship, each of whom observed the whole episode beginning with the initial move to crossover. The accident progressed as reported, but their theory about the cause was quite different from the official one, and theirs makes sense.

The conclusion of the official accident investigation reported the deaths of "the eleven man crew and three instructors." It also defined the mission as a "high altitude, Formation Interception and Camera Bombing First Training Mission." I mention this only in an attempt to identify the type of instructors on board and establish their positions in the airplane. If they were either pilot or bombardier instructors, which was probable, then one or more of them would have been riding on the flight deck with the pilots and flight engineer.

Passengers riding on the flight deck had no seats into which they could be strapped—they sat on the edge of the aisle stand without restraints or sat or crouched on the floor, again, without restraints. Passengers would also sometimes ride sitting in the astrodome or stretched out in the tunnel running over the bomb bays. However, if I am correct in identifying the function of these instructors, then they would have been on the flight deck, probably between the pilot and copilot.

The "bounce" after hitting the prop wash of the lead plane could have thrown one of these "loose bodies" into the control column—literally into the lap of the pilot or copilot—thus wedging the control column into its full forward position. The abruptness of the vertical nose-down position would indicate that something of this nature did happen. One other theory advanced by one of the witnesses was that the crossover was made too close to the lead ship, and so when the prop wash was encountered, the pilot may have perceived a sudden danger of hitting the tail of the other airplane and violently thrown the control column forward. However, if this had been the scenario, control should not have been lost, and recovery should have immediately followed. Once in a vertical or near vertical nose-down position, gravity as well as the entanglement in cockpit apparatus would make it difficult if not impossible for the pilot or passenger instructor to extricate himself so that control of the aircraft could be regained. Or either the pilot or copilot could have been flying without having his seat belt fastened. This is unlikely, but possible. All of this is speculation, of course, but it is a more logical scenario than the official one. Further, the witnesses did not report any pieces of the structure departing the aircraft at the time of the radical change of attitude.

Over the next two and a half months, we flew many practice missions in B-29s and a few in a B-17. Some were to practice formation flying—an exercise for the pilot; to practice instrument flying—another exercise for the pilot; to practice bombing—an exercise for the pilot and bombardier. But most were long-range simulated bombing missions providing practice for the navigator and cruise-control and fuel-management practice for the pilot and flight engineer.

We flew one of these missions to "bomb" Washington, D.C., at night as weather was deteriorating across the Midwest. We found our "target" in Washington and then reversed course for the airbase at Pratt. As we proceeded west, the ceiling kept getting lower—much like my Victorville-Kingman-Victorville flight a year earlier. As we crossed the Mississippi I found all the Kansas B-29 airbases closed down. I was flying through intermittent snowstorms. I needed a B-29 base since they were about the only ones that had the 8,500 foot runways necessary for B-29 operations. Jim was on the radio getting reports for me, and he found Grand Island, Nebraska, still open, so we altered course. As we crossed the Missouri River, I was mentally reviewing the procedures in preparation to fly an instrument let down and approach to Grand Island. I had practiced this sort of thing many times "under the hood" and in the Link Trainer, but this would have been my first "real life" instrument landing approach. However, as I descended, there were holes in the overcast here and there, and lights on the ground were visible. At about 1,000 or 1,200 feet, I broke out of the clouds to the lights of Grand Island and the runway beyond. The landing was without incident, and a truck met us as I parked in the transient area. I closed my flight plan and asked that Pratt be notified of my landing. The truck took us to temporary quarters.

It was then about two o'clock in the morning, it was cold, and we just wanted to get warm and get some sleep. We arose in the morning to a cold, blustery day, but the storm had passed, and it was clear. We were anxious to get back to Pratt as we had not been prepared to remain overnight—we had no toiletries or change of clothes. After breakfast, we caught a ride out to the ship, preflighted it, and tried to start the engines. We tried and tried but couldn't get any one of the four to fire. We finally gave up and I asked the Grand Island Maintenance Section for some help, but they had no time to work on a transient aircraft. Pic and I discussed the problem and finally decided that the spark plugs must have become fouled. We got new spark plugs and Pic and the other enlisted crewmen spent most of the rest of the day changing all 144 of the plugs—in the cold with bare hands. We tried again to start the engines, but without success. We spent another night in the transient quarters and tried again the next morning. *Voila!* We got them all started. The flight back to Pratt was uneventful—we were just glad to be home and get a shower and clean clothes and some sleep.

Among the engine problems experienced in the early engines were ignition malfunctions apparently caused by the pressure difference between the inside and the outside of the various ignition components forcing moisture into certain parts under conditions of rain or high humidity. This may have been the cause of our problem as we had been flying through snow storms and then parked the airplane as the storm abated. However, two days of drying out may have been the simple solution. As far as the manufacturer was concerned, the problem was overcome by changing materials and using filled ignition harnesses.

October, November, and the first part of December passed quickly in this pattern of missions and critiques of the operation of the B-29. During this period I logged approximately 160 hours in the B-29 and had become quite comfortable with it—more than comfortable really: I had respect for it and liked its particular attributes. One of the flying characteristics of the B-29 that I have not mentioned was the ability to fly it "on the step" to achieve and maintain high cruise speeds. It seemed to be a peculiar quality of the B-29 airfoil; at least I knew of no other airplanes with this distinction. I am not enough of an aeronautical engineer to describe and explain the phenomenon—it had something to do with the angle of incidence—but it was like getting a speedboat hull up out of the water and running on the "step" built into the hull about two-thirds of the way back from the bow. With most of the hull out of the water, high speed could be maintained. The process of getting the B-29 "on the step" was to climb 300 to 500 feet above the intended cruise altitude, level out, trim the ship for level flight, then dive back down to the desired altitude. The airspeed of course would increase substantially over that which would be achievable by just leveling out from a climb, and it could be maintained in cruise after retrimming the elevator control. This was part of my cruise control technique.

I was frequently asked whether the B-29 had hydraulic boost on the controls. It did not. The flight controls were activated by cables from the cockpit and were counterbalanced only. The design engineers did an excellent job on this system. The airplane responded to control input instantly and smoothly. The roll rate was not that of a fighter, but it was quite fast for a big airplane.

Also, during this period of training, I tried to check Bud out in the B-29. There might be a time when I could be incapacitated or killed, and he would have to get the ship home. Admittedly, I didn't spend much time trying to do this, but he didn't have the touch to land the airplane. In a regular training environment he may well have accomplished the routine, but with the little time I had to give him, it was not possible. He was not afraid of flying or of the B-29—he just lacked the depth of flying experience. He was laid back and cool as he proved on all the missions he flew with me, but I had to take over on the final approach on each of his attempts to land. I didn't feel that I could let him bumble through a landing and perhaps prang the airplane with disastrous consequences. He was good natured, a good softball player, a good bridge player and was well liked by all the crew. I considered him an asset—I just hoped there would never be an emergency when he would have to land the ship.

After we had been in combat for a while and had some missions under our belts, I heard that the crew had a deal with him. If I was dead or wounded, and if he and Freddie could get the ship back over Guam, they would throw me out, pull my ripcord, and then they'd all bail out over the island and let the airplane go on to crash. They didn't want to risk a landing with him at the controls. Years later, after the war, I asked a couple of the crew about this, and they denied it. Perhaps someone said it as a joke. Perhaps there was no "deal," but I heard of it.

Early in December the eleventh crew member joined us. He was Thomas A. "Tom" Henry from El Paso, Texas. Tom had been trained as a navigator with the additional specialty of radar observer. Our combat airplanes would be equipped with the AN/APQ-13 radar system, and this would be Tom's responsibility on board.

On December 21, 1944, I was granted a seven-day leave, which my wife and I spent visiting my father in Omaha. We knew that the group would be overseas within a month or six weeks, so we were grateful for the Christmas holiday at home. Our return to Pratt coincided with the New Year's celebration, so on December 31, I invited my crew to my apartment for the evening. It was probably the last opportunity to have a party since our training was nearly complete, and we knew we were close to leaving for combat. There was plenty of whiskey and everyone took on a load—one of the gunners to the point of being so thoroughly snockered that his wife had to take him home and put him to bed. Everyone but me, that is—I drank soft drinks because we had a mission scheduled for 8 A.M. the next day, January 1. I figured that, even hungover, if Pic could start the engines, and Bud could muddle through the checklist with me, I could get off, and once airborne, all the others could doze and nurse their swollen heads, so I let everyone drink.

The whole crew reported to the airplane on New Year's Day, more or less directly from the party. We accomplished the preflight, and after the engine run-up, the tower cleared me for takeoff. I responded with "Roger, tower, rolling," as I turned on to the runway and advanced the throttles to full power. Bud started calling out the airspeed as he always did through acceleration and rotation: 90, 110, 130, but we were not about to fly. I knew immediately and instinctively what the problem was and yelled, "Flaps!" Bud calmly and nonchalantly turned around in his seat and said to the flight engineer, "Hey, Pic, close your cowl flaps." I yelled, "Wing flaps, goddammit!" Bud uttered a surprised "oh" as he hit the wing flap switch. By then we were going 150 mph or so, and the airplane literally jumped into the air as the fence and a cornfield at the end of the runway streaked by under the wings. Bud was so chagrined about his mistake that he could hardly sleep after that, but it was really my fault—I had inadvertently failed to match the command with the action when the word "flaps" came up on the checklist. Or maybe Bud failed to read it—I'm not sure. We completed the mission without further incident and by the time we returned at the end of the day, although tired, most of the crew had stolen enough sleep to cure all their hangovers.

On January 7, 1945, the whole 29th Bomb Group was transferred to Borenquin, Puerto Rico, along with other groups from Kansas and Nebraska for the final phase of training in navigation and long over-water flights under simulated combat operating conditions before challenging the Pacific. Our flight was to be non-stop, clearing through Customs and the North American Air Defense Command at Miami by radio while in flight.

As we departed Pratt on January 8, 1945, the squadron formed up into a loose formation and set course for Miami. The flight to Florida was uneventful; typical January weather for the Midwestern U.S. prevailed—various layers of clouds, but good visibility between layers all across the Midwestern and southeastern states. Upon our arrival over Miami, the lead ship completed the required radio clearance for the whole group, and we turned out over the Atlantic on course for Puerto Rico. Minutes after leaving the Florida coast, we entered what appeared to be a light fog bank but turned out to be much denser—so dense that we could not see each other. I was flying the number two position in the lead element, and I rolled off to the left to avoid the possibility of a collision, and started to climb out of it. Climbing was usually the way to get out of a weather system, and I had an airplane that would go to 35,000 feet, so up we went. I reached almost 30,000 feet and still wasn't completely in the clear as there was a high layer above us. The navigator however was able to get a fuzzy shot of the sun and established our position to give me a new course to Puerto Rico.

We had been blown over a hundred miles north of our course. We proceeded on the new heading over most of the weather, and about two hours out of Puerto Rico, I lost the number four engine. We arrived at Borenquin just about dark, and I landed in visible approach conditions with an outboard engine out—the second time for me in a B-29. After turning off the runway, I taxied onto an area that appeared to be part of the taxiway apron, but it was not. It was water soaked from the day-long rain, and I sank in up to the hubs. I couldn't power out, so we climbed out and walked to operations.

Our preflight weather briefing had not disclosed anything about storms in the Atlantic or the Caribbean, nor were we advised of any when we cleared Miami Radio. This storm, however, was a major one and thoroughly soaked the West Indies.

The next day we learned that Irving Ward of the 6th Squadron in our group was lost in the storm en route. So, for the next few days, the whole group flew search missions of eight or nine hours each of ever-widening grid patterns covering the area between Puerto Rico and Florida. No wreckage, debris, rafts, or oil slicks were ever sighted by any of us, and after three days, the hunt was abandoned. This was the second loss for us—the first being Earl Cannon in a crash near Dallas on a training mission in October 1944. There were four B-29 aircraft lost during our training in Puerto Rico—the other three being from the groups based at Great Bend, Kansas, and Grand Island, Nebraska.

The weather cleared up the day after our arrival, enabling us to fly the search missions and the training missions that were the object of the Caribbean exercise. We flew everyday for four or five days after the search for Ward ended and completed our scheduled over-water training. We flew east over the Atlantic and southeast as far as Barbados and Trinidad. They were not romantic destinations for us, just simulated bombing targets.

The base at Borenquin, situated on a cliff at the northwestern corner of the island overlooking the ocean, was the most lavish I had ever seen. Facilities were housed in modern poured concrete buildings, no doubt designed to withstand hurricane winds. They housed quarters for the personnel, a bowling alley, and clubs for both officers and enlisted men. There were swimming pools and an excellent eighteen-hole golf course. We didn't ever leave the base to see San Juan or the rest of the island, but I did fly the circumference of Puerto Rico one day touring at about 500 feet just off the surf line. It looked idyllic. Much of it was mountainous, with green valleys containing small villages nestled in the center. The flatter areas were cultivated with sugar cane fields and orange and palm groves. A ground tour might have revealed poverty and squalor, but from the air it looked like paradise.

I spent the last two or three days on the island resting, sunbathing and playing golf while the Army was deciding how to get us all back to Pratt. After all, we had left a Kansas winter, and I wanted to take advantage of the warm tropical weather while I could. Originally, I was scheduled to fly one of the B-29s back; then it was rumored that most of the B-29s would remain at Borenquin for the training of other crews to follow us, and we would be transported back to the U.S. by ATC (Air Transport Command). In the midst of these and other rumors, I was summoned to operations one evening from the officers club where I was having a nightcap. Operations told me that they had a B-17 that was needed at the navigation school at Batista Field outside Havana, Cuba, and I was to ferry it there. I said, "OK, let me round up my crew," to which the operations officer said, "No, you don't need your crew—just get your copilot." So, about midnight, Bud and I took off for Cuba by ourselves in the empty B-17 with instructions to report to the commanding officer there. We landed at Batista Field about seven the next morning to a beehive of activity on the field. They were moving the whole installation "lock, stock, and barrel" to Jackson, Mississippi, by air.

I reported to the commanding officer, a bird colonel, as instructed, and he said to me, "Get some breakfast, lieutenant. They'll load and gas your airplane while you eat, then take off for Jackson."

"But sir," I protested, "I haven't had any sleep for twenty-four hours, and I've been flying all night!"

"Lieutenant, if you feed a man enough, he doesn't need any sleep. Get some breakfast and takeoff."

I responded, "Yes, sir."

We later heard that the colonel's less than cordial attitude—and his apparent disgust with life and especially second lieutenants who talked back to him—was because he was formerly a general in England, where he allegedly committed an indiscretion with a bedded lady regarding the European invasion. As a result, he was busted down to colonel and sent to the Caribbean, where he could do no harm. I didn't know if the story was true, but I did know that I was the object of his ire.

So Bud and I found the officers club and ordered breakfast. While we were eating, I noticed that the club had a well stocked bar, and I opined that we should see what we could buy to take home. After breakfast I bought two cases of Seagrams V.0., and we carried it down to the flight line. I had paid the mess officer $1.00 per bottle—no tax, no customs, no anything—best booze buy I ever made in my life. I stopped at operations to file my flight plan, and then walked out to the airplane to be greeted by twenty people and all their baggage. I inspected the ship and found a spare engine and two landing gear struts complete with wheels and tires secured in the bomb bay, and various and sundry other cargo stuffed wherever it would fit. A sergeant handed me an aerosol can and told me to return it to operations after I had de-bugged the airplane. As I went through the waist compartment and the cockpit all the while holding the button down on the can, effectively fogging the whole interior, I kept thinking and hoping that the ground crew knew what they were doing when they loaded all this stuff because there was no way I could figure the weight and balance requirements. Obviously the spare engine and the landing gear were in the right place in the bomb bay, but most of the other stuff was a mystery to me. I hoped the center of gravity envelope was not too far off—and then there were those twenty people! The can sputtered out, and I took it back to operations wondering why they wanted an empty can back in the office. Well, I found out—they told me in no uncertain terms that three to five seconds was all it took to fumigate the aircraft, and I had used all of their last can! How was I to know? Well, at least if the ship wouldn't get off the ground, we'd all burn in a sterile crematorium.

I returned to the airplane and distributed the people as evenly throughout the fuselage as I could, still trying to keep that center of gravity envelope within limits. Most of them had to stand, or at least take turns sitting, because there just wasn't a place for everyone to sit. Bud and I each had a passenger hanging over our shoulders the whole way, and I had either two or three in the nose in the bombardier's position.

With everybody on board, I cranked up the fans, we did the engine run-up while taxiing to the runway and I had full power on coming out of the turn as I lined up. The airplane accelerated slowly as it was obviously heavy, but the tail came up at the normal point in the takeoff roll, and we lifted off as I had one hand on the elevator trim tab—just in case. The B-17 responded normally to control input, so I was satisfied that we were OK on weight and balance and center of gravity—the unusual load not withstanding.

I climbed to about six thousand feet, and when approaching Miami, I cleared inbound through the North American Air Defense Command, confirmed my flight plan to Jackson by radio, and proceeded up the Florida Peninsula, across the northeast corner of the Gulf of Mexico, the Florida panhandle, Mobile, Alabama, and into Mississippi. The flight was uneventful until I was somewhere southeast of Jackson when a big red fuel warning light started flashing on the instrument panel. I didn't think that I could possibly be low on fuel, although I had not supervised the fueling of the airplane, leaving that to the line crew as we usually did in the Air Force, but this was a strange airplane to me, not having flown it before this assignment. Even though all examples of the same model are supposed to perform alike, there are individual variations or exceptions; or I could have a fuel flow malfunction or a fuel leak, or be siphoning gas over the top of the wing from a loose or missing cap, or the engines could have had a lot of time on them.

The situation really got my attention, and I began silently reviewing emergency procedures and other options. I had all these people on board with no parachutes for them, so abandoning the airplane was not an option. If fuel exhaustion really was imminent, I'd have to put it down somewhere, preferably under full control. All I could see below me was heavily wooded rolling hills—not good. The weather was clear, but there was a lot of haze and I was flying into a late afternoon low winter sun so visibility ahead was practically nil. I could see straight down, but not forward. I could hear Jackson on the radio, but I couldn't tell whether I was five miles out or fifteen or fifty, just that I was close. Bud wasn't saying anything, but I could see him glancing over to the light on my panel every minute or so. I don't know what the two passengers standing behind us thought, but they didn't say anything either. I was not about to declare an emergency—I was not sure I even had one. In the next few minutes, as I got closer, Jackson radio became more audible and more distinct and at my request they cleared me for a straight-in approach. I stayed right on the beam to the station and then turned toward the field. We quickly completed our landing checklist, and I slid down a long final approach, waiting for the engines to quit, but obviously they didn't. I greased it on, and everybody probably breathed a sigh of relief. Bud congratulated me on the smooth landing and I told him that I did that out of concern for the possibility of the spare engine and landing gear going through the bomb bay doors. As every pilot knows, you try for a "grease job" on every landing, but despite your best efforts they don't all turn out that way—any more than your ball always goes straight down the fairway when you hit it. Sometimes you arrive with a thud, and sometimes you arrive twice; they are not all grease jobs.

I taxied up to operations, and everyone deplaned. I wrote up the malfunctioning fuel light and headed for the BOQ (bachelor officers quarters) to get some sleep as we were scheduled to make one or two more trips between Havana and Jackson the next day. For some reason though, that extended assignment was canceled, so back we went to operations to hitch a ride on something going west that could be detoured for a stop at Pratt. We found a couple of pilots willing to take us to Pratt, so off we went again in another B-17.

We took off in a hurry without a preflight weather briefing, intending to get it once we were airborne. As we proceeded northwest past Little Rock, Arkansas, and Springfield, Missouri, we began picking up reports of a major winter storm making its way across Nebraska and Kansas, so as we approached the Missouri River, with reports of Wichita and Pratt being closed in and the ceiling lowering ahead of us, our friends wanted to return to Jackson. I prevailed upon them to dump us off at Kansas City, which was still open, and then they headed back to Jackson ahead of the storm.

A train was the only transportation available that might get us to Pratt, so we took a taxi from the airport to the railroad station in town. This was when the raised eyebrows and suspicious stares began. When we left Pratt bound for the Caribbean, we left our wool olive drabs and greens behind and wore tropical khaki uniforms. So here we were, back in Kansas, in January, with a winter storm blanketing the state, and we were in tropical tan with no neckties. In addition to that, we each had a B-4 bag, a parachute, a Mae West life preserver, our headsets, and some other miscellaneous flying equipment—and the two cases of whiskey we were trying to conceal under the other stuff. Carrying it all from the taxi into the railroad station and depositing it on a bench took about three trips, and we couldn't decide whether to take the whiskey first or last. We finally decided to take it last with newspapers wrapped around it to disguise it as best we could. Then it went under the Mae Wests and parachutes on the bench.

Leaving Bud to guard our loot, I learned at the ticket counter that a Chicago to Los Angeles train was due in Kansas City in about two hours and would make a stop in Pratt. After stopping at the Western Union office in the station to wire my wife to meet us, I bought two tickets and rejoined Bud on the bench for our long wait. It was then that I noticed the MP detail eyeing us from across the station and apparently discussing their next move. In a few minutes, two of them approached as I stood up and returned the salute of the noncom in charge when he asked, in a very questioning tone of voice, "Ah, lieutenant, are you traveling on orders?" I answered that I was not and explained the sequence of events from Puerto Rico, to Cuba, to Jackson, and then getting bumped in Kansas City because of the storm. I had no orders and no identification except my War Department Adjutant General's card in my wallet, which I showed him along with the tickets to Pratt. He seemed somewhat doubtful but accepted my story, and after a suspicious look at our equipment, saluted again and departed. After about an hour, the MP shift changed to another squad, and I went through the whole explanation again with the same results. Apparently, the first contingent didn't explain to the second shift that we had already been queried. We might have looked less suspicious to the second group because they had not seen us come in with the cases of booze (albeit camouflaged), and by then we had them buried under our equipment.

When the announcement was made on the public address system that our train was arriving, we went into action to get our stuff aboard. Each of us hung a Mae West around our necks, tucked a case of whiskey under one arm, picked up a B-4 bag with the other, and ran down the long flight of stairs to the tracks below. We deposited the whiskey on a double seat, put the Mae Wests and B-4 bags on top, and ran back up the stairs to get our parachutes and other paraphernalia and ran back down to the tracks again. The MPs watched us go through all of this but said nothing. I imagine they just wanted us out of there, and once we were gone their surveillance responsibility was ended— probably to their relief. A couple of wayward pilots were not what they needed. The train chugged through the night, and we cat-napped all the way to Pratt, arriving at 5:00 A.M.

As we descended the steps from the railroad car, there were four girls standing on the platform, tits up, in heels, their most attractive coiffeurs, dressed to the nines in their Sunday best dresses and with eager, love-starved smiles on their faces. Bud and I immediately embraced our wives, and when we came up for air, the other two girls, looking anxiously at the train, asked, "Where are our husbands?"

"Oh, they are still in Puerto Rico—they'll come back later on with another crew," I replied.

Well, I'll tell you—talk about "mad as a wet hen"—those two could have torn me apart limb from limb with delight; but they restrained their anger and frustration, retained their composure (more or less), and I escaped their scorn. They then looked at my wife as if to say, "You got us up at 3:30 in the morning for nothing?" Of course, it wasn't her fault—I'd said in my telegram, "Will arrive in Pratt via train at 5:00 A.M.—meet me." She assumed that meant the whole crew—weren't we always together? I proceeded to my apartment and, after a lover's tryst, fell asleep in a bed for the first time in three days, sleeping all day.

A day or so later, the other crews in the group began arriving back at Pratt in several B-29s. The tower advised one crew not to deplane. The MPs arrived, boarded and searched the airplane, and discovered the cases of booze aboard (which was not difficult). The crew (or the aircraft commander, I don't remember which) was charged with having contraband aboard (no tax or customs stamps on the bottles) bringing it into a dry state, and bringing it onto a government reservation. They called it smuggling. Well, well, fancy that! What do you know? Smuggling, you say!

I gave away some of my contraband to a few of the influential people in Pratt who had befriended us and whom we had come to know while living there—like the mayor and the postmaster. The rest of it I stashed away for some future emergency. The unfortunate crew that was caught had their booze confiscated. I don't know whether there was any punishment doled out to them beyond a chewing out—we were all about to depart Pratt for staging and transfer to an overseas destination, so perhaps that was the end of the incident for them.

Our stay at Pratt was coming to an end. Our training was complete, and as individuals, as crews, and as a group, we were as ready as we would ever be to go to combat. We were eager to implement the offensive that, we were convinced, would end the war in the Pacific.

Aside from our flying preparation, we were completing other requirements to depart the U.S. I had a couple of wisdom teeth pulled, preferring to do it on the U.S. side of the Pacific, and over the previous two or three months, our immunization schedules were being brought current. We got booster shots for typhoid fever and tetanus as well as original shots for yellow fever and cholera. We did not get any kind of malaria preventive because we were told that there was no malaria where we were going. That increased the speculation about our destination, although the rumor was that we were headed for Guam. We were given the usual six-month physical exams for pilots and aircrew members, and then we completed a bunch of legal stuff: making a will, authorizing allotments of our pay to dependents or for the purchase of war bonds, purchasing National Service Life Insurance, designating joint signatures on bank accounts, and signing a power-of-attorney. We organized our clothes and personal possessions, and on February 2, 1945, we were ordered to our staging area at Herington, Kansas.

My wife and I drove to Herington and quickly found a room and bath in the home of Lelia Munson, an elderly widow. This was adequate as we were to be at this station only a week or less. Upon our departure, this woman wrote a nice letter to my father addressed simply to "Mr. Robertson, Omaha, who has a son in the Air Force." Needless to say, it reached him.

The purpose of the staging area was to pick up a new airplane, test fly it, and depart for our overseas destination in it. The process moved rather quickly. I was assigned airplane number 42-93945—a brand new B-29 just manufactured in Wichita and with only ferry time on it. It was like getting a new car—it looked new, it smelled new, and everything worked. It was equipped with all the latest modifications and new "combat" engines. We took it on its maiden flight as a crew. We were out about two hours testing all its systems, and when we returned, I signed an acceptance for the airplane. The next day, I receipted for dozens of items of portable personal and airplane equipment which was issued for the flight to the western Pacific. These included such diverse items as a .45-caliber pistol with three magazines and a shoulder holster, a knife (bayonet) with scabbard, eleven headsets and throat mikes, eleven oxygen masks, eleven three-piece flak vests, eleven helmets, eleven Mae West vests, flashlights, and airplane equipment including axes, first aid kits, fire extinguishers, binoculars, oxygen bottles, thermos bottles, pyrotechnic signals with pistol, life rafts, dinghy radio, crewchief kit, radio spare parts kit, special radar operator's kit, armorers kits, tool kits, emergency sustenance kits with 165 "K" rations, nacelle ladders and nacelle support pads, wheel chocks, landing gear locking devices, engine covers, five-gallon gas can with flexible spout, jack pads, mooring eyes, and a lot of mechanical equipment for the bomb bays like trusses, shackles, half moon supports, and so on. In theory at least, we had everything on board to maintain the airplane (except oil and gas) and ourselves in the event of a landing at an airfield not equipped to handle B-29s, or in case of a forced landing at sea. We stowed all the equipment together with our clothing and personal things we had brought with us from Pratt.

The evening before our departure was a chance for the crew members to telephone their families at home and say their good-byes, then maybe have a few drinks. For my wife and me, it was dinner out with smiles and a lot of small talk, neither of us inclined or willing to discuss what the future might hold. This was the onset of the real war for me, an intermediate culmination of everything I had worked toward and done since Pearl Harbor. We slept in each others' arms all night.

At the scheduled departure time the next day, we stood on the ramp next to my new big shiny bird locked in an embrace that we wanted to go on forever. Wartime military life included a lot of farewells, but we were both silently wondering whether this would be the last farewell for us. With a final kiss and tears welling up in my eyes, I walked over to the airplane and with a wave and a last glance back, ducked into the nosewheel well to join my crew on board. The girls we were leaving behind were on the other side of the airplane out of my vision as I lifted off into a gray, sullen winter sky for the trip southwest across Oklahoma, the Texas panhandle, New Mexico, Arizona, and then up the San Joaquin Valley to Mather Field, our jumping off point for the Pacific.

CHAPTER 6

The Blue Pacific

The journey from Herington to Mather Field near Sacramento, California, was uneventful as far as the trip was concerned—visual flight conditions all the way under a high overcast. It gave me an opportunity to test the airplane. I concentrated on monitoring airspeed and controlling fuel consumption as I had many long overwater flights ahead of me, and I wanted to have all the expertise possible to conserve fuel and "make miles." There were other flying techniques, of course, that contributed to long range—like finding an altitude with favorable winds and flying as high as possible—but in combat we would be assigned certain altitudes at which to fly, so the only range and duration procedures available to us would be strict cruise control. The airplane flew and performed beautifully, and everything worked. I had no qualms about setting out across the Pacific in this new ship.

We landed at Mather Field late in the day and remained overnight. The following day, the line crews refueled the plane and added oil to the engines. We puttered around arranging our own stuff inside, but we really spent the day just killing time until evening when our takeoff for Hawaii was scheduled. Night flight was the preferred routine so that we could navigate by the stars and so that we would have an early morning landing in daylight—always preferable when arriving at a destination for the first time.

We took off at about midnight into a moonless sky. With a "goodbye and good luck" from the Mather tower, I headed down the Sacramento River Valley to Suisun Bay and on toward San Francisco Bay and the Golden Gate. As I approached the bridge, I thought about flying under it but soon abandoned the idea as it was late at night. While that in itself didn't pose any additional danger to me—there was ample room—I wondered who would see us. The thrill of showing off wouldn't be there, so I went over the top. We entered a black no-man's-land atmosphere where we could see neither the horizon, the water below, or the sky above. As I set up the autopilot, I unsealed the orders I had been given just before takeoff with instructions not to open them until we were well off the coast. We had been hearing rumors for several weeks that our destination and new base of operations would be the island of Guam in the Marianas. I keyed the mike button and told the crew that we were indeed being ordered to Guam. None were surprised. We proceeded off the coast at moderate altitude, and while the marine layer remained below us for several hours, within an hour or two the overcast above disappeared and Freddie could navigate by the stars. In the Pacific area we also had a new navigational aid called LORAN (long range navigation), a radio system that enabled us to triangulate our position as a check against other methods of navigation. Our first checkpoint was a weather ship permanently stationed in the Pacific about halfway between San Francisco and Hawaii. Freddie hit this pretty much on the button, and we continued on toward Hawaii.

About seven hours out of Mather, just after daylight, in clear weather, one of the blister gunners called "Flak at two o'clock!" I scanned the sky on the starboard side of the ship, and sure enough, there were little black puffs of smoke appearing rapidly just off our wing. We hadn't been briefed about any Navy target range or Navy maneuvers along our route, but that must have been the reason for it. I banked away to the south to avoid any more of it from the ships below, and then a couple of Navy fighters pulled alongside to look us over. They stayed with us for a few minutes and then, satisfied that we were friendly, disappeared as quickly as they had come. This was the first indication that we were in a theater of war.

After the morning light enabled us to see the water below, I began watching for a glimpse of our landfall at Diamond

Head and tuned the radio in a search for the range station on Oahu. As I recall now, Freddie was a little off on his ETA (estimated time of arrival) but right on the money as far as our course was concerned. As soon as it became audible, I rode the beam toward Oahu, and in due time, Diamond Head appeared dead ahead. As always, when approaching a destination after a long flight, I felt reinvigorated. As I descended from our cruising altitude, my copilot and I completed our landing checklist, and I got landing instructions from the tower and circled south around the island for my approach to John Rodgers Field. Once again, a couple of P-47s came up to have a look at us as I turned on the final approach to the runway. The flight had taken just ten hours. The logistics of this segment of our flight constituted a precursor to some of the missions to come: up all day in preparation, flying all night, and landing the following day in sunlight.

After securing the ship, we hit the mess hall on the field for breakfast, and I ran into Don Purdy, my classmate from Yuma. He was on his way back to the U.S. after nearly two years flying B-24s in the South Pacific campaigns. He was another example of a fighter pilot detoured to heavy bombers. We talked about the two airplanes, the B-24 and the B-29, and he said that the B-24 was not a pilot's airplane—it flew like a truck, you kicked it around the sky. However, he had nothing but good to say about the Pratt & Whitney engines. He said you could run them wide open all day long and they'd hang together and take the punishment. I had always had the same opinion about Pratt & Whitneys. After all, I had about 1500 hours behind them, and they had never let me down. Contrast that to the big Wright engines we had in the B-29s, which required very careful operation and handling and were limited to not more than five continuous minutes at full "combat power" and still frequently let you down. I was glad I had four of them. However, even with the engine problems, my enthusiasm for the B-29 was not diminished.

Don was both homesick and lovesick. He said he was going to get married as soon as he got home, but he didn't seem to have anyone in particular selected. In his frame of mind, I was afraid he would marry the first white girl he saw upon arrival in the U.S.

We got a few hours sleep and then went into Honolulu sightseeing. The weather, of course, was delightful, but I was not favorably impressed with the city. The stores were tourist traps. I tried to buy a mumu or kimono or something for my wife but gave it up when the labels revealed the garments were made in Brooklyn. Waikiki Beach was pretty, but not unlike some beaches in California or Mexico or the Caribbean. The traffic—both foot and vehicular—was very heavy; a part of the fleet was in port, so there were hordes of boisterous sailors everywhere. I didn't begrudge them their shore leaves, but their presence made me feel like I was in San Diego, not Hawaii. We had dinner in a local restaurant, but again it was a tourist trap; the prices were substantial and the food not that good. We returned to our quarters at John Rodgers, and I had the feeling that towns, no matter where, were basically the same. We wanted to catch up on our sleep so we could prepare for the second leg of our journey—a daylight flight to Kwajalein in the Marshall Islands.

We still had some things to do to the ship. The machine guns had to be cleaned and loaded and put in battery (operating condition). On the next portion of our flight to the Marianas, we would pass over some Jap held territory, and although no airplanes had been attacked or fired upon for some months, we were supposed to be ready to defend ourselves. It was only a few weeks later that one of our aircraft with General Harmon on board was lost in this vicinity. It was suspected that this mishap was due to enemy action. With the balance of our preparations accomplished, we loaded our personal equipment on board again and made plans to take off the following day.

With a good breakfast and lots of milk under our belts (Hawaii was probably the last place we could get milk until we got back), we made an early morning takeoff and skimmed out over the masts of the ships in Pearl Harbor. With a last look at the towering green mountains of Oahu, I climbed to cruising altitude and headed west for Kwajalein.

We hit all our checkpoints ahead of time. Johnston Island drifted by, then Jap-held Wojte Atoll, and once again, Freddie hit our destination right on the nose. We approached bleak, dusty, and treeless Kwajalein Island. Kwajalein, the world's largest coral atoll, was about seventy-eight miles long and was composed of about ninety islands arranged in a boomerang or crescent disbursement. Like the first leg of our flight, I was pleased with the performance of the ship, strengthening my confidence in the superior characteristics of the B-29.

When I stepped out of the plane, I thought of the Marine lives that were lost taking this forlorn little spit of land—hardly a half mile wide and less than three miles long. There wasn't a tree left standing after the pre-invasion bombardment, and the fine dust which blew constantly was a nuisance to people and machinery alike. I wondered if it was worth it. However, it would play a strategic part in the Pacific War and, at this point in 1945, provided us with a refueling stop on our way to the Marianas.

We were to find out that Kwaj was a very busy place though. ATC planes buzzed in and out all day long as well as ships bound for combat and others coming home. There was always activity. In their spare time, the boys based there had built rafts and sailing boats from discarded Jap equipment and our own droppable gas tanks, and they sailed them around the lagoon just lazing in the sun or trolling for fish.

As we checked in at the transient personnel quarters, we smiled at the sign over the door stating that the Kwajalein Hilton was open for stags only and the rates were payable in advance. This was undoubtedly installed before WAACs, nurses, and USO entertainers began going through there, but it became a familiar landmark in the Pacific to thousands of people traveling to and from the combat areas. We were to see many such bits of Americana on other islands far from our own Pacific shores.

We showered in seawater that night. Fresh water was scarce, and it was for drinking, cooking, and brushing teeth only. Our dinner was exceptionally good, and we turned in that night on mattresses, sheets, and pillows. We all thought the same thing:

that if our quarters on Guam were as pleasant as these, we certainly wouldn't complain.

The following morning we departed for Guam and arrived there six hours and ten minutes later. It was now February 23. We had flown into the start of a new day by crossing the international date line between Hawaii and Kwajalein. As I requested landing instructions and dropped down to pattern altitude, I looked down on twin runways nearly two miles long and thought that this field looked every bit as good as the fields in the States that I was accustomed to. I was amazed at the amount of development that had been accomplished in the scant few months since we had retaken the island from the Japs. In addition to the runways I could see paved hardstands (individual parking/servicing spaces) for over a hundred B-29s, and more were under construction.

As I turned off the runway, a "follow me" jeep picked us up on the taxiway and took us to our hardstand. I had expected concrete or sandbag revetments, but apparently there was no longer any serious threat of Jap raids on the field so open hardstands were all that was needed. I also noticed bombs and other armament stored in the open as well as the scaffolding, cranes, and other equipment the engineering section needed to work on the B-29 engines.

The old standby Army six-by-six truck met us and transported us and our equipment to our quarters—standard Army eight-man wall tents with dirt floors. It was obvious that our last taste of civilization for a while had been at John Rodgers Field in Hawaii. After selecting a cot in the tent, I reported to Lt. Col. Joseph G. Perry, 43rd Squadron commanding officer, and Maj. Harry L. Evans, 43rd Squadron operations officer, both of whom had preceded me to Guam. They briefed me on the status of squadron activity, and I then proceeded to get settled in. The officers of each crew were billeted in one area and the enlisted men in another, but each group followed about the same routine trying to get comfortable. We made up our beds, which consisted of Army cots with pneumatic mattresses and rectangular netting to keep the bugs out. Our clothing and

other stuff went into footlockers. Quonset huts were being constructed, but we expected to be in the tents for a week or two.
The problem with the tent quarters was the dirt floor—it was
difficult to keep anything clean. There were no showers, so we
bathed under a sprinkler truck. Food in the 43rd Squadron
mess was good, and there was plenty of it. A few weeks later,
the officers' mess was completed and became operational, but
the food there was terrible. Different cooks, I guess, and maybe
they didn't like officers.

We learned some of the history and bio-diversity of the
island. Excepting where it had been cleared for our operation,
the jungle was very dense and its trees were unique. Because
there were only twelve to eighteen inches of topsoil on top of
solid coral, the root structure was shallow and broad with roots
actually supporting branches several feet out from the trunk.

The island had been thoroughly sprayed from the air with
DDT prior to the construction of the field and its environs, so
there were no mosquitoes and thus no malaria. The clearing of
the jungle and grading of the coral, however, created another
problem. It was the dry season, and although hot and humid,
there was nearly always a breeze which stirred up the red coral
dust, and it got into everything, including our eyes and noses.
My eyes were red rimmed and I had a ruddy complexion from
a coat of it. Some of the mechanics and others on the flight
line were forced to wear goggles much of the time. Even
though it was the "dry" season, there was a rain shower from
time to time, and then the problem was mud. It was like the
clay back home—it stuck to everything in great gobs. I hoped I
could fly all my missions and be back in the States before the
wet season arrived. I was beginning to empathize with the poor
Marines and foot soldiers who lived in these circumstances all
the time without benefit of tent and cot. Our living conditions
notwithstanding, within the first week on Guam, we came
under the spell of its tropical nights. Our arrival coincided with
a full moon, and with the ever-present fluffy cumulus clouds
floating over us, the outline of the palm trees against the radi-
ance of the sky, and the balmy temperature, the nights were

truly beautiful. They also made us long for the girls we'd left behind.

We were not allowed in the jungle since there were still numerous hold-out Jap soldiers there and the Marines were rooting them out. During the first few weeks after our arrival, one or two a day were captured and others killed. Presumably the reason we were prohibited from the jungle was because the Marines were trigger happy and shot anything that moved. We didn't have any great desire to explore the jungle anyway. One day in one of the lines for a mess hall, there was a slouched figure shuffling along with his head down and his U.S. Army fatigue hat pulled down over his face. Someone in the line didn't think he looked just right and jerked his hat up to reveal—you guessed it—a desperately hungry Jap soldier. He was unarmed and immediately captured and turned over to the intelligence boys. At least he accomplished his objective—in U.S. captivity he would eat well.

During our first days on the island, I listened to frequent explosions around the perimeter of our area and deduced that they were the Marine patrols using grenades as they mopped up the jungle. Not so, it turned out—it was the Army Engineers dynamiting the coral for their construction projects. Shows what a tenderfoot I was.

The day after our arrival Tokyo Rose broadcast the names of all the recently arrived crews, ours among them. This bothered me not because the Japs knew I was there—I couldn't have cared less about that—but because there must have been a traitor somewhere in the States divulging our overseas orders.

About the third day after our arrival on Guam, we lost our new airplane. Operational losses on Saipan had been so severe that Bomber Command was forced to transfer new airplane arrivals there from Guam. 29th Bomb Group crews were then doubled up—two crews were assigned to each aircraft and would alternate flying missions. We shared an airplane with Don Yates and his crew.

On February 25 I flew a practice mission to Maug, a small island in the Marianas chain that contained nothing but an abandoned Japanese weather station. The mission lasted seven and a half hours and was practice for the real thing. We flew formation from takeoff to landing—the longest continuous period of formation I had ever flown, and I had the sweat to prove it. At this time it was anticipated that our bombing technique against the Japanese home islands would be the same as the strategy practiced against the Germans—high-altitude daylight formation precision bombing.

That evening, twenty-one 29th Bomb Group planes took off on the group's first operational mission, together with the 314th Bomb Wing. The target was the urban area of Tokyo, and all 29th Bomb Group aircraft returned safely. Because I was not scheduled on this one, I knew that the next one would be mine. Over the next ten days or so, I flew a couple of short test and training flights, one of which was on a gorgeous moonlit tropical night. It was a beautiful night to fly, but I returned early with engine problems and one engine feathered. Most of my time, however, was spent helping to build Quonset huts. I was anxious to get into one and out of the tent with its dust and dirt.

One day I made a jeep trip to Depot Field in the center of the island to pick up some item of airplane equipment and had a chance to see a couple of native Chamorro villages and a couple of battlefields. The villages were comprised of small thatched huts, and the local mode of transportation—a water buffalo hitched to a cart—was much in evidence. The battlefields looked just like many of the pictures I had seen of the earlier Pacific campaigns—burned out hulks of tanks and devastation everywhere with the tops of all the trees blown off and scorched earth throughout the area. This was the result of the naval bombardment prior to the landing of the Marines.

On March 5 we moved into a Quonset hut with the officers of two other crews. What a pleasant relief! It was up off the ground out of the dirt, had a plywood floor, a front porch, and a screen door. This eliminated the necessity for mosquito netting. We had electric lights down the transom at the top of the hut, the sides of which were ventilated and screened. We eagerly busied ourselves arranging our stuff and getting comfortable. I made up my bed with a couple of sheets that I had scrounged somewhere. Thin as the sheets were, they seemed to make the air mattress more comfortable. The mattresses were a pain—if you blew them up all the way, they were hard and uncomfortable; if you inflated them only part way, then there was no support at the body contact points. You couldn't win. The kit for each Quonset hut came with a few extra sheets of plywood, and I requisitioned a couple of these at the midnight supply and built a desk and chair so that I would have a place to write. All in all I created about as functional and cozy a spot for myself as could be had under the circumstances.

At about this time we were getting down to the serious business of war. On March 7 we flew a local night mission for the specific purpose of practicing radar bombing runs—an important technique we would use to bomb an obscured target through an overcast/undercast. The next day the whole crew worked on the ship in preparation for a mission in which we were to participate on March 9—to Tokyo.

Over Fujiyama en route to the target. USAF

B-29s departing Guam for the Japanese empire. LOOMIS DEAN

The author as a brand new
second lieutenant, April 1943.
USAF

Training bomb approach pilots and bombardiers near Victorville,
California, 1943. DUSTY WORTHEN

The author as a new fighter pilot
at Yuma, Arizona, 1943.

"Home" for the B-29th Bomb Group: North Field, Guam, 1945.

500-pound general-purpose composition "B" bombs loaded in a B-29 bomb bay.
LOOMIS DEAN

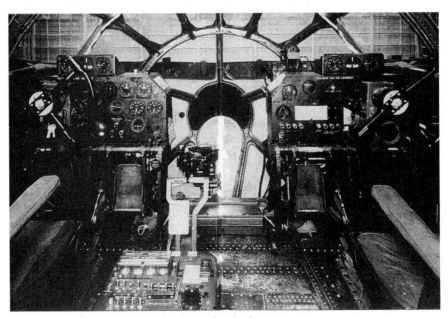

B-29 flight deck. USAF

29th Bomb Group approaching Japan in formation, 1945.
LOOMIS DEAN

Tight formation over Japan, 19th Bomb Group. USAF

World's biggest gas station: North Field, Guam, 1945. LOOMIS DEAN

Crashed B-29 at Iwo Jima with P-51s peeling into landing pattern above. LOOMIS DEAN

P-51s on our wing enroute to Japan, viewed through the left gunner's blister. LOOMIS DEAN

"Mother hen and her chicks"—B-29 leading P-51s to Japan from Iwo Jima. LOOMIS DEAN

Escorting P-51s to their strafing target in Japan, 1945. LOOMIS DEAN

29th Bomb Group ship mortally wounded over Kobe, June 5, 1945. This was the Joseph Franklin crew. USAF

29th Bomb Group "formed up."
USAF

Leaving the initial point for the target, Japan, 1945. LOOMIS DEAN

"Home at dusk"—after 15 hours and 3,200 miles. LOOMIS DEAN

The Robertson crew and the *City of Bartlesville* on Guam, May 1945. Standing, left to right: Robertson, Preuth, Schneider, Rothman, and Henry. Kneeling, left to right: Piccirillo, Kingston, Sampley, Ranker, Seelig, and Retlewski.

"Formidable Formation"—29th Bomb Group, Guam, 1945. LOOMIS DEAN

Otake mission, May 5, 1945. This is an example of the smoke and thermals that the B-29s often flew through. USAF

Starting the long trip home with number one engine feathered. LOOMIS DEAN

Debriefing after the mission.
LOOMIS DEAN

Changing a 3350
on Guam, 1945.
LOOMIS DEAN

"Engine
Junkyard"—acres
of 3350s. LOOMIS DEAN

Tire change: don't try this on the side of the freeway. LOOMIS DEAN

B-29 after ditching on return flight from Japan. The crew was rescued by the Navy. LOOMIS DEAN

Approaching North Field, Guam, from the southwest, 1945.
LOOMIS DEAN

"Going In"—Japan, 1945. LOOMIS DEAN

29th Bomb Group
over the Pacific.
LOOMIS DEAN

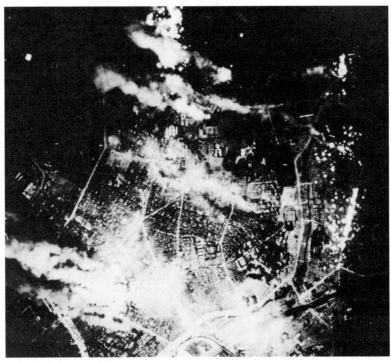

Tokyo mission, May 5, 1945. USAF

Ground crews lived with the planes. LOOMIS DEAN

"Bombs away!" 19th Bomb Group hitting their target. USAF

Koriyama chemical plant after bombs away, April 12, 1945.
The target was completely destroyed. USAF

Gen. Paul Tibbets (*left*), pilot of the *Enola Gay*, which dropped the
atomic bomb on Hiroshima on August 6, 1945, with the author at
the dedication of the B-29 Memorial at the Air Force Academy in
Colorado Springs, Colorado, September 2000.

CHAPTER 7

The Missions

After the March 9–10 Tokyo mission, I had a much better idea of what to expect—not only over Japan, but of B-29 operations in general. Combat operations in any theater and with any airplane resulted in some experimentation to maximize their effectiveness—doing things, either intentionally or unintentionally, that were dictated by circumstances or necessity. For example, in all of my time in the B-29, I had never before taken off with the gross weight that I did on that mission. My takeoffs up to then had probably not exceeded about 115,000 pounds. I had a full fuel load many times, but the bomb bays were always empty, so I was never near maximum gross weight. The B-29 as we flew it in training and as it was delivered to us for overseas duty had a specified maximum gross weight limit of 125,000 pounds. However, once in combat, we loaded them routinely to as much as 140,000 pounds and, in one or two instances, to 142,000 pounds. These high gross weights were not a problem on takeoff if there was enough runway and/or enough headwind, but depending on air temperature, field elevation and other factors, the heavy airplane strained the engines—particularly if you were dragging it all up to 30,000 feet or so. Today, these weights sound minuscule when compared, for example, to a Boeing 747, which weighs, at takeoff, about 750,000 pounds. However, in 1945 the weight we dealt with flying the B-29s was considered tremendous.

There were some other minor modifications made to save weight after we got to the Pacific. For example the inch-thick bulletproof clear glass "windshields" mounted on top of the instrument panels in front of the pilots' and copilots' positions were removed as well as, I understand, some armorplate. Every bit of weight saved allowed for more fuel, more bombs, or both.

After we had more missions under our belts, I became inured to the whole process: the original alert to the scheduled mission; the actual preparation of the aircraft and our equipment; the briefings (one for pilots, one for bombardiers, one for navigators, one for radar observers, and one for radio operators); the short truck trip from the briefing hut to the airplane; and, finally, the beginning of the flight itself. It was a long haul to Japan—a minimum of seven hours with all the attendant possibilities of the effects of severe weather and mechanical malfunctions a long way from home; then the bomb run with the attendant possibilities of getting shot up (or down); then the long flight back with concerns about having enough fuel; and, finally, the release and relaxation of the tension and anxiety, some of which was quite intense, upon landing and telling our stories to the debriefing teams. This included a couple of shots of whiskey from either the doc (flight surgeon) or the debriefers. I noticed that, at the start of the mission cycle, the crew was quieter than usual with some men writing a letter home and each going about his preparations alone with his own thoughts. At the conclusion of the mission, it was sleep for some, perhaps a beach party for others, and, for still others, kickapoo joy juice.

The shots we got at debriefing may have been the best liquor we had during our combat tour except for a few bottles that I had brought with me and stashed away for some celebration. As officers we received a ration of a fifth of booze a week. However, we had no selection—we took whatever came in. Sometimes it would be rotgut rum, sometimes an unknown brand of gin or vodka, sometimes Scotch made in Kentucky, and sometimes Kentucky whiskey that was all of three or four weeks old. I asked a Navy friend at Agana Harbor about this, and he said, "We bring the stuff over here, so we take what we want, and send you guys what's left." Figures. Anyway, we couldn't drink the stuff straight or in a cocktail, so we would get a couple of one-gallon jugs, dump a fifth of whatever in each one, and then fill the jugs with GI grapefruit juice. We had no refrigeration, so we took the jugs on the mission, carrying them in an unpressurized section of the airplane, and when we returned—presto!—we had cold fruit cooler. We called it kickapoo joy juice.

There was another process for beer, which was also rationed. It was saved up and then cooled by the ingenious boys on the flight line. They would fill a fifty-five-gallon drum with bottles or cans of beer, then the drum was partially filled with gasoline, the top tightly secured, and the drum pressurized with air through a tire valve installed in the top. Slightly opening the valve to vaporize the gasoline out of the drum cooled the beer. The lid was removed, and everybody grabbed one. It tasted a little like gasoline, but it was cold.

I've made it sound like we were all alcoholics—quite the contrary. Many passed up the shots offered by the doc or the debriefers and drank little or not at all except at an infrequent party. In my case, I seemed to have lost my taste for beer, and so my drinking was limited to an occasional mini-binge on kickapoo joy juice or imbibing at one of the parties we had.

SECOND MISSION: KOBE, MARCH 16, 1945

We had a few days rest after the Tokyo raid and then flew our second mission, this one to Kobe, one of the leading industrial centers in Japan and at the time the most densely populated city in the world with over 104,000 people per square mile.. This was also a night incendiary mission where we made individual bomb runs. The weather was more or less clear with only broken clouds at our cruising altitude all the way to Japan and over the target. We bombed by radar to insure hitting the target properly; however, the cloud cover was only about six tenths so we could have bombed visually. While this was only our second mission, we were to learn later that such cooperative weather was unusual. A fighter picked us up on the way in but did not attack. We learned that this was not an uncommon occurrence—the fighter would fly along with us out of range of our guns and radio our course, altitude, and airspeed to the anti-aircraft batteries on the ground so they could zero in on us. As we started our bomb run, we saw quite a bit of flak up ahead, but when we got there, we were not shot at, nor did they pick us up in the searchlights as they had when we were over Tokyo. We dropped our bombs and turned away from the city, heading back out to sea. Our observation at bombs away looked like the damage was extensive. We began picking up news broadcasts from the States about the raid on our way back to the Marianas, and while news broadcasts as a rule were not particularly accurate, they were reporting destruction of the target.

The Jap night fighters, except for the one monitoring and pacing our approach, were not in evidence until we had completed our bomb run and banked away from the city; then sixteen of them picked us up and followed us for over an hour. However, none pressed an attack. I attributed this to their inability to see us clearly. The engine exhaust was all that was visible to them as we flew without navigation lights. I cautioned the gunners not to fire unless we were under direct attack and the fighters were within range (theirs and ours) as I didn't want the flames from our gunfire revealing our position. I also considered their lack of aggression as proof that their night fighters were not equipped with any sort of radar to pick up a target at night, so unless it was moonlight, they could not see well enough to attack.

I was particularly tired when I returned to Guam. I don't know why, since this raid was a "milkrun" as far as enemy opposition and weather were concerned. It might have been because of an extended period of "pre-mission jitters" and stress. We had been scheduled for a mission on the thirteenth, but the ship was out of commission at more or less the last minute so we didn't go on that one. Then we were immediately scheduled for Kobe on the fifteenth, but then the mission was postponed for twenty-four hours shortly before takeoff because of weather over the target. Then finally we pulled it off on the sixteenth. Four days of "readiness" was the only reason I could think of for the exhaustion. On the nineteenth, our boys went back to Nagoya to finish incinerating the city. Everyone returned, but flak was heavy. One of our ships had over forty holes in it, but others went through without damage just as we had at Kobe.

Between missions I frequently flew short hops of an hour or two to test repairs that had been made to an airplane or to "slow fly" a new or repaired engine to break it in. On one of these flights I took five Marines along who were visiting the field looking for a ride. I figured that after all, they were the guys who had recaptured these islands so we would have airbases, and the least I could do as a slight token of my appreciation would be to take them up in the big silver bird. Also, they didn't have much to look forward to except the invasion of Okinawa, so I felt they were deserving. Three of these boys had never flown before. During the flight they crawled all over the ship and talked to every crew member. They had a million questions for us, and they had a barrel of fun. I took them on an air tour of the whole island as well as a little buzzing over the Navy in the harbor and the nearby ocean. After we landed, they thanked me profusely, and one of them said he would like to go on a mission with us. That, of course, was not possible, but it was nice to have had such an appreciative bunch of passengers.

THIRD MISSION: NAGOYA, MARCH 24, 1945

It was our turn again with the airplane. We were alerted on the twenty-fourth for a mission to destroy the Mitsubishi engine plant at Nagoya, so we began our preparations. Nagoya could be a tough target—its defenses were on a par with Tokyo and the mission planners always seemed to route us directly over them. Throughout the course of our offensive against Japan, Nagoya missions accounted for a high proportion of 20th Air Force losses. This mission was planned as a night precision bombing raid rather than a general saturation of an area. The plant had been attacked four times previously but had eluded destruction. It was important because Mitsubishi produced about 40 percent of Japan's aircraft engines. The technique to be used was to illuminate the target with flares, bomb the target with incendiaries, then saturate it with demolition bombs to obliterate it.

We took off at 1704 hours loaded with incendiaries to mark the target for the ships behind us. As on the Kobe mission a few nights before, the weather favored us; except for passing through a weak front, we were above the clouds the whole way. It was bright moonlight, a beautiful night to fly, and the airplane was performing perfectly. As we passed Iwo Jima unseen beneath us, I began to be concerned about what I thought could be ahead. Our approach to the target would take us right up the length of Ise Bay, then over the breadth of the whole city before we would even see the target. We would be flying over all their defenses before the actual bomb run was initiated. Why couldn't the planners have had us approach the plant from the land-side where anti-aircraft batteries were not so concentrated? There was no point pondering this question—we were going up the bay and across the city. My other concern was that, if the clouds under us broke up at the coast, it would be a wonderful opportunity for the Jap fighters to have a field day with us. It looked like it might be a tough and costly mission.

As we approached the coast, the clouds did indeed break up, and it was clear over the land mass. There was a total black-out of the city. We were flying at only 7,300 feet so we could see the outline of the bay and as we flew up it, searchlights began to flicker along its shores, and here and there in the dark of the city itself until, as we were over the dock area, there were at least forty or fifty probing the night sky. It was clear and light enough for us to see the dock area, Hori Canal, Nagoya Castle, the aircraft plant, and the river beyond it. As we crossed the city, one searchlight found us and immediately ten or twelve locked on to us. I was once again subjected to the intensity of light in the cockpit as I had been over Tokyo, and I began to worry and sweat—all those lights on us, and nothing happening. I thought that every gun in the city must be tracking us and that at any moment all hell would break loose.

Miraculously, it didn't. One battery put five shots right on our nose and one of those shattered a panel of glass and put a few holes in the skin of the airplane on the top of the fuselage. I didn't see the burst, just heard the glass tinkle at my feet on the flight deck—and then nothing more. The rest of the flak that we saw was meager and inaccurate.

There were Pathfinder B-29s ahead of us dropping flares to illuminate the target for us. We continued our approach, and at bombs away at 0106 hours, twelve of them went out and hit squarely on the roof of the factory, starting the first fires. Al was right on the money. The other eleven hung up in the bomb bay and it took five attempts to get them out. By then we were just off the Jap coast, but the first twelve did the job of lighting the target for the following ships. There was no point in trying to get back into the stream of B-29s again just to get these last eleven on the target. On this mission, each ship had been assigned a specific moment in time to hit the target, and we hit ours to the minute. Any attempt to make another run would have disrupted the flow of aircraft and posed a collision hazard. Because of the ideal night flying conditions, the fighters were up in force, but again, none pressed an attack—at least not on us. I then settled in for the long flight back and landed, tired, at 0845 hours—15:41 hours total flying time.

The next day we got the recon photos, and the plant was still there. A minor percentage of it had been damaged. A paper mill and some other adjacent buildings were destroyed, but not the engine plant. How could that be possible? We could see so well! Intelligence analysts figured that not more than 50 ships out of the 300 on the mission actually hit the factory. Where were those guys looking? We had marked the spot for them with our incendiaries. Five B-29s—none from our wing—were lost on the raid, and we would have to go back and do it again.

A day's rest was in order after this mission, and following that, I finagled a truck and some food and sent the crew on a picnic at the beach. I didn't accompany them, wanting to work on some furnishings for my corner of the Quonset Hut. I previously had been to the beach where they were headed, and on a couple of jeep trips, I had had the opportunity to see parts of the island which they had not. We had still not finished all the Quonset Huts needed to house the crews, and I spent a fair amount of time working on those. In one of my letters to my wife, I said that when I returned home I would be a qualified cabinet maker and construction engineer.

We had a four-hole latrine now, so the slit trenches were passé, but the new latrine didn't afford much privacy. I could read a letter or a magazine over the shoulder of the guy next to me while listening to the groans of encouragement being made by the guy on the other side. I really missed a good, comfortable, flushing toilet. We still didn't have showers, and I don't know what happened to the sprinkler truck, but bathing out of a helmet was what we were doing at this point. That meant carrying a couple of gallons of water from the mess hall up to the front of the hut (or maybe five gallons if you were really ambitious and wanted lots of rinse water). You would then strip to the buff, and using your helmet as a basin, start at the top and work down. Brushing teeth was first, then washing your face, then shampooing, then wetting yourself with half the water left, then soaping up, and finally, rinsing off with the remaining water. Shaving was a separate exercise. I had a little pocket survival stove that burned small tablets for fuel, and using the metal cup out of my mess kit canteen, I'd heat water for shaving. Thus a helmet full of water would make you somewhat more acceptable to yourself and your crewmates.

I was thus engaged one day when Colonel Storrie came by the hut in an open command car with two girls. They had to have been nurses from the Navy hospital in the middle of the island. I don't know where else he might have found women. Anyway, like some other situations in life that you see coming, but cannot stop or avoid, you instinctively and quickly decide to exploit the incident and make the most of it you can. So when I became aware of them almost in front of the hut, I turned and faced them and gave them a full frontal. I guess I thought that, as long as I was caught and he was giving them a tour of our area, I might as well be one of the sights—maybe the high point of the tour. However, if in fact they were Navy nurses, then I probably was not the high point of the tour—probably more like the low point.

The senior officers as well as a lot of others (especially all the wolves in the outfit) were eager to get the officers' club built when the crew quarters were finished. I think that is what the colonel was doing—showing the girls the location of our proposed club. They wanted a place for elbow bending, for the officers to gather and relax and, of course, for parties and some musical entertainment. Part of the plan in support of the club was to dispatch a B-17 on a more or less regular liquor run to Australia so that there would be good stuff to drink rather than the rotgut we were getting from the Navy. The cement for the club's foundation had been acquired—surreptitiously I think. This project was next on our list when the crew quarters were completed. Colonel Storrie tried to motivate us by telling us that the 29th was in solid with the Navy nurses—we were their favorite outfit on the field (I don't know why), and they wanted to come see us, our airplanes, and our club, so hurry up and build it.

Another extracurricular duty to which we were assigned from time to time was censoring the enlisted men's mail. We usually spent a couple of hours in the evening on these assignments, and the objective was simply to insure that no military secrets were being divulged about our location, equipment or operations. So we read letter after letter, and if we found something prohibited or questionable, we would simply snip out a word or two with scissors and send the letter on through. It was often difficult to read the letters—it seemed that penmanship was not an accomplishment of the average airman. Beyond that, the content of the letters was quickly forgotten. We, of course, didn't know the individuals involved anyway, so the letters meant nothing to us. However, after doing this a few times, I could not escape a few general impressions.

First, the great majority of the letters were to wives and sweethearts, and they were, pure and simple, love letters—expressing the writers' love and loneliness and seeking an expression of love and support from the woman. My own letters to my wife were not exceptions. All this was perfectly normal, of course, but I wondered if those women really understood and appreciated how absolutely important their letters and reciprocal expressions of love were to these guys, wherever they were. Walk through any Quonset Hut and over every bunk was one or more pictures of a pretty wife or girlfriend. More were pasted inside the lids of footlockers. More were carried in wallets. More were pasted at crew members positions in airplanes. And how many airplanes were named after the woman in the pilot's life? The morale of the men and, to some degree, the dedication to what they were doing depended on these women.

Another thing that stuck in my mind was that in a very significant number of the letters, after the expressions of love, were stern admonitions to the women to behave themselves. The guys didn't trust them. As one writer put it, "Keep your panties on, your skirt down, and your legs crossed until I get home." Some of the admonishments were even more graphic. I guess I was naive, but I couldn't imagine in my worst nightmares the necessity to caution or admonish my wife regarding such errant behavior.

Occasionally, a censor got out of line and overstepped his authority and the bounds of propriety, appropriateness, and good taste. We had one of those incidents one evening. A young lieutenant was reading a letter and started muttering: "Oh my God . . . for Christ's sakes . . . Jesus!" And then: "Get this sergeant in here." In a few minutes, the sergeant showed up, and the lieutenant started berating him about the contents of the letter. The rest of us were sitting there in ignorance of what was going on—we thought the sergeant had divulged some highly secret military information or something. But no, the lieutenant was infuriated and offended because the sergeant had gone into lengthy, minute, explicit, meticulous, specific, and exquisite detail about what he was going to do to this woman when he got home. The lieutenant, who was perhaps twenty-one or twenty-two years old, addressed the sergeant, who was an old-timer of perhaps thirty-two or thirty-three years and who may have been in the Pacific for a long time. "You can't talk to someone like this," the lieutenant said. We could see the resentment building in the sergeant's face that this young shavetail, this ninety-day wonder, this whippersnapper of a lieutenant, should be sharing his intimate letter and challenging him when there had been no wrongdoing. He responded vehemently, "Why not? She's my wife." And the sergeant was right—it was none of the lieutenant's damn business what he said to his wife, and the incident should never have occurred. The letter went through intact.

Just before the last week of March, the wing was given a few days' rest in recognition of its contribution to the offensive against Japan, which had started with the mission of March 10. There were letters of commendation from General Arnold and General LeMay, and one from General Power to the 29th Bomb Group. It read:

> We have just finished eleven days of all-out effort. The result of this effort has made history. Terrific damage has been inflicted on the enemy's vital manufacturing and shipping centers. Your effort has shortened the war and saved American lives that would have been lost if this damage were to be inflicted by any other method of attack. You have operated under primitive conditions that taxed your ingenuity and resourcefulness. Your tireless effort and fighting spirit have exemplified the highest traditions of our Armed Forces. I am humbly proud to be your Commander.
>
> > Signed: Thomas S. Power
> > Brigadier General

Also during this rest period, there were some individual events worth a celebration. Marchesi received the DFC (Distinguished Flying Cross), my promotion to first lieutenant finally caught up with me after following me around for two months, and Marc was promoted to 43rd Squadron operations officer after Harry Evans was promoted to assistant operations officer for the group. So Marc and I pooled our hoarded good liquor and threw a whing-ding. Besides Marc, me, my crew, Major Evans, and both of the flight surgeons, most of the aircraft commanders of the 43rd Squadron were in attendance. It was just about the end of my V.0.—that well-traveled liquor that was made in Canada, bought in Cuba, smuggled to Kansas, and finally drunk in the Marianas.

ABORTED MISSION TO OMURA, MARCH 30, 1945

We prepared for our fourth mission—this time to Omura on Kyushu just north of Nagasaki with a staging area and repair facilities as the target. I was to fly the number three position in the lead element. We were to take off, assemble at South Iwo, and hit the target in formation in the morning. We were loaded with GP (General Purpose) demolition bombs containing a new explosive known to us only as "Composition B." It was supposed to be very touchy stuff and reportedly the bombs would detonate if dropped on any hard surface from a height of ten feet or more whether they were armed or not.

We had preflighted the ship and were all on board with all four engines running just waiting for some other 29s to clear the taxiway as Bud read the last item or two on the checklist. One of those was to close the bomb bay doors. I responded with "bomb bay doors coming up" and reached down to the aisle stand between us to throw the switch. There were two upright switches next to, and in line with, each other—one marked, "Bomb Bay Doors," and the other, "Bomb Salvo." Don't ask me how or why, but I mistakenly and inadvertently hit the Bomb Salvo switch, and the whole load dropped on the tarmac of the hardstand, rolling and tumbling all over the place under the airplane. At the drop, a red light came on at the top of the bombardier's panel, and Al, eyes big as saucers, and, in a falsetto voice about three octaves higher than usual, whirled around in his seat and exclaimed: "Gordon, you dropped the bombs!!!" I had been watching my crew chief, "Little" John Miller, who was standing in front of the nose waiting for me to taxi. I saw the startled look of fear on his face as he started running down the taxiway when the first bomb appeared—even before it hit the ground. If it had been possible to clock him, I'm sure he would have been recognized as the new world's record holder for the hundred-yard dash. The rest of the crew and the other ground crews on the adjacent hardstands also set some kind of record getting the hell out of there. They were headed for "anywhere-but-here" with a determination and dispatch never before known even to themselves.

All of this, of course, took only seconds to transpire, and I immediately shut down all four engines and scrambled to get out of the airplane. Not everyone on board realized what had happened. Either Jim or Freddie, I don't remember which, appeared on the flight deck saying something like "What's going on? Why did you shut the engines down?" Bud or Al or Pic said something like "We dropped the bombs." Whoever said it, I guess, didn't want to indict me—at least not right then.

We got out of the airplane, and the armorers were already wheeling the dollies toward the bombs to round them up, and people from the ground crews were hesitantly drifting back towards us. I was standing in front of the ship when a jeep came roaring down the taxiway at top speed. It had two flags on the front bumper and a star on each flag. The driver nearly turned it over while veering into the hardstand, both wheels on the inside of the turn lifting about six inches off the ground. The passenger came boiling out of his side of the jeep in a half crouch drawing his Colt .45. He had it about halfway out of the holster when he looked at me and shouted, "Lieutenant, are you going to shoot that goddamned bombardier or do you want me to do it?" I replied, "General, he didn't do it—I did." The general froze in that crouch for a few seconds, staring at me, then shoved his .45 back in its holster, got back in his jeep, and drove off. I don't know whether he figured that bombardiers were expendable and pilots were not, or whether he was just so completely dumbfounded and disgusted that a pilot would do such a stupid thing that he didn't want to acknowledge it or discuss it, so I didn't ever hear another word about it.

My crew said nothing to me about it either—they kept their thoughts to themselves—at least in my presence. I don't know whether they were disgusted or understanding and forgiving—or just glad to be alive under the circumstances. If those bombs had detonated, the whole north end of the island would have been obliterated. There were a couple dozen other B-29s loaded as we were, and God knows how many more tons of bombs stored on the field in addition to hundreds of thousands of rounds of .50-caliber ammunition and millions of gallons of gasoline. It would have been immensely tragic.

A six-by-six truck picked us up and returned us to our quarters. I knew each of the crew members were disappointed at not having made the mission—we were at about the bottom of the list for number of missions flown at that point anyway because of having to share an airplane, and we were eager to fly every mission we could. We went to bed without any incriminations—I don't recall that I tried to make excuses or apologize—and the matter was laid to rest and not mentioned again. Tomorrow was another day.

The rest of the group went on to carry out the mission, and they had quite a time. They assembled at South Iwo as planned and flew on to Omura in formation. As they approached the target, they got some flak, but it was sparse, intermittent, and inaccurate. There was a new development, however: the Japs tried air-to-air bombing. The fighters were up in force, flying above the formation dropping phosphorus bombs hoping to set the B-29s on fire. No 29s were hit, though, and as the fighters then pressed attacks, at least three of them were shot down. There was only minor damage to the 29s, and no one was hurt. All the ships returned safely to Guam.

After my faux pas, an order was issued and distributed throughout Bomber Command and back to the factories in the U.S. that the bomb salvo switches on all B-29s were to have a half-moon guard installed on them, and the toggle switches safety wired so this couldn't happen again. The safety wire could be broken if the intent was really to salvo the bombs, but it would be enough of a deterrent to prevent an unintentional activation of the switch.

Writing a letter to my wife the next day, I started out by saying, "Well, I know now that God is my copilot, and he gets on board before I take off . . .," and then I related the incident. I said nothing more about it for nearly fifty years, being ashamed, I guess, to admit to such a stupendous blunder. Then, at the Boeing party in Seattle in 1992 celebrating the fiftieth anniversary of the B-29, another pilot related his story of aborting a mission on the hardstand one night. When he finished, I said, "Yeah, I aborted a mission on the hardstand one night, too." After telling the story, one of the group said, "I remember that! Was that you??" So the story was out at last, and I've been asked to repeat it many times since then. The 29th Bomb Group Association even has it on tape. I guess that's my punishment—having to tell the story repeatedly.

At the reunion of the 29th Bomb Group Association in Kansas City in 1995, we were guests at Whiteman Air Force Base. On one of the tours, the whole association was standing in front of a B-2 Stealth Bomber listening to a colonel on a scaffolding platform explaining the mission of the airplane and reciting its specifications. After a short question and answer period, he said that the group could form a double line, ascend the scaffolding, and look in the cockpit—"all except the guy in the cowboy hat with the white beard back there. We have switches in this airplane and we don't want him in the cockpit!" Harry Mitchell, our president at the time, had put him up to it by telling him my story.

One other incident relating to this event: while I was inspecting the B-2, a fellow came up to me, introducing himself as being a member of my club—maybe the only other member. He was Ron Jacobs, a technical services representative for Northrop Grumman's B-2 Division. He had committed a very similar act to mine, except that it was about twenty years later and in a B-52, not a B-29. His had also taken place on Guam. Ron was not a member of the military but was on board as a civilian tech rep. He was in the bomb bay as the airplane was taxiing and had his headset on listening to the chatter on the intercom when he heard the word "salvo." It sounded like a command to him, so he reached up and mashed the button, dumping them all out. But enough about all this—I've paid my dues and served my time.

FOURTH MISSION: SHIZUOKA, APRIL 4, 1945

After the rest period of the last few days of March and the aborted mission on the thirtieth, we were anxious to get on with the strikes. That's what would win the war and get us home again.

We were having a little morale problem because the Air Force had not decided how many missions we would have to fly to be eligible for rotation back to the States. There were rumors that it would be twenty-five—the same as in the European Theater. Then that number was questioned because the missions in Europe were tougher since England was socked in most of the time and the Germans were better shots than the Japs. The counterargument was that our missions averaged almost three times longer flying time, and it was all over water—an inhospitable environment if you had to bail out. The uncertainty went on for a few weeks, and finally the number was set at thirty-five. At least now we had a goal. Although it seemed excruciatingly slow, every time we flew a mission we could mark one more off on the calendar, and the day when I could point the nose of the old 29 east instead of north crept a little closer.

On April 2 we were alerted to fly a mission—our fourth—but there was a typhoon in the area, so all flying was canceled until the storm passed. The next night, we flew a mission to Shizuoka to destroy a new Mitsubishi aircraft engine plant. This effort was to be carried out like the Nagoya mission—visual bombing with flares. Forty-eight B-29s of the 314th Wing conducted the raid. This was a difficult mission because of the weather. The typhoon had spawned some wicked fronts between the Marianas and Japan. There was so much harsh, relentless, severe turbulence that at times I wondered if the wings would hold together. I could see the wingtips flexing violently, and I was amazed that something constructed of metal could be that supple and bendable. It was so rough that everything and everyone had to be tied down. Out of a total flight time of 14:27 hours I logged just over seven hours on instruments.

The target was obscured by an overcast with tops at 7,000 to 8,000 feet, so radar runs were made individually by each ship. Radar bombing techniques did not insure the accuracy of visual approaches, however, so results were not precisely marked. The flare ships ahead of us were also locating the target by radar, so there was some question about whether they had dropped in the right place; if not, they would perhaps mislead the ships of the main force. It all combined to make a difficult problem. From the image that Tom had on his radar scope of the ground below, and from what little I could see, I was reasonably sure our bombs hit the target. Also, other B-29 crews who saw us make our bomb run claimed that we hit the buildings, but I had some doubts. Because of the weather we encountered no fighters and saw no flak, although one ship returned with some minor flak damage. My biggest worries were the weather and the possibility of collision with other B-29s.

On the flight home, mentally reviewing the circumstances of the mission, I was concerned that if we had missed the target, Bomber Command would go back to daylight formation bombing in clear weather, and I much preferred the nocturnal excursions. In many ways they were much safer—at least as far as enemy action was concerned. My doubts were resolved later when the recon photos were received and analyzed. They showed 83 percent of the target destroyed. This kind of news was always a relief: the loss of the facility would hamper the Japanese war effort and thereby shorten the war—and we would not have to go back there again.

Well, Bomber Command did go back to daylight bombing the day after we returned from Shizuoka. It was against the Mitsubishi engine plant at Nagoya that we had previously bombed at night, and it was a rough mission. Four B-29s were shot down—two by fighters and two by anti-aircraft fire. A fifth ship was badly damaged and ditched between Japan and Iwo Jima. Two of the four shot down were from our outfit—Crowcroft and Buttfield were lost over the target. Several other badly damaged ships went into Iwo and Saipan.

This was the roughest mission yet for a daylight formation raid—the fighters were very aggressive and the Japs had learned to put up barrage type flak. This meant that instead of shooting at a particular airplane or even at a particular formation, once the B-29s were on the bomb run and irrevocably committed to the prescribed course and altitude to the target, the Japs would simply fill the sky in front of the formations with a continuing barrage of flak. Some pilots said that it was so thick they could have put their wheels down and taxied on it. I also encountered this kind of flak on some later missions that I flew. It gave you a helpless, ill-fated, foreboding feeling when you flew through it because there was nothing you could do about it. You could not fight back, and you could not take evasive action—you just had to sit there and take it—and hope they would not get an engine or knock you down. This time 90 percent of the target was destroyed, so we wouldn't have to go back there and do it again. We had paid a heavy price however for this consolation.

Following this mission, we finally got our own brand new airplane. A replacement crew brought it over and, like our arrival at Guam in February, immediately lost it to us. We, of course, were happy to have our own airplane—no more sharing—and we began talking about what to name it. Each crew member contributed his suggestions and thoughts, and we finally settled on *Grand Slam*. It seemed appropriate for the biggest bomber in the U.S. arsenal. The naming was also influenced by the activity of the officers on my crew—they started a game of bridge shortly after our arrival in the Pacific, and it went on until we completed our tour and were headed home. When we left on a mission they simply put each hand down on the table, and when we returned they would just pick up the cards and continue the game. It lasted six months. *Grand Slam* meant the winning of all thirteen tricks in a deal or the winning of all the events in a competition such as golf. The double entendre for me was that I fully intended to win them all and to slam the holy shit out of the Japs with my big bird. They were going to know and remember that I had been there.

A couple of weeks before getting our own ship, Bomber Command had decreed that each airplane was to be named after a U.S. city. There seemed to have been some complaints by the media correspondents about the difficulty of writing a story to be published in hometown newspapers relating a heroic accomplishment by the crew of the *Vicious Virgin* or the *Nipponese Nemesis* or *Cherry, The Horizontal Cat* (with an appropriate picture) or a crew who identified themselves as the *Hairy Horndogs* or the *Raunchy Rapscallions* or *The Saltpeter Resisters* or any of numerous other examples of crew originality. The noble idea was that dispatches could be made to the papers of the various cities about "their airplane" and thereby promote their interest and a following among the residents of that town. There was another reason for Bomber Command's edict and it may have been the most compelling, notwithstanding what we were told about names and noseart. Eleanor Roosevelt had either seen some airplanes, or pictures of them, and complained to FDR about the vulgarity of the names and illustrations. So it could have been a direct order from the White House.

Not having a ship of our own when the order came down, we were left out. We were a couple of weeks late in the process, so well known cities were already taken. I tried to register my hometown, Omaha, but it was gone; then I tried my wife's hometown of Glendale, but it also was gone. We then just went down the crew list by rank and when we hit Freddie, our navigator, we hit paydirt. Our ship became, officially, *The City of Bartlesville* (Oklahoma). We took some ribbing about that: "Bartleswhat? Where the hell is that?" So, on the right side of the forward fuselage, the standard insignia of a map of North America in a circle with a flag exhibiting the city name was emblazoned in color; but on the left side under my window, in foot high letters was "GRAND SLAM" along with the record of missions flown—each represented by a small bomb.

Freddie and his father were prominent in Bartlesville (or so he said) and were friends of Frank Phillips, president of Phillips Petroleum, the town's preeminent industry and employer. Fred thought Phillips would sort of "sponsor" us and see that we got a lot of publicity, but I don't recall that we ever heard from Phillips or anybody else in Bartlesville except Fred's father who, a couple of weeks later sent navy blue baseball caps for the whole crew. We promptly painted little silver bombs on the bills and front of the caps and wore them for a couple of official photographs.

FIFTH MISSION: KORIYAMA, APRIL 12, 1945

April saw the beginning of another concentrated blitz or offensive against Japan, and our next mission, on April 12, was to bomb a chemical tetraethyl lead plant at Koriyama, 130 miles north of Tokyo on the island of Honshu. Our preparations for this mission included the installation of an extra fuel tank in the bomb bay as this was to be a long flight—over 3,800 miles—and would challenge my fuel management skills. We took off at about 2:00 A.M. and flew singly to a 10:00 A.M. rendezvous at a rock off the coast of Honshu, where we were to form up into three-plane elements and proceed up the coast. I was to fly the number three position in the lead element.

As this mission was just getting under way, a dramatic and almost deadly incident took place. While not lethal, it was tragic for one man and resulted in his becoming the only Medal of Honor recipient in the Twentieth Air Force. Those of us who flew the mission were not aware of what had happened until we returned to Guam, where the story was already circulating. We heard about it in bits and pieces.

When we flew daylight formation missions, it was our practice to fly individually to a rendezvous point somewhere near the coast of Japan, relatively near the target where we would assemble into formation. A formation leader and a deputy leader were designated for each mission, and the other participating aircraft were each assigned positions to fly in that formation. With takeoffs at approximately one-minute intervals, the stream of airplanes would converge at the assembly point and the leader, circling the island or other recognizable spot, would identify himself by firing a flare or dropping a phosphorus smoke bomb from his aircraft as a signal to the others to form up on his ship. Twenty-one aircraft from the 29th Bomb Group conducted this strike, and it was during this assembly procedure that the mishap occurred. While unobserved by me or my crew (we may have arrived at the rendezvous point after it happened), the leader aborted the mission, and the deputy leader fired a flare. The rest of us thereafter formed up on his airplane, and we proceeded to the initial point in formation ignorant of the absence of the original leader.

The original lead plane was flown by Tony Simeral of the 52nd Squadron, and the heroic behavior that saved the crew and the airplane was performed by Henry E. "Red" Erwin, his radio operator. His story has been told over and over and published in the official records of the Air Force, in newspapers and magazines, military organization newsletters, and in various veteran and retired military personnel organization publications. Rather than telling it in my words, I quote from the report written by Lt. Col. Corey Ford and Maj. Alistair MacBain:

We were with Colonel Carl Storrie, the B-29 Group's noted leader, when Erwin's plane returned to the base that night, and we heard the story in faltering sentences from the stunned, incredulous members of his crew.

It had happened about an hour off the coast of Japan, Captain Tony Simeral, the pilot said. Simeral's hands were dotted with burns, and there were deep holes burned in the hands of Lieutenant Colonel Gene Strouse, the Squadron leader, who was flying copilot. But they paid no attention to their burns; what Sergeant Erwin had done put everything else out of their minds.

They were lead ship in the formation, Simeral said. An hour off the coast they were supposed to drop a phosphorus smoke bomb to assemble the other B-29s into position. Dropping the bomb was the radio operator's job: at a signal from the pilot he was to release it through a narrow tube with a flap valve at the bottom. Simeral gave Erwin the signal; but there was a malfunction in the tube. The sputtering bomb hit the jammed valve, bounced back into the ship and exploded in Erwin's face, tearing off an ear and blinding both eyes.

You know how phosphorus burns, with a furious intensity that makes fuselage metal blaze like tinder. The bomb at Erwin's feet was eating its way through the deck, and there was a full load of incendiaries below. He was alone; the navigator had left his table just before and gone up to the astrodome to get a star shot. There was no time to think. He stooped, picked up the white-hot mass of flames in his bare hands, and started forward toward the cockpit, feeling his way with elbows and feet.

The navigator's folding table was down and latched, blocking his way. Erwin's sleeves were rolled up. He placed the blazing bomb under his bared right arm, hugging it against his side while the fire ate into his flesh (you thought of the Spartan boy and the fox), and with the remains of his left hand fumbled with the spring latch until it opened. The loose skin came off his hand onto the table as he lifted it. We looked over the plane next day; you could see the imprint of his whole hand seared onto the table. He took the bomb back in his hands, and he held it out in front of him, and stumbled forward again. He passed the engineer's compartment, a walking torch. The engineer turned a fire extinguisher on him and smothered the flames in his clothing, but the phosphorus was burning into his flesh as intensely as ever. He reached the copilot, and gasped, "Is the window open, sir?" and leaned over and tossed out the bomb. Then he collapsed on the flight deck.

The smoke had blotted out the instrument panel, the plane was out of control; Simeral's wingman, following him down, reported that he was less than 300 feet off the water when he righted it. Simeral radioed the formation that he was turning back, jettisoned his bombs, raced for the emergency field at Iwo Jima. The crew applied first aid to Erwin, gave him plasma, smeared grease on his smoldering flesh. He never lost consciousness; halfway back to Iwo, he asked another question, the only other time he spoke: "Is everybody else all right, sir?" When they removed the unguent pads at Iwo a couple of hours later, and exposed his flesh to the air, it began to smolder again. He was still exhaling smoke, they said, and his body and limbs had become so rigid that he had to be eased through the engineer's window. He could not see or feel, but he could know—he could always know—that he had saved the lives of the ten men of his crew.

As we passed through Pearl Harbor a few days later, we heard about an urgent request for a Congressional Medal of Honor. They wanted to make the presentation to a critically injured Sergeant in Guam. There was just one Congressional Medal in the whole Pacific, as it happened, in a display case at General Richardson's headquarters. They broke open the case, and flew the medal by special plane. We knew it was for Sergeant Erwin; and we knew that no American had ever deserved the Congressional Medal more."

I certainly cannot add to this eloquent report of heroism.

This was the first time I had seen Japan in daylight, and it reminded me very much of California from the air. The topography was similar to parts of California—there were wooded hills with snow-capped mountains behind them, green valleys, and the long irregular coastline. It looked as peaceful as California, too—we could see a few automobiles driving along the roads, and everything appeared very much as it would have had we been flying in the States. I don't know exactly what I expected to see, but surely there was nothing to indicate a war in progress or the destruction we were about to start.

Formation flying is a discipline that takes a lot of practice and a pilot with a deft touch on the controls and keen perception of the most minute changes in the airplane's position and progress. If a pilot is leading a formation, it is imperative that he fly perfectly straight and level and initiate course and altitude changes very smoothly and gradually. The leader must think in terms of the whole formation, not just himself. If he doesn't, his wingmen have a difficult time maintaining their positions. It takes as much skill to be a leader as it does to be a wingman—maybe more.

The whole purpose of flying formation in combat is to achieve and provide concentrated firepower against enemy fighters, and the tighter the formation, the more formidable it is. A tight formation not only concentrates the firepower of all the aircraft, but prevents the fighters from diving through the formation, thus eliminating one favorite form of attack.

On this mission, we had an extremely poor leader, and I was working hard to stay in formation. He was all over the sky, requiring abrupt and large control and throttle changes to stay in position—never a contribution to well-maintained and tight formations. It was also, to some degree, hard on the engines. Constant retarding of the throttles and quickly slamming them forward to an overspeeded condition was not conducive to long engine life. A few days after the conclusion of this mission, I told the pilot of the lead plane that I would never fly as his wingman again because of his poor formation flying techniques. Even his crew felt that his flying ability left a lot to be desired. As it turned out, I didn't ever have to—he was sent back to the States for more "lead crew" training, and our paths didn't cross again.

We proceeded up the coast and finally turned inland on what seemed the longest bomb run ever. We droned along, peacefully, as if we had been on a practice mission in the States. I was tense. I was apprehensive because the weather conditions and our low altitude of 8,000 feet provided an excellent opportunity for Japanese opposition. I was waiting, expecting something—flak, fighters, anything—but there seemed to be neither, just the country spreading out below us and the target coming up ahead. I stuck my tongue out to wet my lips and my mouth was like cotton. It was chilly up there, and yet I was perspiring freely from the anxiety of the expected opposition. It was different from the night missions: we could see, of course, and we were in formation, so we felt that if there was to be any trouble, we would have a lot of company. We felt more secure with the other ships near to help us if fighters did come. But none did—and there was no flak. That always astounded me—on some flights we went through hell and on others we had little or no opposition. This was one of those. We went straight in, dropped our bombs—scoring a perfect hit and completely destroying our target—turned for the coast again, and flew on out. Only then did a couple of fighters show up, but they did not press an attack—they flew over us dropping a few phosphorus bombs without damaging us.

I thought at the time that the reason for the lack of opposition on this mission was that we took them completely by surprise despite the clear weather. They apparently didn't detect our coming, and when they found out, it was too late. I also suspected that they didn't think we could make it that far north of the Marianas and therefore neglected to have defenses there.

On this type of mission, only the bombardier in the lead plane used his bombsight on the bomb run. All the other bombardiers kept their eyes glued to the lead plane, and when they saw the first bomb come out of its bomb bay, they released theirs. Thus, if the lead bombardier was properly on the mark, the whole formation's bomb load hit at the same time and place, obliterating the target—usually a military installation, a factory, or other vital industrial facility. Conversely, if the lead bombardier was not on the target, then the whole formation's explosives were wasted, and the mission would have to be flown again. "Dropping on the leader" also served another purpose. If the formation was under attack from enemy fighters, the bombardier was freed to become the nose gunner—an important station as many fighter attacks came from head-on at twelve o'clock. In such a case, the pilot, whose eyes were already glued on the lead plane to stay in formation, dropped the bombs when he saw the pattern start to emerge from the leader.

Bombs were away at 1230 hours, and I started the long flight back, conserving all the fuel possible. When I arrived at Guam, the weather was horrible with a storm over the island. I flubbed around in the soup at 500 feet fearing collision with other ships. I decided that this was no place for me so I dropped down to the deck to avoid the traffic and flew down to the center of the island to land at Depot Field after 18:12 hours in the air. This was the longest mission flown in the Pacific Theater in World War II. B-29s made longer flights after the war ended, but this mission set the record up to that date. In a few hours, meteorological conditions improved enough for me to take off and return to North Field. I arrived there about 1:30 A.M.—almost twenty-four hours after I had left. Two airplanes were lost by the 314th Wing on this mission, but none from the 29th Group. One ditched, and one crashed on landing as a direct result of the storm over the island and pilot error on the approach to both fields. In his let-down off the approach end of the runway at North Field in almost zero visibility conditions, the pilot descended too low and hit a tree. He immediately slammed the throttles to the firewall and pulled up, but the ship had sustained considerable damage in the encounter with the tree. He then flew down to Depot Field in the middle of the island and made an approach behind us. Almost to the threshold, but short of the runway and only a few feet in the air, he chopped the throttles to start his landing flare; however, because of the lack of power and the damage to the wing, the 29 stalled out and crashed. It exploded immediately and burned. Only one man—the tail gunner—survived. We witnessed it, and once again, the event had a personal twist for me. Among the crew members who were killed was a boy from Omaha. I had not known him, but his father was a business acquaintance of my father's, so I was called upon to supply details of the crash for the bereaved family.

After my return to the States, and while on leave for a week or so in Omaha, this man met with me in my father's office to hear the details of the crash that had taken his son's life. I repeated those details almost verbatim from the letter I had written about it following the crash. He asked a number of questions which I answered as best I could. It was not a long meeting—perhaps fifteen or twenty minutes—and was somewhat awkward and strained because of the subject matter and because we were strangers. When he rose to leave, I shook hands with him and expressed my sorrow for his loss. He then turned to my father to shake hands and thank him for arranging the meeting, and I thought his face expressed anger and resentment, as if to say, "You still have your son—mine is gone." As I stood by my chair when he went out the door of the outer office, I thought, "I have not brought this man comfort, but only renewed turmoil." I hope I am not being callous or unfair, but this was the impression I had at the time.

I was learning that, for many parents and other family members, acceptance of the death of a soldier or airman was tempered or influenced by the circumstances of his demise. Crass as it may sound, they would like to report to others, and themselves believe, that their loved one died in heroic defense of his country and not as a result of his driver hitting a tree or some other non-enemy-action disaster or accident.

Many families had no place to go to establish a parting with their loved one, no overseas grave that they could visit, no remains sealed in a box that they could rebury at home—indeed, for many, no knowledge of the how or where of the departing of their flesh and blood. They could only live in the shadow of their loss, and recall memories that had no connection to the event of the loss itself. Unfortunately, this was part of the tragedy and misfortune of war.

SIXTH MISSION: TOKYO, APRIL 13, 1945

I had been without sleep for forty-two hours at this point but found myself scheduled to fly again almost immediately. I didn't think I was physically able to go another thirty or forty hours without sleep, but there was no time to think about it. We were going—period!

We grabbed about seven hours of sleep while the ground crew prepared the airplane for another mission, and we took off again that evening for a night strike against what most of us considered our roughest target, Tokyo. I always felt that we were safer up there at night than in the daytime, but still, the anxiety and apprehension were intense because you were alone. You wondered all the way to Japan what you would encounter, and you hoped and prayed that you would make it to the target and complete the bomb run without being hit.

As we turned from the IP onto the bomb run, the searchlights began to probe the sky. We prayed again that they wouldn't find us, but then one did, and immediately others swung over to us. Then I knew it was coming, and in a few seconds I felt the rumbling of the flak exploding and heard the shrapnel raining off the ship. They had us spotted, and the ship started to bounce and lurch from the thermals and the concussions. That's when you really begin to feel lonesome. You are there all alone in the night and it seems as though the whole world is fighting you and you wonder how you can stand such odds. You have a terrible urge to start climbing-climbing faster and faster—until you are out of earth's bounds and nothing can reach you; but you have a job to do, so you just stay the course, sweating and hoping, and each second seems like an eternity. You bore on through, and finally the bombs go away and you turn for the quickest way out of the inferno and conflagration below, seeking the safety of darkness and altitude and clouds and ocean between you and the enemy. And when you reach it, you stop to realize what you have gone through and a sort of ecstasy grips you because you are alive and unhurt, and it buoys you up because there were times when you didn't know whether you were coming out of it or not. And then you realize how tired and exhausted you are, and you drowse and wait for the long hours to pass so you can put your wheels down on your home base again. You say a prayer of thankfulness, and then when you get home, you wonder why your prayers were answered and someone else's were not—they are still in the target and they won't be back. And you wonder again—maybe next time it will be different—but you are too tired, so you just sleep, and the next mission seems as far away as the ones behind you.

This mission was not as bad for us as some others though. The aiming point was the Tokyo Arsenal. We went in at 9,500 feet in clear weather and obliterated the target as well as most of the surrounding area. B-29s from all three wings participated, and thus the bomb loads varied. Some ships carried incendiaries, some carried 500-pound general-purpose demolition bombs and others carried 1,000-pound general purpose demolition bombs. 10.8 square miles of the city were burned out. Tokyo was slowly becoming a wasteland.

Seven B-29s were lost, including another from our outfit—Fritschel went down into the inferno. We went through unscathed again, but we witnessed ships on both sides of us taking a hell of a beating—flak was heavy and accurate. The arsenal was somewhat obscured by smoke so we used radar as a back-up to insure that we hit it. We landed at 0840 hours, logging 14:18 hours of flight time. I was greeted with the news at debriefing to get some sleep as I was again scheduled to go right back up there that evening. I really needed some rest but on second thought decided, "What the hell, let's fly the damn missions and get them over with so we can go home." I had nothing to say about which ones I flew anyway—as long as I was upright and the body was warm, they kept scheduling me. But that's what I was there for—to destroy Japan and win the goddamned war.

SEVENTH MISSION: KAWASAKI, APRIL 15, 1945

So back we went. We took off about 4:00 P.M. for Kawasaki, which, along with Yokohama is a part of the Tokyo metropolis located on the west side of Tokyo Bay. This was another night low-altitude incendiary mission. We were pathfinders this time, expected to mark the target for the main force following us. We managed to get through the first searchlights without being detected, but then they caught us as bombs were away at 11:55 P.M. in the midst of flak that was murder. The Japs had moved a lot of 40mm guns into the area, and with our altitude and airspeed nailed down, they were very effective. We went through there like a broken field runner—turning, dodging, leveling out, turning again, and still we couldn't seem to get away from it. One shell went completely through the left wing and exploded above us, and others were exploding so rapidly that it sounded like hail on a tin roof. I had a new airplane commander along who wanted to see what it was like before he started flying missions himself, and he really had a show. We saw three B-29s shot down before we got out of the target area, and we were full of holes ourselves. However, apparently nothing vital had been hit. We knew we had some hits but, of course, didn't know the extent of the damage until we landed.

Then we counted up—one big hole and five smaller ones all the way through the left wing; a hole in the flap; a hit in the number one engine; a hit in the number three engine; a big hole in the belly; a hit in the nose, which broke the glass again; and several small holes in the tail. Yet all four fans kept turning and took us home. When I looked back on it, I wondered how we flew through all that lead without more happening, but we did. Others, however, were not so fortunate. Eleven ships were lost: two more from the 29th—Watson from the 6th Squadron and Russell from the 52nd Squadron—didn't make it back. The original crews of the 29th Bomb Group were rapidly being thinned out.

This was our seventh mission, and I was convinced that I had the best damned crew in the outfit. They sit up there on every mission and take it and function perfectly as a team. I don't think they react to the pressure as noticeably as I do— Bud said he looked at me once on the bomb run and my face was glistening from sweat pouring off it. I'm busy on the bomb run and in the target area, so every man helps me. They spot flak batteries and watch for fighters and other B-29s, and their voices on the intercom are reassuring and a great help. In one of my letters to my wife, I said, "I wouldn't swap them for any other bunch."

At this time we learned of the death of President Roosevelt on April 12. I noted it without much emotion one way or the other. The country and the war machine were cranked up and in high gear. The momentum of the war effort would carry things on, and I couldn't see how our lives would be affected in any particular regard. I had not liked Roosevelt because of events in the early and middle '30s when I perceived his actions to be ruthless, tyrannical, and vindictive. Throughout his terms in office, I also believed his programs were leading us down the road to socialism. My thoughts were more about what sort of president the new man, Harry Truman would prove to be. I had missions to fly, and that was my immediate concern.

After this mission, I began to think about what I might do—for example, what flight tactics I could change—to increase the probability of getting through the target area without damage. There was nothing I could do about barrage flak, but that was used primarily against formations in daylight. On the night missions where B-29s were overflying the targets singly, it was the pilot's discretion how he flew as long as he didn't impede or hinder the mission plan. We were never criticized as long as we put our bombs on the target. However, we were assigned specific altitudes at which to bomb, and I didn't want to change that—if I was lower, I risked having another B-29 drop its bombs on me, and if I was higher, I risked dropping on another ship. Of all of the computations needed to hit us, the Japs seemed to be most inaccurate with elevation. I remember one instance when we got a burst about 100 feet below us followed by a burst 100 feet above us. I feared the next one—after those bracketing shots—would be right on our nose but it was not—it was 200 feet below us. Elevation then might be the most vulnerable computation for the Japs and the least dangerous for us. But what about airspeed? The Japanese anti-aircraft batteries usually had our altitude and airspeed and course cranked into their computations to track us, so what if I threw one of these computations off to confuse them? I decided to try it. It would not be absolute insurance, of course, but it might be the one element to save us from being hit on some occasion. I decided to fly faster. The Japs were accustomed to our usual airspeeds of 230 to 250 miles per hour, so what if I flew 300 miles per hour? It would get us in and out faster and throw the anti-aircraft gun batteries off. By then we'd be gone. I resolved to make this a part of my future tactics.

I talked to some of the intelligence boys a day or so after the Kawasaki mission, and they said that we would probably not be scheduled for some time for more missions like the last two because we had destroyed so much of Tokyo that the mission objectives had been pretty well accomplished and also because the increased opposition was making it tough on our crews. They added, though, that a new all-out offensive against Japan was about to start, and they were betting, along with the Navy, that the war would be over by September.

The day after that conversation, we were put on the alert to fly a mission every other day for the next ninety days. To me, that meant only one thing—a huge air offensive coordinated with the Navy to precede the invasion of Japan. Many of us who were flying the B-29s were of the opinion that an intensive enough bombing offensive would bring Japan to its knees without an invasion. On every mission, we were witness to the destruction of their cities, and even at this point in the war, we were able to put several hundred B-29s up for a strike. Despite our losses, the XXI Bomber Command was increasing in strength. We would soon be able to launch as many as 750 or 800 ships to hit various targets in Japan simultaneously. Adding credence to this knowledge was the news that production of B-29s was being curtailed and some factories were being shut down because, after the big offensive, there would no longer be a need for B-29s. Moreover, a couple of bombardier instructors whom I had known during my assignment at Victorville showed up on replacement crews and told me that nearly everyone from Victorville—both pilots and bombardiers—were now in B-29 outfits either in the States or on their way to the Marianas.

The thought of the war possibly being over in six months was heartening and encouraging, but in all major military efforts, whether on land, or on the sea, or in the air, the risks were intensified and the losses were inevitably multiplied. The generals planning them had to be concerned with the ultimate objective and the accomplishment of that objective—and not be overly concerned with losses unless their plans indicated annihilation of their own forces. B-29s and their crews, of course, were the tools of the planners, and as a pilot, I was well aware of my function and responsibility in their plans. As line officers and airmen, we had to carry out those plans. At the same time, I was also aware of my vulnerability. I hoped we would survive it all.

I wondered if I could physically endure a schedule calling for a mission every other day. Flying three missions in four days as we had just done had almost made a zombie out of me. I couldn't unwind. The few hours of sack time that we were able to get between flights was not restful and regenerative sleep.

We slept as if we were doped and then forced ourselves to function against the will of our bodies. On the missions themselves, some crew members could catch up on a bit of sleep, but for the pilot, navigator and flight engineer, consciousness and attention at all times was, almost without exception, a necessity. There were a few times when I just couldn't keep the lids up, so after taking off and setting up the autopilot, I'd tell Bud to watch everything and to wake me up at Iwo if I was asleep; then I'd doze in my seat with my chin on my chest as we droned on. But, as I have previously said, there was a war on, and our steadfast allegiance to the cause was necessary. We hadn't forgotten why we were there.

Rumors were flying thick and fast. The latest was that the enlisted men on Saipan had been issued ODs (wool olive drabs) in anticipation of a move to Russia. The expected scenario was that the war in Europe would soon be over, then Russia would declare war on Japan and grant us airbases on the west side of the Sea of Japan, putting the B-29s within an hour or two of any target in the Japanese Empire. I'd have to see that to believe it. Where did all these latrine-o-grams originate anyway?

EIGHTH MISSION: KANOYA, APRIL 18, 1945

The invasion of Okinawa had started on April 1, and by the middle of April, the Navy was catching hell off its shores, including Jap kamikaze attacks. They inflicted major damage, beginning with the aircraft carrier *Franklin*, on which 724 men were killed and 265 wounded, followed by the aircraft carrier *Wasp*, on which 101 were killed and 269 wounded. As April progressed, the attacks were stepped up until about fifty ships had been sunk or so badly damaged that they had to withdraw from the battle. These included the carriers *Intrepid* and *Hancock*, the battleship *Maryland*, and twelve destroyers. These losses were considered by the Navy to be of sufficient concern to warrant asking the B-29s to strike Kyushu airfields. It was not a mission for which the B-29 was designed, but although we could probably not accomplish much more than a disruption, the XXI Bomber Command's schedule was diverted to help the Navy.

I had a soft spot in my heart for the Navy and felt we owed them a great deal. I was glad to fly a mission in their support. They had a "Dumbo" (PBY amphibian) flying off the end of our runways every time we took off in order to pick us up if we went in the drink. A submarine picked up one of our ditched crews, took them on the sub's mission, and then, three weeks later, sent us a TWX from Pearl Harbor to come get them. To us, it was a crew returned from the dead. There were other courageous submarine commanders who surfaced right under the Japs' noses on their coast to pick up our guys. So if I could return the favor, I was all for it.

On April 18 I participated in a mission to knock out the airfield at Kanoya on the island of Kyushu. Some of our ships carried 500-pound HE (high explosive) bombs to crater the runways making them unusable, and the rest of the aircraft carried fragmentation bombs to destroy aircraft on the ground and anti-personnel bombs (similar to the frag bombs) that were booby trapped to go off at intermittent intervals over a period of about twenty-four hours, thus rendering the airfield inoperative for that period of time. This was a daylight formation mission flown at 18,000 feet. No fighters were encountered and the flak was moderate but accurate, and several ships suffered damage. One of the 29th Group's aircraft was hit several times; an engine was knocked out and the navigator was wounded. They went into Iwo for medical and mechanical assistance. We, once again, suffered no damage and no injuries.

The next several days were spent resting and relaxing including one day at the beach, where we found a secluded inlet with high cliffs on each side, white sand, and calm water. There were not many people there—a few officers and Navy nurses—so it was not like Coney Island. I had some goggles and a snorkel tube and swam among the rocks and along a reef looking at interesting plants as well as varieties of sea urchins and sea anemones that I had not seen before. It was beautiful, and for a little while, I was able to forget all about the war.

EMERGENCY LANDING ON IWO JIMA

As we were winging our way across the Pacific from Mather Field in the last weeks of February, the invasion of Iwo Jima was just beginning. Both General Marshall and General Arnold had deemed the capture of Iwo Jima essential to the defeat of Japan. A line drawn from the Marianas to Japan ran right through Iwo, and it would provide an emergency landing spot for B-29s returning from missions to the Empire low on fuel, damaged beyond the probability of making it home, or with wounded on board needing immediate medical attention. It also would function as a base for P-51s to provide fighter cover for the B-29s on daylight formation missions. The campaign waged by the Navy and the Marines to capture the island was one of the most grueling, bitter, bloody, and hard fought of the Pacific War. It was the most costly fight in Marine Corps history. It had cost more in lives lost per square foot than any other battle. Occupation of the island was achieved only with appalling casualties.

The story of the Iwo Jima campaign is a fascinating and enthralling tale in itself—but not to be told here. What can be told here is that the nearly 6,000 Marines who lost their lives securing the island and its airfields ensured and made possible the survival of thousands of B-29 crew members who landed there between March and the middle of August 1945. I was one of those, and the Marine Corps has my respect, gratitude, and an undying feeling of indebtedness and appreciation for their sacrifice. They truly died that we might live. I doubt if there is any B-29 crewman alive today who does not feel as I do.

The first B-29 to land on Iwo Jima did so on March 4. The aircraft was on a return flight from a raid on Tokyo and had experienced malfunctions that would have prevented it from reaching its home base. The emergency was open bomb bay doors and an inoperative gas valve. The open doors had created so much additional drag that fuel consumption had been substantially increased and the stuck valve prevented fuel flow from the reserve bomb bay tanks. It was Iwo or nothing.

A successful landing was made on the dirt fighter strip adjacent to Mount Suribachi, after which the doors were closed and the fuel valve repaired. This was what capturing Iwo was all about. Thousands of cheering Marines had just preserved eleven lives and a B-29 for the Air Force.

My first experience landing at Iwo Jima came only a few weeks after the island was declared secure on March 18. We were returning from a mission that had turned out to be a nightmare—not from enemy action, but from weather, logistic, and mechanical problems.

We had taken off about two in the morning and flown to a rendezvous point at Tanega, a small island just south of the southern tip of Kyushu. Our target was the airfield and military installation at Miyazaki on the east side of Kyushu. The weather was good virtually all the way to our landfall, and then it socked in solid. We were supposed to get into formation at 16,000 feet, but we were all on instruments at 16,000 feet. From the chatter on the radio, I concluded that everyone was going on top, so I started up too. It was as thick as pea soup, and there were sixty-six airplanes milling around in it. We were fortunate that we had no midair collisions among the B-29s. I accumulated a lot of ice on the way up and finally broke out in a hole at 23,000 feet, but I had to go to 29,000 feet to clear it all. There were a lot of ships up there—spread out over a wide area—and after chasing some of them around without finding any of our own, I elected to bomb a secondary target by radar alone. The radar image, however, was so poor that we had to make two runs at it to drop our bombs. Then the bomb release mechanism malfunctioned, only eight bombs went out, and the bomb bay doors would not close.

What followed was about forty-five minutes of flying around getting the rest of the bombs to drop and, finally, using emergency procedures to get the doors closed. These chores involved Al running through his procedures several times, checking his circuit breakers to be sure all were closed, then trying to drop them through the salvo circuit, and finally, going into the open bomb bay and—hanging on to the catwalk framework—physically kicking the bombs out or tripping each mechanism with a screwdriver. Hal Seelig, one of the gunners, went in the bomb bay with him to help, and then they hand-cranked the doors shut.

I no longer have a distinct recollection of our having done so, but at 29,000 feet, the procedure to accomplish all this would have been to depressurize the airplane so the door to the bomb bay could be opened, then have everyone don oxygen masks to survive while the two crew members were in the bomb bay using portable bottles and masks. The cabins would have been repressurized after their reentry. I do recall that on other missions when we had similar malfunctions, we were either at an altitude below 12,000 or 15,000 feet, or descended to moderate altitude before entering the bomb bay so oxygen was not required. I must assume that on this occasion we descended to an altitude permitting entry into the bomb bay, because I do not recall depressurizing the airplane. Another of my crew members, Tom Henry, recalls experiencing bitter cold during this incident but, like me, has no recollection of depressurization. By this time, of course, I had burned so much fuel that there was no chance of making it back to Guam. It had to be Iwo.

As I approached the island, I got on the Navy's radio frequency and, after explaining that I did not have enough fuel to reach the Marianas and that it was either land at Iwo or ditch, I received that universal, widespread, constantly encountered military command: "Stand by."

I circled the island at low altitude and reduced speed, observing the destruction and utter desolation of the landscape as well as the traffic between the U.S. armada and the beach. There must have been 150 vessels of various types anchored or standing off the western beachhead unloading supplies to be transported ashore. The dozens of lighters, LSTs, LCMs, and DUKWs plying the waters back and forth reminded me of streams of ants on the march. This went on without pause, day and night.

I decided that if I could not land, I would ditch the airplane right there in the middle of their anchorage where they could pick us up, but I really didn't want to ditch—I preferred to land. The Navy came back on the air telling me that they had no gas on shore, so again, "Stand by." After more "holding pattern," they radioed instructions to land at the small number one airfield just by Mount Suribachi. They also said to land to the southwest, as there were still Jap infantry troops at the east end of the field and they would be potting at me on my approach. Better to end my landing roll at the friendly end.

They had sent gas ashore in fifty-five gallon drums in a DUKW and four or five marines or sailors were waiting for me as I braked to a hard stop at the end of the dirt strip. I had the window open, and one of them yelled, "Don't shut them down" as he and another man scrambled up on the wing, opened the cover, and removed the gas cap to the main wing tank. I told them to put it all in one tank, as, once airborne, I could transfer fuel from one tank to another. The men on the ground then end-rolled the drums up to the trailing edge of the wing and, after handing the hose up to the two on top, started pumping madly. As arms tired, they would spell each other, and as a drum was emptied, they quickly unscrewed the pump, screwed it onto another drum, kicked the empty over the cliff, and again pumped madly. When the last one was empty, it too went over the cliff, the gas cap and cover were replaced and secured and they jumped to the ground, yelling, "Get the hell out of here!" As they slid down the cliff, I turned around and opened the throttles taking off to the northeast as we again took small arms fire, but without damage, from the Japs.

I no longer remember how long we were there or how many gallons of fuel they gave me, but it was enough to get home. I also no longer remember how long the strip was, but light as we were, I made it in and out O.K. My guess is that it was about 3,800 or 4,000 feet—about half what the usual B-29 runway was. It was shorter than the field in the center of the island and had been used as a fighter strip by the Japs. The flight back to Guam, at low altitude, was uneventful, and we landed a couple of hours after all the other 29s had returned from the mission.

NINTH MISSION: SUZUKA, APRIL 22, 1945

After the rest and the day at the beach, I was called to operations and told to prepare for another mission the next day. I was not told much about the mission or its objectives—just that I would not be carrying bombs, and I was to fly to Iwo Jima, where I would get a further briefing.

Accordingly, the next morning about seven, we departed Guam and arrived at Iwo at about eleven in somewhat stinky weather, although fairly good for Iwo. We had lunch and then attended a briefing to learn that we were to take a bunch of P-51s on a strike against the naval airfield at Suzuka on the west side of Ise Bay, just south of Nagoya, the following day. The fighters did not have the navigational capability to make a 700-mile flight over open water, but they could follow us, and we would take them to their target. We would also monitor their radio frequency and be a "listening post" for them although their leader would direct the attack on the airfield.

As B-29 aircrew members, we had no opportunity to collect war souvenirs ourselves; we could only barter liquor for them from Marines sent to Guam for rest and recuperation between campaigns. (I acquired an Arisaka rifle and a small automatic pistol this way.) We had a good part of the afternoon left and concluded that this might be a good opportunity to find some relics to take home with us. One of the Marines to whom we spoke suggested that we follow a bulldozer which was working along the edge of the island somewhat inland from the beach. "He'll turn some things up for you." Well, he did—first a live bomb that had failed to detonate, then numerous other things like parts of vehicles and other miscellaneous war materiel, and then the bodies of two Marines killed in the assault on the island. That ended our souvenir hunting—we no longer had the stomach to follow the bulldozer. The bodies were retrieved and identified for burial.

This incident emphasized the differences between the way footsoldiers and airmen lived and died. The Marine or footsoldier was in the battle all the time, living in miserable conditions day and night, whereas we lived in fairly comfortable circumstances and faced battle only intermittently. In our situation, it was pretty much a case of returning from a mission or not—there was usually not much in between. There were exceptions, of course—some crews ditched and survived, some crews were able to make it through to an emergency crash landing in crippled, badly damaged aircraft. A few were able to abandon their aircraft and parachute to an unknown fate on the ground—to be taken prisoner perhaps—but many still died. However, most of the time, it was a few last minutes of unmitigated sheer terror and then obliteration: no identification, no burial—just gone.

We learned more about the island that day. "Iwo Jima" means "Sulfur Island," and the name was apt, as fumes from sulfur springs permeated the air at all times. It was one of the Volcano Islands chain only 660 miles from Japan and had been considered a part of the Japanese homeland. It was created by twin volcanoes that rose above the surface of the sea. At the southern tip of the island, one of those volcanoes had risen about 550 feet above sea level and created Mount Suribachi (literally a cone shaped mountain), a landmark visible from many miles at sea. The island was small—only about five miles long and perhaps two and a half miles wide at its widest point. It comprised approximately eight square miles. The other volcano was on the northern part of the island and had created a rocky plateau about 300 feet above the ocean. Sulfur bubbled to the surface from the lava below making the ground hot in many places.

It was one of the most desolate places imaginable—just rock covered with about two feet of volcanic dust. The personnel stationed there wore goggles all the time. There was no vegetation whatsoever and no water. Water for drinking and cooking was imported or distilled from seawater. The sulfur-laden water that came out of the ground could be used for bathing as it was hot—almost too hot for bare skin—but it could be used if you didn't mind smelling like sulfur. The wind blew all the time, compounding the problem of aircraft maintenance. The volcanic dust was very abrasive and it took its toll on all machinery. We learned that numerous airplanes crashed because the dust raised on the takeoff run clogged filters, killing engines just as the airplane became airborne. Iwo became known among the troops as the "Asshole of Creation." If they were going to give the world an enema, this is where they would stick the hose.

Weather was also a severe problem around Iwo. It was usually bad and made aircraft operations very difficult. The night before we arrived, five P-61s (Northrop night fighters) and three B-25s were lost in bad weather in the vicinity of the island. Iwo was a very busy place. Besides the water traffic between the fleet and shore, the airstrips handled a lot of traffic. In addition to the aircraft newly based there, the island was a haven for crippled B-29s returning from missions to Japan. Parking space was at a premium. While we stood by the runway watching all the activity, a returning B-29 with its bomb bay doors open touched down almost in front of us and a 500-pound GP demolition bomb dropped out of the bomb bay. We all hit the dirt, but fortunately it didn't explode.

We were billeted in tents for the night with cots to sleep on. We slept in our clothes and were not too comfortable—but we slept. We had been warned not to leave the tents during the night as the sentries would shoot anything that moved and investigate in the morning to see what they had shot. They were dead serious about this. A week or ten days before our arrival for this assignment, and only three days after the arrival of the 15th and 21st Fighter Groups, a Japanese infantry detail boldly penetrated the 21st's bivouac area about two o'clock in the morning and, charging into their tents, began throwing grenades and slitting the throats of the sleeping airmen and other personnel. Most of the invaders ultimately were killed, but not before the 21st Group suffered forty-four fatalities, including nine or ten P-51 pilots who had just arrived that day by air transport. The wounded numbered nearly a hundred.

This was an ironic event—the detail was led by a Jap sergeant who had lived in the U.S. and spoke English. He reportedly was counting cadence in English as he led his men into the area. Why this didn't alert the U.S. troops is still a mystery—who would be marching and counting cadence in the middle of the night in a combat zone? Strange things happen. The Japs were secreted in caves and an elaborate system of tunnels which had withstood our pre-invasion bombardment. The final operation for their extermination was to go into the caves with flame-throwers and incinerate them—which the Marines did over the weeks following the incursion.

We took off the next morning to escort the fighters to Japan. There were 6 B-29s and 124 P-51s headed for six airfield targets. We took our group to the tip of Ise Bay, where they peeled off and went in to strafe the target. We then went off the coast a few miles and orbited over a "lifeguard" submarine which was surfaced and going around in tight circles creating a wake that could easily be seen from the air. It took a lot of guts for that sub commander and his crew to do that right under the Jap's noses. During the strike one P-51 came off the bay heading out to sea, the pilot radioing that "they got my radiator—the engine will seize in a minute." I asked him if he could see the sub, and upon his affirmative answer, I instructed him to bail out or ditch as close to the sub as possible. Then we watched as he threw the canopy back and hit the silk. His ship crashed, and he hit the water in his chute. The sub started after him immediately and picked him up exactly seven minutes after he jumped. It was perfect coordination, and we were relieved to see him rescued. This was the sort of thing that endeared the Navy and the Air Sea Rescue Service to me. The fear of a ditching episode was ameliorated by the knowledge that the Navy would risk their subs and ships and men to try to pluck us from probable death.

The P-51's fuel capacity only allowed approximately fifteen minutes over the target if they were to get home again, so as they started coming out, we picked up about twenty-five of them and headed for Iwo. One B-29 and twenty-five fighters—

like a mother hen with her chicks. The fighter pilots seemed
elated. They looped and rolled around us until Iwo came into
sight when they again peeled off and dove for home. Our
radio equipment had failed as we were leaving the Japanese
coast, so on the way back my gunners made a couple of crude
signs and held them up in the blisters. The P-51 jocks would
then slide between our wing and tail and read the signs, which
were only two or three words, like "how was it?" or "good
show?" The response was affirmative head shaking and the universal "AOK" sign with circled thumb and forefinger. Sign language was not a very good system, but we gathered that the
raid was a hot one and they shot the hell out of the Jap airfield
and their aircraft.

Leading the fighters from Iwo to Japan and back required
a higher than normal cruise speed for the B-29 so that the 51s
would not overheat and so that their fuel burn and performance would be efficient. We were light, enabling me to fly those
legs of the mission at 300–315 miles per hour. I throttled back
during our orbiting off the Japanese coast and between Iwo
and Guam, but still set a record of five hours and fifty-five minutes from Ise Bay to Guam.

The incident involving the rescue of the P-51 pilot on this
mission brings to mind the story of another rescue by a brave
and gutsy submarine commander. A fighter pilot—we heard a
P-51 pilot, but it could have been a Navy aviator—had been
shot down over Tokyo, and he had bailed out over Tokyo Bay
and was floating there in his one-man life raft taking small
arms fire from the shore. The submarine entered the Bay submerged but with its periscope up. It proceeded to the downed
airman who wrapped his arms around the periscope and hung
on as the sub retreated out of the Bay where it quickly surfaced, took the grateful pilot on board, and submerged again
for its escape.

I always wondered how the sub managed to find its way
through the nets across the entrance to the bay and back out
again and avoid any mines in the process. Years later, I was told
by a Pacific Navy veteran that there were neither nets nor

mines across the entrance to Tokyo Bay—that it was too wide. Even if the sub commander knew this, it took a lot of guts to do what he did. I have related this story to at least a half a dozen people over the years whose response was, "Yeah, I've heard that story, too." However, no one has been able to verify it. Perhaps some reader can do that for me.

One of the little known P-51 disasters of the war occurred about a month after we flew our guide and navigation mission with them. On June 1 fifty-four P-51s left Iwo to provide fighter cover for B-29s on a mission to Osaka. They were led by a navigational B-29. An extensive cold front lay between Iwo and Japan. The P-51s, in formations, entered the front at 20,000 feet. With no sign of breaking through, some formations tried to return to their base. Chaos reigned in the clouds as those formations trying to return flew through and into others causing a series of mid-air collisions that brought down twenty-seven P-51s with only five pilots surviving. The other twenty-seven exited the front and completed the mission. This fiasco had a dampening effect on morale and it was several days before the units were back to strength and flying again.

After the Iwo escort mission with the P-51s we had a couple days off, which was welcomed and appreciated. Crew morale as well as my own individual attitude improved considerably with two or three days without having to think about a mission. Sleep became undisturbed and restful again and we could just putter around, play softball, go to the beach or the local outdoor evening movie, write letters or whatever.

The relaxation however didn't apply to everyone. While we were resting, the other squadrons in our group, along with two crews from our squadron, flew a daylight formation mission against the Hitachi aircraft factory at Tachikawa west of Tokyo, and it was the toughest one yet. Flak was very intense and very accurate, and the fighters were aggressive. All the ships from our group returned but were badly damaged—one was to be junked and another would need a new wing it was so full of holes. All crew members, however, survived. The 19th Group (also based at North Field) was first over the target and sustained very heavy losses. Three of their ships went down over the target—two from flak and one from flak and fighters; two more couldn't maintain their position in the formation because of damage and mechanical problems caused by that damage. They ditched just off the Jap coast, and others were reported to have ditched. That made five for sure, plus those that were unaccounted for—and all out of one group. They went over the target at 13,000 feet—in the opinion of most pilots, a suicide altitude, especially in daylight.

The next day another mission was flown by the group to Kyushu, and one B-29 was lost out of our formation, but it was not one of our boys. A 39th Bomb Group ship, apparently unable to find his own formation had pulled into our formation at the rendezvous point to fly the bomb run. There was little opposition, but as the flight turned from the target after bombs away, a few fighters showed up dropping phosphorus bombs, and one of these hit the unfortunate 39th Group ship and set it on fire in the air. We had been alerted for this mission but were not scheduled to fly it.

The next several days were the same: we were alerted for two missions, prepared for each, and were on "stand by" as a spare, but didn't fly either one. We would have gone only if someone had aborted. This was somewhat difficult—going through all the preparation, losing a night's sleep, suffering all the pre-mission anxiety, and then not going. But it was sometimes part of the routine.

ELEVENTH MISSION: TACHIARI, MAY 3, 1945

On May 3 we were scheduled for a daylight mission to Tachiari, and it turned out to be one of the tough ones.

We had been assembling our formations right on the Jap coast and, until this mission, had gotten away with it, but this time the tables were turned and the Jap fighters were waiting for us—we were caught with our pants down.

We had a hell of a cold front to fly through on the way up—in fact, the mission had been postponed for five hours because of it. We broke out of the clouds right over the assembly point, and there were ten Tony fighters waiting for us. Several other B-29s were there only minutes ahead of us, all trying to form up. Being alone, we were all attacked repeatedly by the Tonys. I slid up to Harry Hayes's starboard wing to concentrate our firepower, and as the Tonys came after us, my gunners—and I'm sure Hayes's gunners—responded immediately and warded them off, shooting two that appeared to go down. During the attack, Hayes took a 20mm shell in the prop hub of the number three engine. The oil, of course, drained out, and the prop ran away. The usual sequence of events when a prop ran away was that the hub would, in a matter of a couple of minutes, turn red hot from the friction, and then, in another two or three minutes, turn white hot and twist off entirely. At the moment of departure from the engine, the danger was that it could spin into the fuselage and cause severe damage, particularly if it was from an inboard engine. From my position on his wing, I could not see the prop hub and so could not predict the moment of its separation, but I could perceive the overspeeded revolutions of the prop. This time, fortunately, when it did let go, it spiraled out more or less straight in front of the airplane and went down. Hayes, now without his number three engine, salvoed his bombs and aborted the mission, heading back to the clouds and out to sea. The Tonys had succeeded in damaging several B-29s.

The rest of us finally got into place and the Tonys backed off, apparently not wanting to face the concentrated firepower of a formation of B-29s. One of the 43rd Squadron ships got lost (presumably) and did not make the party. Our hurried and pressured assembly resulted in some of us flying in unassigned positions. This was not too important as long as we got into formation, but it points up the effects of fate. I flew the number two position in the lead element and Anderson took my scheduled position in the number three position in that element. After we left the assembly point, about twenty Nicks (twin-engine Jap fighters) moved in on us and worked us over for about a half hour. They were much more aggressive than the Tonys were and inflicted considerable damage to several B-29s. The 29s however put up a good fight and shot down a number of the Nicks. We claimed one destroyed, one probable, and one damaged. Shooting from the bombardier's position, Al claimed the kill and the probable. He thought the probable was also a kill, but he didn't see it hit the ground—a requirement in order to get credit. He was too busy shooting. He had the four-gun top turret right over my head in action all during the attacks. On the first one he scored multiple hits, and as the Nick started down trailing smoke, he yelled, "I got him! I got him! I got him!" But the yelling stopped almost immediately as he concentrated on the next attack. At the same time, Rich, the left blister gunner, was scanning the sky and spotted a Nick in a climbing attack from below and behind us, guns blazing. He quickly fitted the Nick's wingspan into his sight and let go with a long burst. The Nick started smoking, rolled on his back, and disappeared. This was the one we claimed as damaged.

The Nicks withdrew as we turned on the bomb run, and the flak batteries took over. There wasn't much of it, but what there was, was accurate. Anderson, who was flying the position we were supposed to be in sustained two direct hits—one in the forward bomb bay and one in the rear unpressurized compartment. None of the crew was injured, but Anderson had a difficult time flying back to Iwo and landed with the help of the C-1 Autopilot. The ship had suffered so much damage that it was shoved into the scrap heap to be cannibalized for parts. Hayes and Jolink were both at Iwo with their damaged ships when I landed there short on fuel. Hayes discovered upon inspecting his ship that he had sustained two other 20mm hits—one in the number two engine nacelle (which did not hit anything vital) and one which had entered the fuselage and was stopped by a sheet of armorplate. The crew that "got lost" landed behind us, also short on fuel. Who knew where they had been?

For some reason, fuel was not available to us when we landed, and we had to spend the night on Iwo. We spent it in the airplane, but it was very uncomfortable and almost impossible to sleep. The next morning, I got several hundred gallons of gas and proceeded back to Guam, thinking some very uncomplimentary things about the mission planners who always had us assembling right on the coast. When would they learn? When the strike reports began to filter in from other ships returning to Guam indicating that the raid had been a rough one, an intelligence officer remarked that it looked like we were going to lose some crews. It was reported that one of our squadron COs said, "To hell with the ships and crews, where did the bombs hit?" Perhaps that was not meant to get back to us, but it did, and it certainly didn't do anything for our morale, and it furthered the destruction of any respect we had for him. With a rare exception, we had always destroyed our target, and this mission was no different. Despite the damage to aircraft on this flight, I am not aware that any returning crew members suffered injuries.

Over the next several days a number of missions were scheduled and then canceled—mostly on account of weather either enroute or over the target, so we had not gone out. The 6th Squadron, however, did get off during this period on another strike to Tachiari on May 5. They lost two ships to fighter attacks—the Ralph E. Miller and Marvin S. Watkins crews—and missed the target as well. The lead bombardier forgot his target folder, and instead of the airfield, they hit the parade ground of a nearby military academy. Then the 58th Wing went back to Tachiari to do the job the 6th Squadron bungled, and they lost four ships to fighters. That made us wonder, now that we had P-51s on Iwo, why we didn't have fighter protection on our daylight missions.

A few weeks after my wife returned to California following my departure from the U.S., she went to work for United Airlines in the dispatch office at the Burbank, California, airport. United had contracts with the U.S. Army Air Force to fly Military Air Transport (MATS) routes including the Pacific run to the Philippines. This flight followed the same route that we had—Hawaii, Kwajalein, Guam, and, for them, termination in the Philippines. She became acquainted with some of the flight crews and prevailed upon one crew in particular to carry "care packages" to me on their trips. So once every few weeks, a United crew delivered a box of goodies to me: mostly snacks like dried fruit, cheese, crackers, dates, raisins, olives, cookies, candies, nuts, lunch meats, canned goods, and so on—stuff the mess hall didn't serve and which was available when the mess hall was closed.

About the end of April or the first of May, one of the United pilots traveling to North Field to locate me was Jay Plank, who visited me several times while I was stationed on Guam, including the day the war ended. We have been friends ever since. I took him for a ride in my big bird one day when I was test flying it. Jay spent his entire flying career with United—from first officer in the early '40s to 747 captain in the years before mandatory retirement. He had an enviable and successful career, and we still talk airplanes and flying when we see each other.

On May 8 we learned that the war in Europe was over at last. We received the news quite calmly and without celebration. While we were certainly glad and relieved, we realized that our Pacific War was far from over—we had a long way to go yet. Still, there was a lot of speculation about the immediate future—like when Russia would get involved, whether they would attack the Japanese homeland, and whether, with the collapse of the other two Axis Powers, Japan would be motivated to seek peace in an effort to cut a better deal for themselves. Then we heard the rumor to top all rumors: General MacArthur was on the island with Admiral Nimitz, who had Japanese envoys with him.

I personally did not believe that the Japanese would ever surrender unconditionally even though it was most obvious that they had lost the war. I felt that their fanaticism would push them to fight bitterly to the very end as they had on Iwo Jima and the other places we had met them. I felt that the bloodiest battles, particularly on land, were yet to come.

TWELFTH MISSION: OTAKE, MAY 10, 1945

Well, all those wonderful rumors were false, of course. MacArthur was still in the Philippines, Nimitz was in Washington, and the war was still on—so we flew another mission, our twelfth.

Before we took off, it looked as though it could be the toughest one yet, but it didn't turn out that way. In the target area it looked to us as though some other people were catching hell, but once again we came through unscathed and uninjured. We hit Japan's biggest oil cracking and storage plant at Otake in daylight formation. Bombs were away at 1108, and from all the smoke and fire it looked like we did a good job. This was the biggest single B-29 strike to date—over 450 ships. Flak was moderate but we didn't catch any, and there were no fighters sighted. This was something I couldn't understand. A couple of days earlier, we were up there to bomb a dinky airfield, and they had all kinds of fighters up to meet us; then on this mission we went after one of their most important industrial targets, and there wasn't a fighter in the sky. The 314th Bomb Wing didn't lose a single ship on this mission. We all wanted more missions like this one.

On the way back, I was thinking about the massive force we had in the air—and this was only the beginning: before long we would be sending out a thousand planes at a time as they had in Europe. I hoped the Japanese would realize this and spare themselves the annihilation that was bound to be their lot, but I really doubted that they would. The longer I spent at this business, the more convinced I became that regardless of the destruction we poured on them, their fanaticism would impel them to resist to the very last man. Despite this feeling, I couldn't help wondering what the Japanese people below thought when they looked up and saw us. Their government had promised and convinced them that the war was being prosecuted to the fullest and, indeed, that they were winning the war. Yet there we were, four hundred strong, deep into Japanese territory and there wasn't a single fighter up to defend them. Couldn't they see what was happening? Did it matter?

The sight of so many B-29s in the air was quite impressive. In every direction that I looked, there were swarms of them and I thought of the old adage: "In numbers there is strength." Maybe that's why there wasn't a single Jap fighter to challenge the might of our air armada.

Again, the rumors started—this time to the effect that the Japanese were sending peace feelers to the U.S. through the Swiss, and that the Japanese Navy had put a surrender bill before the Cabinet, but the Army turned it down. Then to top it all, the island of Guam was put on the alert for a suicide attack from Jap carrier-based planes. I didn't see how an aircraft carrier could get down to Guam from Japan without being detected, so I dismissed the whole idea. It didn't happen. I talked to a couple of Navy boys just back from the Okinawa campaign and they had a compliment for us—they said we helped them tremendously with our airfield attacks on Kyushu. I was glad we did, for at the time it didn't seem like we were doing much good.

THIRTEENTH MISSION: NAGOYA, MAY 14, 1945

Bomber Command's ability to send more and more B-29s to Japan was being realized, and on May 14 we participated in the largest strike yet—over 600 B-29s in a bold, show-of-force, daylight-formation incendiary mission to destroy the city of Nagoya. It was our thirteenth. We were not in the first wave of ships to bomb, but as we approached the target, we heard the radio chatter from the first groups reporting heavy flak and fighters and B-29s going down. Later, on the way back, we heard others going into Iwo Jima with wounded on board, with two engines out, and God knows what else. Our bomb run, however, was completed without opposition, and we flew back out to sea undamaged. We saw no fighters and no flak, but the thing that saved us was that by the time we arrived there was so much smoke from the fires already started that we were obscured from the gun batteries on the ground. The fighters must have been busy with other formations.

The official reports about this raid state that 472 aircraft actually hit the target with the loss of 11 B-29s. The 314th Bomb Wing lost 4—1 to enemy fighters and flak, 1 to mechanical causes, 1 ditched, and 1 to unknown causes. Gunners claimed 23 fighters shot down, 16 probables, and 31 damaged. The Japs claimed 20 B-29s shot down, 9 damaged, and inconsequential damage to the city. Tokyo Rose was on the radio after we landed back at Guam saying that our raid was a failure—that they had all the fires out within two hours of the time we dropped our bombs. However, we didn't believe her because we were scheduled to go right back to Nagoya the next day, and the mission was postponed because smoke still obscured the city.

When we landed after this mission, we learned that the 29th Bomb Group had lost all but three members of another crew, but it had nothing to do with enemy action—Bedford lost an engine about an hour out of Guam and crashed upon returning to North Field. The three survivors were gunners in the rear of the aircraft.

Also, when we returned from Nagoya, we were advised that we had been officially credited with the fighter kill on the Tachiari mission, so we painted a Jap flag on the side of the ship under my window alongside the rows of bombs showing missions completed.

FOURTEENTH MISSION: NAGOYA, MAY 17, 1945
On May 17 we went back to Nagoya for a night burn job—our fourteenth mission—to incinerate the lower part of the city and the dock area. After completion of the mission, I was of the opinion that we should not have to go back there again. The target was well hit—first fragmentary reports had the dock area 40 percent destroyed and 7 square miles burned out of the city.

This mission rivaled the previous one on the fourteenth. Four hundred and fifty-seven B-29s were launched from all four wings, and the pathfinder technique was used to drop over 3,600 tons of bombs to finish off Nagoya. We were one of those pathfinders—about the second or third airplane over the target. We could see what we would be getting into long before we got there because the weather was unusually clear over the city. As we neared the Japanese coast, we donned our helmets and flak vests in preparation for the bomb run. No smoke this time to obscure us. Being first over the target, I flew as fast as I could—Al being apprised in advance of my intended technique so he could adjust his aiming procedure. The tension and anxiety was such that, the engine noise notwithstanding, you could have heard a pin drop in the cockpit. One of the reasons for this feeling was that we were all well aware that frequently the lead planes on a mission were the ones to suffer damage or get shot down. We were as alert as it's possible to be. Sweat trickled from my forehead and my shirt was wet. I thought that our voices on the intercom sounded unnatural.

As I turned on the bomb run, I could see searchlights starting to flick on, probing the sky, hunting for us. Several came close and I held my breath, but they went on by. Then one caught us, and instantly a dozen more came on. The blinding glare made me duck in the cockpit to see the instruments. There was no way to get out—I was committed to the bomb run, and all I could do was stay on course and bore on through, hoping that we would make it safely. Then the big stuff started coming and the ship rocked from the concussions, but I was not aware that we were being hit. The next instant the bomb bay doors popped open, and the bombs were away. I turned sharply and started the old game of weaving and dodging to confuse their aiming, but that straight bomb run in the lights had given them time to compute our altitude and speed, and they had us well bracketed. The shrapnel rained off the ship like hailstones, and once, in a turn, I heard the sickening crunch of metal being torn and crushed. I thought the number one engine had been hit, but the old fan kept turning and everything on the panel looked O.K. as I climbed, gratefully, into the darkness. We left the Jap coast behind us, as the main force hit the area we had marked for them.

I turned to the course Freddie had given me for the flight back, set up the autopilot, and throttled back for the most economical airspeed and cruise control as Pic adjusted the mixture and prop controls and began monitoring head temperatures. We settled in and relaxed for the trip home.

After we were about four hours off the coast of Japan in the long slow descent to the Marianas, the post-anxiety fatigue of the mission had overcome the whole crew, and most were asleep—or nearly so. I looked at Al in his bombardier's seat, and he was leaning to the side against the bulkhead with his head down. I looked over at Bud, whose chin was on his chest. Pic was dozing; perhaps Freddie was awake—I couldn't see him—but he was probably the only one besides me. My own eyes were heavy as I was lulled by the steady drone of the engines in the blackness. Slowly, I became aware of the sky above me just beginning to be light—the dimmer stars disappearing as the dawn began to break, barely illuminating the tops of the mountainous cumulus build-ups towering above us to 30,000 or 40,000 feet. The sea below was black and the lower bases of the clouds a dark, dull gray. Then, almost as if in response to a drum roll, there was an explosion of color: streaks of red and orange began to shoot heavenward into a pale, azure canopy high above. The intensity built to a crescendo, a silent cacophony of color until the whole eastern sky was aflame, backlighting and illuminating the cumulus around us. I touched the intercom button, alerting the crew, and, after a couple of moments, quietly said, "Everybody . . . look out the left side of the airplane." There was a muffled response or two: "Jesus!" or "Christ!"

The show continued as we slid down through the deep canyons created by the cumulus. The reds gave way to lighter orange, yellows, and pinks as Aurora, the goddess of dawn, conquered the night and drove its darkness to the west. The spectacular display slowly dissipated as the sun gained the horizon, flooding the atmosphere with light and turning the clouds from gray to white as whitecaps became visible on the water below. The immense cloudscape through which we were flying gave me a perspective of size. I felt my airplane was as of a grain of sand on an endless beach, and I, individually, no more significant or obvious in the world scheme of things than that grain of sand. My brief excursion into one of God's wonderlands and the entrancing reverie in which I had been immersed was over. Emerging from the fear and anxiety of the raid and the blackness that followed into the birth of the new day brought catharsis and promise of a new beginning and ultimate dominance in our struggle.

I sat up in my seat, thankful to be alive with my hide in one piece and have one more behind me—another step closer to home. I stretched as best I could and went back to the routine of checking instruments and fuel burn in anticipation of arrival at our base.

After landing, I found what made that sickening crunch over the target—a direct hit in the leading edge of the wing just inside the number two engine. How it missed the prop, I'll never know. There were also a number of small holes in the left wing. In broad daylight it all seemed like something in the far distant past, but at the time it was very real, something that you feared and hated, but you kept at it because each time you did it, you knew that it brought you that much closer to home and the end of the war. Others of the pathfinder group were also shot up, but only one of the main force behind us suffered any damage, and no ships were lost.

About the nineteenth or twentieth of May, I was advised that my crew and I were second in line after Jolink to be put on detached service and sent back to the States for "lead crew" training. We would then return to the Marianas to finish our tour of thirty-five missions (or more?) as a "lead crew." I had ambivalent feelings about this. For one thing, I wondered what

I could learn (or be taught) about being a lead crew that I didn't already know. I had been the pathfinder (i.e., first over the target) or in the pathfinder element to mark the target either with flares or incendiaries for the strike force following me on numerous night missions, and I had flown the number two or number three position in the lead element of a box formation numerous times on daylight missions. I thought that with eighteen or twenty missions under my belt, I could probably teach the Stateside Training Command some things rather than the other way around. I was strongly inclined to stay and just finish my tour—then when I returned to the States, it would be permanent, and I wouldn't have to sweat missions anymore. However, it would, more than likely, be a headquarters decision, and I was not sure that I could decline the order even if I wanted to. There would probably be a promotion involved—at least for me if not for others on the crew—but I was really more interested in preserving my hide than in a promotion. Everybody on the field would think I'd lost my mind if I turned it down, and my crew might be inclined to skin me alive. Then there was the strong emotional allure and attraction of going home and being reunited with wives and families, but what if we had to return to the Pacific? Wouldn't that be deja vu and even more heartrending and difficult than the first time? After wrestling with this for a while, my thoughts, as expressed in my diary, indicate that I finally decided that if the opportunity presented itself (or I was ordered) to return to the States, I would go and take my chances on a return to the group; I might be reassigned in the U.S., or the war might end and there would be no more need for lead crews.

However, as it turned out, about six weeks later, I had changed my mind. One day, all the aircraft commanders were requested to meet with squadron COs to discuss the subject of rest leaves. By this time, we had twenty-three or twenty-four missions to our credit, and they were coming at a fast enough rate that I could see the possibility of completing our thirty-five mission tour in August, so I told the CO that we didn't want a rest leave. We just wanted to fly the missions and get it over with. None of my crew members were complaining about fatigue or exhaustion beyond what was normal under the circumstances anyway. I was probably as tired as anyone on the crew because the demands of the missions on pilots could be more critical and exacting than on other crew members, but even so, I didn't want to decelerate or interrupt the process of completing our tour. Therefore, no orders were forthcoming. As a matter of fact, we were more eager than ever, because we could see the end, and home, looming on the horizon.

FIFTEENTH MISSION: TOKYO, MAY 24, 1945

So it was on with the missions. Some of the group's crews participated in a mission to Tokyo to bomb an airframe assembly plant, but it was solid overcast, so they bombed Hammamatsu by radar instead, with unobserved results. Four B-29s were lost on this mission, but none from our group. Then Bomber Command started concentrating on Tokyo again. We were scheduled for a night incendiary mission on the twenty-third, and I was concerned that we might not be able to go because Bud was in the hospital recovering from the removal of a couple of wisdom teeth. However, we had an as-yet-unassigned pilot in the group, and he flew the mission as my copilot. He was Jerry Theisen, soon to become a member of another crew in our Quonset hut.

We took off before sunset and, like the March 9–10 Tokyo mission, flew to Japan at relatively low altitude, then climbed to our bombing altitude just off the coast. I had explained to Jerry how I intended to fly the bomb run, and I had also advised Al so that he would be prepared for my technique. Our target was South Tokyo, just north of Kawasaki. We were part of a 520-aircraft effort, with each B-29 overflying the target alone. On many of our all-out-effort raids when 500 or 600 airplanes were launched, the force was divided among as many as seven or eight targets. Tonight, however, we were all going to the same place. The mission planners had scheduled the takeoff and bomb release times for each aircraft on a plan to maximize B-29s, one at a time, over the target—a schedule of three or four planes a minute to thoroughly saturate the area. The Guam-based airplanes took off first (we had farther to fly), then the Tinian groups, and then the Saipan contingent. As we approached the target, we donned our helmets and flak suits. Because of the traffic, I told the crew to watch carefully for other B-29s.

I turned on to the bomb run, and because we were on the bottom of the stack at 7,800 feet (it went up to as high as 15,000 feet), I dove a couple of hundred feet while advancing the throttles to the firewall to cross the target area as fast as I could fly. Fires covered a considerable area below, and the glow was reflected on the bottoms of all the attacking airplanes, so other B-29s, at least over the target, were visible to me. We saw a fair amount of flak and a few fighters, but none came our way, so, after bombs away and the bomb doors popping shut, I followed the briefed withdrawal route back out to sea. There were times on other missions when I used the excess bomb run speed to climb to a higher altitude for the trip back, but on this mission I maintained my assigned altitude as there were several hundred airplanes above me—admittedly strung out in a fairly long line, but still, I didn't want to get into the traffic and pose a collision hazard.

The trip back to Guam was uneventful. I taught Jerry my efficient cruise control procedures, and we landed, undamaged, after 14:45 hours in the air. This was one of the easier missions—the weather favored us; I logged no instrument time on the flight—and, for us, there was no serious enemy action.

The official report on the mission disclosed that out of the total force of 520 airplanes, 500 actually went over the target, dropping 3,646 tons of bombs on the Tokyo urban area between 3:00 A.M. and 4:38 A.M. for a strike rate of 4.3 planes per minute—a very effective logistical accomplishment. Seventeen B-29s were lost or 3.2 percent of the force. Seventeen airplanes and crews sounds like a lot, and it is, but on a percentage basis, our losses were actually going down because of the increased size of the strike force. However, that was no consolation to the families of the approximately 190 men who died.

SIXTEENTH MISSION: TOKYO, MAY 26, 1945

We had a day to get a little sleep, and then we prepared to go right back to Tokyo. We took off the evening of May 25 on our sixteenth mission and our fifth to Tokyo, this time to duplicate what we had done the night before, but on an area somewhat north of the previous target. Jerry was my copilot again since Bud was still in sick bay. The routine was the same, and weather was clear over the target, but a cold front lay between Iwo and Japan. I logged four hours of instrument flight going and coming.

The experience over the target was different for us this time, too. It seemed that the Japs were throwing everything but the kitchen sink at us and the sky was literally ablaze. Flak concentration was intense and accurate when we went over and there were all kinds of weird explosions that we had not seen before including phosphorus shells and "balls of fire." They even had flak boats ninety miles south of Tokyo, and we received fire from them well out to sea. I logged 14:35 hours—just ten minutes less than the night before. Again, our good fortune held, and we had no damage and no injuries.

I was exhausted after this mission. In my letter to my wife describing the strike, I wrote:

> I'm tired—terribly tired—mentally and physically. I don't believe I've ever been so utterly exhausted in my life. I feel like I've been wrung out and then just left all twisted up in a knot after the wringing instead of being shaken out. My eyes feel as though they haven't been shut for weeks and I ache from head to foot. I can't seem to think straight and my actions are instinctive and involuntary—I'm just in a daze. But, perhaps our efforts will put an end to this ghastly business soon and then we'll know it was worth it. The show last night rivaled, if not surpassed, the raid of March 10th. It was all the Fourth of July's in history rolled into one. It was a scene of the most devastating destruction by fire imaginable, and chaos reigned supreme for the

enemy. Stick after stick of bombs poured into the target area, turning it, literally, into a huge blast furnace. The intensity of the fires was such that we could still see them when we were 150 miles off the coast. But the Jap was fighting desperately too, and he threw everything he had into the air. How we flew through it without damage, I'll never know. If anyone had returned from a raid and told me what I had to tell when I returned from this one, I'd have thought him crazy. The sky too was ablaze—with the heaviest concentration of flak and weird explosions conceivable. It was fantastic—like Orson Welles and Superman and Buck Rogers—and then some.

The official report on this mission states that 454 aircraft dropped 3,262 tons of bombs in the target area at the rate of 3.0 planes per minute—one every twenty seconds—again a significant logistical feat. Our might was beginning to show. The fires were so intense that the planes arriving toward the end of the mission exercise had to climb to as high as twenty thousand feet and bomb by radar because of the thermals and smoke. We learned later that, shortly after our fire bombing started, Tokyo was hit by a seventy mile-an-hour wind, obviously profoundly heightening the effect of the fires' intensity and destruction.

Twenty-six B-29s were lost—5.5 percent of the attacking force. Most went down over the target, but at least one ditched, and four damaged ships tried to land at Iwo but could not because of a bad storm in the area. Their crews bailed out in the vicinity of Iwo, in the storm. I presumed they were lost. The report did not indicate that they were picked up by Air Sea Rescue.

On all missions to Tokyo, we were instructed to avoid the Imperial Palace and under no circumstances were we to bomb it. However, on this mission we were attacking areas all around the palace, and while I had no intention of bombing it, I thought that if, somehow, during the raid, the emperor was blown to Kingdom Come, it might be to our advantage. I felt that if this was to occur, it would destroy the myth that he was divine and thus would enable and encourage the Japanese people to agitate for peace. However, he was not killed.

In the two raids, approximately eighteen square miles south and west of the palace were burned out, bringing the total area of Tokyo destroyed by incendiary raids to approximately fifty-six square miles or slightly over half the city. Tokyo was never again the subject of mass fire bombing. Maybe, like the March 10 mission, the results, from a Bomber Command viewpoint, sanctioned the losses—this was all-out war—but it was hard for us to contemplate the loss of 26 ships and 285 or 290 men. That was the equivalent of half a group—and in only one night. Our only consolation was that we were among the survivors and that what we were doing was not in vain, but necessary, and that it would shorten the war and, in the long run, save many more lives than it had cost us.

The "balls of fire" phenomenon that we witnessed for the first time on this mission puzzled us. We reported it to intelligence upon our return, but they had no explanation—it was not a new identifiable weapon that they knew of. The "ball of fire" looked just like its name sounded—a large burning sphere hanging out there in the sky. It appeared to be aerodynamically incapable of flight and, further, had no visible means of propulsion. Sometimes it looked stationary in the sky, and sometimes it seemed to follow us around.

As we were leaving the target on this mission my gunners reported a "ball of fire"—a flaming ball-like object that appeared to them to be about eight to twelve feet in diameter beneath and behind us at about the seven o'clock position. It was, in their opinion, about 200 yards away and climbing toward another B-29 that was on a parallel course with us. The flaming object seemed to be overtaking the other B-29 that was firing at it. My tail gunner fired a couple of short bursts at it himself. The "ball of fire" suddenly broke up into several large pieces and fell onto the roofs of some buildings on a pier jutting out into the bay below, setting the buildings on fire.

Following this incident by only a few minutes, my tail gunner reported another "ball of fire" following us at our altitude. Tom, my radar officer, turned on his equipment and reported a "blip" on the scope indicating something that was approximately one and a half miles behind us and gaining on us. He could not identify it beyond the fact that something was recording on his scope. They reported this to me and I increased our airspeed until they announced that it was receding. The distance was now three to four miles astern of us. I throttled back, and there were no more sightings that night.

A number of crews reported sighting these flaming objects on this and other missions. If the burning spheres were intended to be some sort of offensive or defensive weapon, like barrage balloons from which cables were suspended, they would not work. We certainly would not fly into anything as long as we could see it. The phenomenon was still without explanation. I don't recall whether my crew saw any "balls of fire" after this mission, but if they did, we didn't fire our guns or take any action—we simply watched.

Speculation by the aircrews who had seen these burning spheres provided a possible scenario. The Japs were known to launch high-altitude balloons carrying either incendiary or demolition bombs, which would ride the jet stream across the Pacific and land in the Northwestern U.S. After the war I learned of a couple of these events: one landed in Oregon and started a small forest fire, and the other landed harmlessly with a demolition bomb which later detonated, killing several hikers who examined it when they found it.

Their theory was that what we saw were the burners on these balloons as they ascended. However, there were numerous arguments against this explanation. For one thing, the balloons would have followed a rising trajectory moving with whatever wind prevailed rather than following airplanes around. But the biggest argument against this theory was the unlikely probability that the Japs would be launching balloons in the middle of a fire raid when everything on the ground was burning.

Then, at a briefing some weeks later, we got another purported explanation from the intelligence boys. They said that what we had been seeing was the planet Venus rising in the east.

Their explanation was based on the time of year, the altitude at which the sightings were made, the time of day (night) when the sightings were made, our altitude and course in relation to the position of the "ball of fire" when sighted, and, simply, the fact that no other explanation could account for our observations. However, the explanation offered by the Intelligence Section was another example of people attempting an analysis of something that they had not themselves experienced or seen. Perhaps they thought that they had to come up with something, no matter how bizarre, because aircrews might be afraid of this object that they perceived to be a new secret weapon against them. The aircrews, however, scoffed at this explanation as being absurd and ridiculous, still believing that this was new weaponry, notwithstanding the fact that no airplane had ever been "attacked" or "shot down" by a "ball of fire."

Researchers tried to solve the riddle of the "balls of fire" following World War II. They compiled many reports of sightings, but had no explanations. Several incidents of "balls of fire" observations were reported by crews in the CBI (China, Burma, India) Theater as well as over Japan, and, even to some degree, in the ETO (European Theater of Operations). Descriptions of the incidents in the European Theater, however differed markedly from the flaming spheres seen over Japan. The objects were referred to as "Foo Fighters" or "Balls of Fire."

After the war, I talked to several retired intelligence officers about the stories and sightings, but they said that it was determined after the surrender that Japan did not have any secret weapon, radio controlled or otherwise, that fit the description of what we had seen.

The whole subject is somewhat like the "flying saucer" controversy. There is a lot of visual evidence by seemingly reliable witnesses, but no hard evidence, no proof of what we had seen, only speculative comment. So the mystery persists.

LIFE ON THE BASE

On a comparative basis, our life on the base when we were not flying missions was better than most, but not always peaches and cream. In all groups of people forced to live together by circumstance or edict or, for that matter, even by choice, individual and group relationships become established or destroyed, loyalties forged, and dislikes fostered—some of which are subtle and achieved subconsciously and some of which are conscious, deliberate, and obvious, but all of which affect sensibilities and perceptions and therefore lives, attitudes, and behavior. We were no different except that there was the magnified influence on our group of people of fighting a war— the deliberate, almost constant voluntary risking of our lives in pursuit of a victorious end to our endeavors and coping with the loss of friends, buddies, acquaintances, or just loss statistics, even if we didn't know them. They were just like us.

There was one other significant difference. We were stuck on a small island where we were isolated from life as we had always known it, and we had little diversion. Our counterparts in England, for example, could visit villages and towns where they could associate with people in a society much like their own. Many of the U.S. Armed Forces were scattered over the world in isolated places like ours, so we were not the only ones to suffer from such segregation, but sometimes there seemed to be no past and no future—only the present and only the war. That's why letters from home and loved ones were so extraordinarily important to our sanity and morale. The military establishment did its best to preserve some semblance of normalcy. It provided an outdoor movie theater, an athletic field with a softball diamond, fairly good mail service under the circumstances, U.S.O. entertainment from time to time, and fairly decent food in the mess halls, but it was not home. None of us ever seriously complained. We didn't expect it to be home, and we knew why we were there and what we were doing, but the effect on some was discouraging and disappointing.

One of the effects of this on some individuals was the loss of the ability to cope with it all, and their courage and bravery abandoned them. We had one crew who, after a number of missions, requested and was sent on a rest leave. I don't recall that they ever returned to combat status. We had another crew whose pilot, upon approaching the target, or simply arriving at the coast of Japan, would feign some aircraft malfunction, or fake some excuse to avoid going over the target, and, instead, would drop his bombs on some insignificant little village or in the middle of nowhere. His crew ultimately mutinied for fear they wouldn't get credit for missions flown. They went to their squadron CO requesting a new pilot. The CO told them that their request would not be tolerated, and if they knew what was good for them, they'd better just continue as they were. They were stuck with him.

Others, in an attempt to cope, became fatalists: if your number was up, it was up; if it wasn't, it wasn't. The problem with this was it could lead to carelessness in the belief that if your number wasn't "up," you could survive anything. Personally, this didn't make sense to me, and while "fate," however you defined it, could and did influence various events, and was usually beyond your conscious awareness, I didn't believe in the fatalistic approach to attitude and mindset.

At one point, we had several crews out of commission because one or two members were in the hospital complaining of "combat fatigue." This brought on some lectures by the brass to the effect that there was no such thing as "combat fatigue," and we'd better get it out of our heads. The flight surgeons couldn't find anything physically wrong with the boys in the hospital, but they were tired and scared and just couldn't face doing it anymore. Were they lacking in moral fiber? How could you get their courage back for them so they would be dedicated fighting men again? Or is it possible? Perhaps not for some people.

On the fostering of dislikes, there was one member of the command group that fostered plenty. By the time our tour was over, he was pretty thoroughly disliked by the men in his command because of his absurd pettiness and tyrannical, overbearing, rank-pulling attitude toward his men. He rarely would approve promotions for either enlisted men or officers in his command; replacement crews were arriving from the States with more rank among them than the veteran crews serving under him. He did not recommend or award citations on the order of other outfits on the field. No one was angling for awards—they were just doing their job—but if deeds and accomplishments were being rewarded elsewhere, then they should have been bestowed upon his men also.

There was a signpost outside one Quonset hut with a bunch of arrows on it pointing to and naming the hometowns of the crews billeted there. He made them remove it because it didn't "look military." The occupants of another hut built a coral sidewalk outside their quarters to reduce the amount of mud being tracked in. He told them to remove it—again, it didn't "look military." In Ernie Pyle's writings about American GIs the world over, he made a point of noting that everywhere, unlike other troops, they made their surroundings as "homey" as possible and themselves as comfortable as possible. This, however, didn't hold around our area. This commanding officer got on a binge once of pulling quarters inspections in both the officers' and enlisted men's quarters. This was unheard of under our circumstances in a combat zone. He was down on the line once as the B-29s were returning from a mission. One had a tailgunner who had been killed at his position, and another aircrew was standing by the ship watching the removal of his body when this officer came by and ordered them to leave and go police the grounds around the outdoor movie theater. What the hell kind of behavior was this? I suppose he fancied himself a tough disciplinarian, but what was the violation of discipline in these instances? I think he just liked to pull rank and delighted in making others grovel. Or maybe his military career had not gone as he thought it should have, and he soured and took his disappointment and imagined injustice out on the rest of the world.

I got into an argument with him once. I have no recollection whatsoever about the subject of the discourse, but I do remember, in the heat of the dispute saying to him, "You chickenshit son of a bitch, if you ever fly a mission, don't get in front of me because I'll shoot you down." Of course, I wouldn't have—I would not have risked eleven others just to get at him. I worried about this for a while, thinking he could have me court-martialed for insubordination, but as it turned out, he could not have—he would have needed a witness, and he didn't have one.

We also had a couple of officers who were West Pointers and therefore looked down their noses at the rest of us. This always rather disgusted me; what the hell, I had answered the call to duty just as readily as they had—maybe more readily since I had volunteered and they were already in the military and had no choice. I was flying the missions and doing all the same things they were. I figured that in wartime at least, there should have been some sort of equivalency, but that was not, it seemed, the way it worked in the military. They were the elite, and we were the hoi polloi. I guess I just didn't understand the politics of the military life.

The other side of the coin, however, was that most of the senior staff was liked—some very well liked. There were several of the headquarters and intelligence staff officers who seemed to have a sincere interest in the aircrews and the prosecution of the war and were liked by the pilots. Our operations and group staffs, for example, well liked by all the pilots and crew members, and our group commanding officer, Col. Carl R. Storrie, was held in high regard and esteemed by all. There was never any dissension of which I was aware among my crew members (although I suppose I might not have known about it if there was any, being their skipper) nor was there any among the few other crews I knew well except the two previously mentioned. Some of the friendships forged in war lasted a lifetime—in part just because of the sharing of the experiences and circumstances of the time, a manifestation of the bond that grew and existed among men who regularly shared danger and who depended on each other.

There was really no rank in my airplane. We were all on a first name basis: Rich and Merle and Hal and Chet and Tom in the back of the ship, and Bud and Pic and Al and Freddie and Jim on the flight deck. I was occasionally called "Skipper" by some; Al usually called me by my first name, but mostly they called me "Robbie"—a sobriquet acquired by many people named Roberts, Robertson, Robbins, or Robinson. There was discipline, respect, and cooperation among us without a thought of rank. Obviously, I was in command—I was flying the airplane—but every man knew his job and performed it well and respected the dedication, the capabilities, and the boundaries of the others.

After the Tokyo missions, Bud got out of the hospital following extraction of his wisdom teeth, but he was having trouble with an earache, and the doc was talking about removing his tonsils; however, the infection cleared up in a couple of days, and he was returned to flying status. We knew he would be on the next one with us.

The "next one," however, seemed to be eluding us. We were scheduled for a mission one night, and Freddie got sick at the last minute, so a standby crew flew our airplane. Fortunately, they brought it back with no damage. Then a couple of nights later, we missed another one because *I* was sick. Twenty-four officers went to the hospital with some sort of food poisoning. I didn't go to the hospital, but I was not up to flying. I regretted missing two missions—I wanted to see the number of missions flown keep going up. During this period of crew infirmity, Bud flew a mission as copilot with another crew—he wanted to catch up on the two he had missed.

In this time off, we were back to working on the officers' club again, and it was promising to be the best one west of Pearl Harbor—certainly the most lavish on Guam. Over the previous month, they had scrounged all sorts of stuff for it, including a fancy curved bar made of solid mahogany. How tough can the war be when you can get a mahogany bar in the middle of the Pacific Ocean? I was looking forward to getting it finished so the parties and the all night card games could be there instead of in the Quonset hut where I was trying to sleep.

Then on May 28 we were scheduled for a daylight mission to Yokohama. We went through all the preparations but had a malfunction with the airplane. We got it fixed, but not in time to make the takeoff. Those that did make it suffered some flak damage, and Major Evans, flying with one of the group crews, absorbed a piece of shrapnel over the target about the size of his thumb. He was in the hospital recovering from its removal when I went to visit him. Thinking he would need some cheering up and some distractions, I smuggled a couple of bottles of beer, a cigar, and a copy of *Forever Amber* into the hospital for him, but when I located him, he was sitting on the edge of his bed between two attractive nurses (visiting, not practicing). He was doing all right for himself and didn't need cheering up by me.

While I was there, I talked to a Marine who had just returned from Okinawa and had some interesting stories to tell about the battles there. One of the things he referred to involved the women who accompanied the Jap soldiers, even into combat. They were not involved in the actual fighting, although they might be among the casualties. They were there as "comfort women" for the gratification of the soldiers. He said a company might have as many women as men. They were carried on the company roster as clerks and laundresses and the like, but that wasn't their real purpose. I mention this only because it related to some of the psychological propaganda directed at us and all the U.S. troops in the Pacific. They tried to "rub in" the fact that all of our boys were lonesome (and we were). One of Tokyo Rose's favorite introductory lines in her nightly broadcasts was: "Hello, suckers—I got mine last night, your wives and sweethearts back home probably got theirs— did you get yours?"

The Marine also related a somewhat unusual incident that, at the time, was considered possibly prophetic. Two Japanese officers had been captured, and that being a rather singular incident, it aroused everyone's curiosity. When they were inter-rogated about not having committed Hari-Kari as all the others had done rather than lose face by capture, they replied that Japan was going to surrender soon, so they wouldn't be losing face any more than any other Japanese officer.

Then there were more rumors—some carried by the U.S. newspapers—to the effect that the big industrialists in the Japanese cabinet were trying to overthrow the military clique in power to effect a surrender that would save some semblance of the empire rather than resisting to the last man when nothing would be left.

We heard also that the Japs had considered the battle for Okinawa to be the deciding one of the war for the "Homeland"; nearly all organized resistance there had ended, so why didn't they surrender? I really thought that our terror campaign against their cities—four of the five largest having been destroyed—would force the issue and bring them to their knees, but they fought on.

SEVENTEENTH MISSION: KOBE, JUNE 5, 1945

Our "dry spell" finally ended, and on June 5 we flew our seventeenth, a daylight-formation incendiary mission to destroy what was left of Kobe. Thirty-eight aircraft from the 29th Bomb Group joined nearly 500 ships from all three wings on another massive show-of-force strike. We had a lot of severe weather to fly through on the way up, and I worried more about that than the Japs. It cleared short of the coast, though, and we found visual conditions over the target. The ships ahead of us had the target burning well when we started our bomb run, the smoke was already several thousand feet above us. We could see the formations ahead of us catching a lot of flak. Observed in the same horizontal plane as our view, it looked thick enough to walk on. We braced ourselves for the onslaught of shrapnel we would have to fly through in a minute or two. The bomb doors of the ships ahead of us opened, and the bombs fell from their formations in a classic simultaneous pattern on the city below. We entered the barrage of anti-aircraft fire and repeated the performance of the preceding ships as the low, muffled rumble of the concussions caused by the flak began to affect us. We sustained some minor damage, and then suddenly, the flak stopped. We flew through a wide turn and headed back out to sea. A few fighters buzzed around our formations but failed to attack and did us no harm. We proceeded back to Guam and landed after 15:50 hours of flight time including five hours of instruments. Eleven B-29s were lost on the mission, but none was from our group. Low bombing altitudes ranging from

13,500 feet to 18,500 feet were responsible for the losses and the heavy damage suffered by the 73rd Bomb Wing, which had preceded us into the target area.

EIGHTEENTH MISSION: TACHIKAWA, JUNE 10, 1945

Our next mission was a daylight formation strike against the Japanese Army Air Depot at Tachikawa on June 10. This was our "hump" mission—number eighteen—which put us over halfway to our thirty-five-mission goal. We had more in the book than we had left to fly. We were first over the target, and I was leading a flight as I had done at Nagoya. Thirty-four 29th Bomb Group aircraft hit this target which had been attacked previously on April 30th. One hundred and thirty-eight tons of bombs destroyed it. This mission went off just as briefed—all our plans clicked, and there was little opposition the from the Japs. We returned for the eighteenth time without damage or injury, unless you counted the sprained ankle that Pic suffered the day before sliding into home plate in a softball game. He couldn't walk, but the doc wouldn't ground him, so we carried him down to the flight line and lifted him into the airplane. He didn't need his feet to do his job anyway—maybe the doc thought the same thing.

On the way back, we picked up a radio broadcast from San Francisco saying that the emperor had given Premier Suzuki dictatorial powers in the government, and in his speech following the granting of such power, he acknowledged that Japan was suffering a shortage of food, munitions, and transportation, but that they would never submit to an unconditional surrender—they would fight to the end. This had a deflating effect on my optimism for an early end to the war.

The day after this mission, I was about to go to dinner at the officers' mess when four guys in ATC uniforms showed up on my porch. It was Jay Plank and the other members of his crew. We had dinner and talked for a couple of hours until they had to get back to their quarters at Depot Field. They said that there was a lot of public support for using gas on the Japs to bring the war to an end. I doubted that the Allies would ever use gas in war, except, perhaps, as retribution toward an enemy who used it first. However, unknown to us, there was something else in preparation that would be used against the Japs in about six weeks, and it would influence the ending of hostilities. Jay said that he would be back in the States in three or four days and offered to take anything with him that I wanted to send home. I had nothing to send but my love for my wife, so I sent that.

About a week before this incident (or maybe a week afterwards—my memory isn't that good), we were preparing to have a party one evening to celebrate the cancellation of a mission which was to have been flown that night. Everybody seemed to be in the mood. I contributed my last bottle of good booze, and all the rest of the gang had contributed something—beer or more booze, cups, Cokes, ice, or whatever—when I received a message from a Mr. Wickwire saying he had a package for me. I borrowed a jeep and beat it down to the center of the island. I didn't know who Mr. Wickwire was, but I figured that either Plank or Milstead had brought the package over and left it with local United or ATC personnel. I found Wickwire, and he gave me the package (a fruitcake). I found out that Eddie Hoy of United had brought it over and left it for me. There were several United pilots there, and I stayed and talked to them the rest of the evening. One of them, Lee Duncan, said he flew out of Burbank and knew my wife in the dispatch office there. He also said that he was on a crew once before with Plank, and they had traveled to North Field looking for me, but I was flying a mission. These contacts were great morale boosters for me and very important to me—not only for the receipt of the goodies, but for seeing and talking to people from home still involved in the life that I'd left and so wanted to get back to. And my wife appreciated them, too, just to talk to someone who had actually *seen* me was a thrill for her.

I got back to the party about ten-thirty or eleven and found my whole crew, including the ground crew, on my airplane plastered to the gills—except, of course, Tom and Rich, who were teetotalers. Seelig was celebrating the upcoming birth of Hal Jr. after five years of trying ("trying"?). So he was entitled. Pic's tongue got so tangled that he reverted to Italian instead of English, and nobody could understand anything he was trying to say. They were funny for a while, but I was sober and soon tired of them, so I left and went to bed. I didn't begrudge them the party at all. It was good for them to unwind, and as soon as the hangovers were cured, I knew they'd be ready to go again.

NINETEENTH MISSION: OSAKA, JUNE 15, 1945

On June 15 we were scheduled for our nineteenth mission. The target was the city of Osaka. There were 512 B-29s participating, and radio reports following our departure from the coast indicated that Osaka's industrial area had been obliterated. We were subjected to no enemy action, but the flight was one of the worst we had experienced because of the weather between Iwo Jima and Japan. The storms in those latitudes at that time of the year could be particularly turbulent and vicious. Compounding the rough ride and the strain of flying instruments in that kind of atmosphere was the constant worry of traffic in the clouds—the danger of midair collisions with other bomb-laden B-29s. We flew these missions at moderate altitude, so we were in the middle of the worst turbulence. It was not like flying above the weather at 25,000 or 30,000 feet. While I logged only four hours of instrument time on this trip, in my letter to my wife afterwards, I said, "I'd almost as soon face flak and fighters as weather like that again!"

After the March 9–10 Tokyo mission when the Musser and Johnson crews were lost, Adolph Heyke and Bob Combs had moved into our hut with their crew officers. Some weeks later, Hal Leffler, Combs's copilot, was promoted to aircraft commander and took over the Brady crew. Bob Bigelow then became Combs's copilot, and Jerry Theisen, who had flown with me on two missions, was assigned as Leffler's copilot. The Leffler crew was popular both in our hut and on the field. Hal and Jerry were gregarious and outgoing and their airplane became readily identifiable on the field in part because they painted white sidewalls on the tires. Hal somewhere had acquired an Indian taxi horn—you know the kind, a trumpet in front and a big black rubber bulb on the rear. He would hang it out of his window and honk it like a teenager on cruise night as he left his hardstand and taxied toward the runway. I also heard another story about horns. This apparently predated the Leffler promotion and acquisition of the crew. On someone's sortie to visit the Navy at Agana Harbor, an air horn from a destroyer was acquired and installed in the bomb bay. It was reportedly hooked into the oxygen system for air power and was honked repeatedly on the final approach so the ground crew would know they were landing. However, I didn't ever hear this blaster. The other part of their identity was the official name of the ship: *The City of Grundy Center* (Iowa). They were kidded a lot about that, but the unusual name stuck in everyone's memory. The population of Grundy Center was possibly the smallest of any city represented by a B-29 anywhere in the Marianas. It was Hal's hometown. Heyke was the opposite—introverted and serious, not inclined to participate in the horseplay that sometimes dominated life around the Quonset hut between missions.

When we returned from the Osaka mission, we experienced the same shock that we had on March 10—Heyke had been lost on takeoff for the mission. His was the third crew to be lost out of a hut in which three crews were domiciled. Three out of three. We were told that he blew up off the end of the island moments after liftoff. I distinctly recall a meeting held the next morning down on the line with the Engineering Section personnel when Colonel Storrie really chewed everybody out and read the riot act to them. It was thought at the time that the cause of the blowup or crash must have been a maintenance error—a fuel leak ignited by an electrical spark, or something similar to that—and so the responsibility for the loss lay squarely with the ground maintenance people. That may not have been fair, but the perception persists to this day among many of the 29th Bomb Group Association members. I have asked a couple of them recently if they remembered what happened to Heyke, and their response was, "Yeah, he blew up."

Yet the official records about this incident do not indicate an explosion in the air. That report states that another crew observed the Heyke aircraft in a shallow bank and a slow descent toward the water between Guam and Rota, a small island just north of Guam in the Marianas chain. Perhaps they exploded upon crashing into the ocean, although, if that happened, it would have been a fuel explosion as the bombs were not armed. In any event, they were gone, and only small pieces of debris were ever recovered in the area of the crash.

Official records sometimes differed from the observations of witnesses, and I have no explanation for this discrepancy. Official reports were always published at varying time intervals after the event itself, and by people who were not witnesses, but analysts or interrogators or interpreters or reporters who may have, rightly or wrongly, misunderstood the evidence. I had an experience with this type of situation once myself. I had reported an incident and the circumstance leading up to it to the debriefing team after my return from a mission, but the official report identified the cause as being exactly the opposite of what I had told the debriefer. Was his interpretation different because he was not a pilot and therefore unable to understand where I was coming from? In discussing the official report phenomenon, I'm not trying to change anything about it regarding the Heyke disaster, but I know that all of us in the squadron believed, at the time and subsequently, that he had blown up in the air.

TWENTIETH MISSION: KAGOSHIMA, JUNE 18, 1945

Kagoshima at the southern end of Kyushu was next on the seventeenth and eighteenth and was mission number twenty for us. It was a night incendiary, like the others we had flown against the cities of Japan. The same weather system that we had encountered two days before on the Osaka mission was locked in between Iwo Jima and the Japanese coast. Once again, I flew instruments manually in severe turbulence for over two hours each way. Some of it was so rough I thought it would shake my teeth out. I always worried about the effect of severe turbulence, which wracked the airplane around, on the

outbound flight because of our exceptionally heavy weight. I
didn't like it any better on the way back either, but I didn't
worry as much because the airplane was 25,000 or 30,000
pounds lighter and better able to withstand the extreme gust
loads to which it was subjected in the storm. These conditions
also brought back a worry that I had had on some previous
missions: collision with our own ships.

I thought we would have to bomb by radar, and I alerted
Tom to this possibility. However, as we flew up the Bay of
Kagoshima, a hole opened up over the city, and we were able to
bomb visually. That same hole however made us visible to the
Japs, and they threw up barrage flak in incredible concentra-
tions. I hadn't seen flak like it except over Tokyo. In this
respect, the missions were getting tougher rather than easier—
the Japs were getting more practice and perhaps more desperate, so they were throwing everything at us. We did not,
however, see all the weird stuff in the sky that we saw on the last
mission to Tokyo. No phosphorus shells, no flare bombs, no
"balls of fire"—just a hell of lot of anti-aircraft fire. As we went
in and saw the barrage ahead of us, I wondered how an airplane could fly through all that shrapnel at all, but most of us
did without getting hurt. I tried to pick an easy way in, but that
was almost impossible—you never knew where the stuff was
going to be or when it was going to come. We got through with
no injuries and only minor damage to the ship. I used the
excess speed coming off the bomb run to gain as much altitude
as I could, thinking that I might be able to top the weather and
thereby avoid some of the turbulence on the return flight. But
it didn't happen—we were in it for the duration to Iwo.

After landing and finishing with the debriefers, I crawled
into my sack, dead tired. On this mission, I had not been able
to drowse even briefly, to "rest my eyes," as I sometimes was
able to do. When I awoke three or four hours later, I felt like I
had taken a beating and couldn't get over it. We were always
thankful and grateful to be back from each mission, but even
after we returned, it took a while for the nervous tension
to subside and finally leave us. Sometimes, maybe feeling a
little sorry for ourselves, or at least suffering some pangs of

homesickness, we could only wonder, "why, oh why, doesn't the damn war end so we can go home?" It seemed like such a long time since we had left home, and sometimes home looked a long, long time away. So near, and yet so far.

Back on the seventh of May, a parade was scheduled on the field, something that had not occurred since we were cadets. The purpose was to award the Air Medal to all the crews, ours among them, that had participated in the offensive against Japan during March and April. Photographs were taken of the ceremony to be forwarded to hometown newspapers and distributed among the crews. Then, on the seventh of June, we were awarded an Oak Leaf Cluster to the Air Medal—no parade this time, just the handing out of the citation. By the time the war ended, we received two more. All of the citations read the same:

> For meritorious achievement while participating in aerial flights as crew members in successful combat missions from bases in the Marianas Islands against the Japanese Empire. These missions were flown under rapidly changing and often-times adverse weather conditions. The flights were subjected to intense enemy antiaircraft fire and fighter opposition. There were constantly present difficult navigational problems, danger of engine failure and consequent ditching many miles at sea. Under a prolonged period of physical and mental strain, and undaunted by the many hazards faced regularly and continuously, each crew member displayed such courage and skill in the performance of his duty as to reflect great credit on himself and the Army Air Forces.

Sometime around the end of June or early July, the prevailing easterly wind began to weaken—indeed, sometimes stopped altogether or became a slight westerly. I would imagine that this was a normal seasonal climactic circumstance and not a singular event. However, it posed another hazard for us when we launched. Even a light fifteen or twenty mile an hour headwind was a great help in getting our overloaded airplanes airborne, but a no wind or slight downwind condition added hundreds of feet to our takeoff run. Between the end of our runway and the cliff at the eastern edge of the island was a half-mile or so of jungle which we had to overfly. I often wondered why the Seabees and engineers building the runways didn't bulldoze this area to clear a path all the way to the edge of the island, but they had not.

On these takeoff runs, it seemed that I levitated the airplane into the air by fervent concentration as much as I flew it off. The runway was slightly downhill for the first one-half of its length, and then slightly uphill for the final one-half. In that agonizing uphill struggle to reach 125 or 130 miles an hour or so, I physically strained along with the engines to achieve the speed to produce the lift needed to raise that gargantuan roaring behemoth into the sky. As the labored gradual liftoff was achieved, my copilot retracted the gear, and I flew over that width of jungle at twenty-five or thirty feet, throttles still wide open, almost on the ragged edge of a stall, for the five or ten seconds it took to traverse the distance to the cliff. A runaway propeller or an engine failure during these critical moments would, in all probability, mean an instant crash with all of us becoming ash and detritus in a huge cloud of black smoke.

When the cliff edge was passed, it was like a sudden cool breeze in my face. I could dive two or three hundred feet down to the water, gaining flying speed, slowly raising the flaps as I did so, and reducing power thereby relieving the engines of much of the strain and heat to which they had been subjected. At that point, the first hurdle of the mission was behind me. Which, I guess is true of every takeoff, but these mission launchings seemed to have their own special hazards.

The rainy season was also approaching, and there were periods when it would rain in monsoon torrents for a couple of days at a time, creating puddles and mini-lakes around our living area. This brought about a local biological peculiarity indigenous to our tropical island. The local amphibians were suddenly everywhere, ribbeting and croaking and burping. They had emerged from the mud where they had burrowed and remained, hibernating, as the land dried out after the last rainy season. We were awash in frogs and toads.

When the weather cleared after each deluge, things literally steamed. The humidity was 100 percent, and the heat was stifling. All our possessions started to mildew and rot—including our feet if we were not careful. Shoes were particularly susceptible. I scrounged an extension cord somewhere and kept a forty-watt light bulb burning all the time in my footlocker in an attempt to stop the moldy deterioration of my stuff. Flying was the only escape; we could find comfortable temperatures aloft. On the ground, though, there was no such thing as air-conditioning or other relief. Swimming at the beach afforded some respite, but not much, and it was only temporary.

Flying schedules became somewhat dubious during these tropical storms, and sometimes missions were postponed or canceled, and sometimes we tried to get one off in a lull or when the prospect of clearing by return and landing time the next day looked promising. One of these attempts was the occasion of my only intentional aborting of a mission. I don't remember which mission it was, but it was night and it was raining hard. We had completed our preparations and pre-flight routine, and when I taxied into position for takeoff, it was raining cats and dogs. As I advanced the throttles beginning my takeoff run, I could see the runway ahead, but by the time I had reached sixty or seventy miles an hour, I couldn't see at all. The rain on the nose blotted everything out. It was like trying to fly underwater. I chopped the throttles and braked to make the last turnoff to the taxiway.

I had made a number of instrument takeoffs in my career, but those were not like this. In those instances I was taking off into fog and cloud that was down to fifteen or twenty feet above the ground. Typically, I could see the runway boundary lights fading into the distance ahead, but at least I could see the ground, and the water accumulating on the windshield was only a mist. I would roll ahead a few yards to be sure the nose-wheel was straight (or, in the case of the B-17, I locked the tail-wheel), and advanced the throttles to takeoff power. I went on instruments immediately as the groundroll started, my eyes glued to the gyros as I accelerated.

My copilot quietly called out the airspeed as he monitored my track down the centerline. If the track began to veer in the least, he would apply slight gentle pressure on the rudder pedal and I would accept the correction as my directional gyro was telling me the same thing. At liftoff I was already enveloped in cloud, but by then the instrument discipline was in command of my being, my thoughts and my actions. I was totally concentrated and proceeded into the precise operation of the flight on the gauges.

I even did this once many years later in a single-engine Cessna 182 without benefit of a copilot. I was departing Santa Monica airport about 9:00 A.M. in June when the marine layer typically blankets the Pacific coast in southern California. The ceiling was below minimums for operations except for instru-ment takeoffs. The weather boys had told me that the marine layer was only about 2,500 feet thick, and that it was burning off about three or four miles inland. So, I took off to the east on a special clearance using exactly the same procedures I have described above. The only difference here was that the bottom of the marine layer (ceiling) was probably forty or fifty feet instead of fifteen or twenty. As I recall it was just brushing the tops of all the hangers.

But the takeoff in the deluge was something else. I taxied back to the head of the runway for a second try, but when I reached about seventy miles an hour or so, I made the same decision as on the first attempt, and I chopped the throttles. For some reason, I didn't think I could make it in all that water. If I had been alone, I think I might have continued the takeoff, but I had ten other people to consider, as well as the big bird. My memory is not good enough at this late date to understand and recall all my thoughts and feelings at the time, but I had made a decision after two attempts, so I parked the ship and we deplaned. Every pilot, at the outset of every flight, makes a "go" or "no-go" decision, and this time, justifiably or not, mine was "no-go."

The six-by-six truck picked us up and returned us to our Quonset hut. No one—neither the ground nor aircrew—censured me. There was no discussion about it (to my knowledge), so I don't know what they were thinking: "What's the matter with him? Has he lost his touch or his guts?" "Other people took off, why couldn't he?" Maybe nobody had these thoughts, but I know they were all disappointed at having missed a mission. So was I.

TWENTY-FIRST MISSION: SHIZUOKA, JUNE 19, 1945

Our next sortie—number twenty-one for us—was a night incendiary strike against Shizuoka, a crowded city of about 160,000 people, on June 19. To illustrate the population densities typical of Japanese cities, consider that these 160,000 individuals lived tightly packed in an area of less than five square miles. Their abodes were wood and paper and plaster structures that were exceptionally susceptible to destruction by fire. For example, a fire started in a bakery shop in 1940 and before it was contained, 6,000 houses had been destroyed. Contributing to the potential for destruction was the almost complete lack of either natural or manmade fire breaks. No wonder our incendiary attacks were so devastating. Once the inferno started, there was nothing people could do but evacuate and let it burn.

Our trip up to Japan was plagued with a lot of weather, but I was able to pick my way through or around most of it without experiencing much severe turbulence. It was clear over the city, and I gave them my "rapid delivery routine" right in the center of the target. We observed some flak, but we were not hit, so once again we headed back out to sea undamaged.

Some of our boys came back and said this was the roughest mission they had ever flown. I had learned, however, that particularly on night incendiary raids, the same mission could be bad for some people and relatively easy for others. For instance,

we had been on missions where, before we went in or after we
came out, we could see terrific barrages of flak, but at the particular moment when we went over, there was little or none.
That worked the other way, too: we had been caught in those
barrages when others saw only meager ack-ack. You never knew
what any particular target would be like until afterwards. We
had come as close to being shot down over Tokyo as anyplace
else, and yet we went over once without having a shot fired at
us. I have previously described taking some flak and then having it suddenly stop. Why? Were they reloading? It doesn't seem
plausible. Did they suddenly get hit with some of our bombs?
Who knows? The same mission could spell doom or reprieve.

The 314th Bomb Wing lost two B-29s on this mission, but
they were not from our group. Sixty percent of the city was
completely destroyed in our onslaught. The two losses sustained on this mission were the result of a midair collision of B-
29s over the target, not enemy action.

TWENTY-SECOND MISSION: TAMASHIMA, JUNE 22, 1945

Thirty-six hours later, we were off again, this time on a daylight
formation mission—our twenty-second—to Tamashima on the
twenty-second of June. Our objective was to destroy the Mitsubishi Aircraft Plant. We had clear weather over Japan, and we
achieved excellent bombing results. Recon photos the next day
showed 85 percent of the plant had been destroyed. One hundred and twenty-four B-29s flew the mission, with the 29th
Bomb Group providing twenty-eight aircraft.

I was deputy leader and therefore assigned the slot position
in the lead box element of our formation. We formed up at the
rendezvous, and shortly thereafter, the lead ship dropped out
of the formation and aborted the mission. This was due to a
mechanical malfunction, as we had not yet experienced any
enemy opposition. I moved up into the lead position, and
someone else slid into my place in the slot.

As the formation proceeded to the initial point where we
would turn onto the bomb run, we could see a fair amount of
flak and a lot of fighters buzzing around the groups ahead of

us. As Father Cummings, a U.S. Army chaplain on Bataan had said early in 1942, "There are no atheists in foxholes." Well, perhaps there are no atheists on the bomb run either. This was the moment of greatest anxiety for many crew members and resulted in a lot of believers and nonbelievers alike trying to make a deal with God: "Please, God, see me through this safely, and I promise to work for a better world when I get home" or "I promise to go to church every Sunday" or some similar vow or assurance. I was talking to Him more than praying or trying to make a deal: "O.K. now Boss, let's go through here just like the last time and get home in one piece." But maybe it's all the same, I'm not sure.

We turned to the bomb run heading, and the fighters moved in and made a number of attacks, but without, at least in our view, shooting anyone down. As we approached the aircraft plant, the flak started. It was moderate in volume, but we were not hit, and after bombs away and after we left the target, we were subjected to innumerable attacks. One fighter came from dead ahead, 20mm cannon blazing away. I could see the orange burst of flame each time it fired. He broke off the assault, diving under us and pulling up quickly, ramming the B-29 in the slot position behind us. As it went down we saw two or three of the crew bail out, and then other fighters moved in and shot them in their chutes.

This was not the first time we had observed this, but it was revolting and sickening to see it happen—their bodies jerking violently in their harnesses as they were hit, and then suddenly going limp, like a rag doll, their heads hanging on their chests. What sort of people would commit such an act? It is one thing to meet your enemy on the battlefield where you are each mentally prepared to kill the other—and the fight rages—and quite a different thing to kill your adversary after he has exited the field and is helpless.

At that particular moment, I probably would have given anything to have had a P-51 strapped to my butt—I'd have wiped the sky clean of those goddamned, uncivilized, barbaric, sadistic, subhuman, infidel Jap bastards. But I had a B-29 strapped to my butt, and the responsibility for ten other lives on board as well as the integrity of the formation and the mission objectives. There was nothing I could do for my fellow airmen except say a silent goodbye and fantasize about avenging their deaths. The 29 was not from our group; we didn't know who they were.

When I reported the ramming incident to the debriefers after landing, they recorded it as an intentional ramming. I disputed this theory and argued with them about it. If it had been an intentional ramming, he would have taken me out—why dive under me to ram another airplane? I believe that he never saw the ship in the slot. The ramming had to have been completely unintentional and accidental. Some things in life seem to be determined by chance—being in the right place at the right time or, in the case of the other crew, the wrong place at the wrong time. The incident preyed on my mind—except for the abort, I would have been in the slot. Fate? Or Providence?

TWENTY-THIRD MISSION: NAGOYA, JUNE 26, 1945

After one day's rest, we were preparing to execute our specialty again. The morning saw us at the beach practicing dinghy drill. I viewed that somewhat like a parachute jump—why practice something that had to be done perfectly the first time? Besides, we didn't have a B-29 fuselage in the water there to practice exiting it, and that was the critical part of the exercise if we ditched. Getting in the dinghies was a secondary part of the drill—unless, of course, the seas were running eight or ten or twelve feet.

In any event, it was an absolutely gorgeous day with the water as blue as I had ever seen it, and the sand sparkling like millions of white diamonds. The horizon was not, as was often the case, slightly hazy and somewhat indistinct as it receded in the distance gently blending the transformation from water to air, but rather a clear, hard, sharp line dividing sea and sky into their distinguishing hues of blue. It looked as though we could see a thousand miles. It was the kind of day that made you feel privileged and glad to be alive, the war notwithstanding. The afternoon was spent preparing the airplane and our equipment for a mission scheduled to depart about two in the morning for a daylight strike against the Nagoya Arsenal. Premission anxiety precluded any sleep before engine start: Nagoya could be tough. After our briefing and being transported to the line, we sat around the ship for an hour or so talking about the mission to come and watching an almost complete eclipse of the nearly full moon. As it was ending, once again bathing us in tropical moonlight, we boarded and began the now routine and familiar process of bringing the ship to life. After takeoff, I climbed above the broken stratocumulus layer and it was almost as bright as day. The air was smooth and the moonlight on the clouds below was beautiful and mesmerizing.

The night flight seemed quiet and serene over the gossamer blanket below. The steady sound of the engines was the same as in daylight—they were not muffled—but in some way, it was different. We were suspended in a world bereft, except for ourselves, of any sign or influence of mankind.

Over the vast reaches of the Pacific there were no occasional small clusters of sparkling lights revealing the presence of a community of humans, nor the necklace-like threads of intermittent lights on highways linking the villages together. We seemed suspended in time and space, the ethereal illumination divulging nothing to us except the slow progress of the moon and stars along their path to the west. A gorgeous sunrise a few hours later revealed clear skies all the way to Japan—an unusual situation for us. Typical weather, at least from Iwo Jima to Japan, was a series of fronts requiring, at a minimum, a couple of hours of instrument flying each way. But this trip, we had perfect flying conditions up and back.

Our in-flight routines varied a little occasionally, but on most flights, unless I was manually flying on the gauges (instrument flight), there was communication and interaction among the crew members. That was the case on this mission in the clear weather. I would talk to some crew members from time to time on the intercom, but also, several times during the flight,

I would turn the flight controls over to Bud, get out of my seat to stretch my legs, and walk around the airplane just to say hello to everyone and see that each was all right. Even though he was on the flight deck with me, I would usually stop at the engineer's station first.

"How are the head temperatures, Pic? All in the green?" He would respond affirmatively.

"How are we doing on fuel consumption? Going to have enough to get home?"

"On schedule, Skipper—we should be O.K."

I then would move back to the navigator's position, and the conversation would be something like this.

"Hello, Fred, how are we doing?"

"Fine—we're a little right of course, but I have corrected for that."

"How much drift do we have?"

"A couple of degrees right."

"When will we reach our next checkpoint?"

"On time."

"Going to get to the target on time?"

"Yep, I think so."

"O.K."

After the navigator, I talked to the radio operator. He was stuck behind the upper forward turret in a cubbyhole with no window. He just had to stare at a table full of radio sets. He monitored all the assigned frequencies—that is, the ground station back on Guam, other B-29s in the air, the Navy and air-sea rescue frequencies, and so on. He, too, like the engineer and the navigator, kept a running log, but on all missions radio silence was the rule, so he usually had little to do. Of course, if we or someone else was in trouble, or if the ground station was sending out new instructions, he got busy. He had some other responsibilities as well. He sent a radio message to Guam after bombs away so that Bomber Command would know that we had hit the target, and he was keeper of the flares. If I had to fire a flare or drop a phosphorous smoke signal in flight, Jim was my man. Consequently, because of the inactivity, he carried a good stock of reading material to pass the time. If anyone else wanted a magazine, he crawled to the radio operator's table. Jim was also custodian of our water jug and in-flight lunches. He dispensed food or drink upon request.

I'd always ask him if he had any new dope, and he never did, so I moved on through the tunnel to the rear of the airplane to talk to the gunners and the radar man. This also gave me an opportunity to inspect the engines from the rear—to observe the exhaust flame and to look for oil or fuel leaks. The scanners monitored these things for me on an ongoing basis, too, but on my "tour" I always looked out each blister.

We hit the coast, were met by Jap fighters, and the battle was on—at least until we were well off shore again. The beautiful clear weather was to their advantage, too. Fifty-eight B-29s from the 314th Bomb Wing conducted this raid, and the heavy fighter opposition notwithstanding, the only B-29 lost was due to a direct hit by flak over the target.

We were subjected to many fighter attacks as we proceeded from our rendezvous to the initial point and turned on to the bomb run. One Tony scared me half to death. He suddenly appeared out of nowhere directly ahead and bore down on us in a classic frontal attack. I was looking right down his gun barrels, and hunkering down in my seat, convinced that his shells were coming right into the cockpit, but they didn't—or I wouldn't be here to tell about it. It was a very short attack. The closure rate was probably at least 600 to 650 miles per hour, and I could clearly see the grinning sonofabitch in the cockpit as he flashed by. My gunners were firing at him, but other 29s in the formation behind us shot him down moments later.

In the usual predictable pattern, the fighters backed off as we approached the target and the flak batteries took over. As we tightened up our formation, Nagoya spread out before us, its burned out areas quite prominent in the morning sun. The flak concentration became heavier. It seemed to be everywhere—above and below, to each side, and ahead of us. It was intense barrage type and as we penetrated it, we could feel the rapid concussions as it exploded all around us. The sky was black with it. Nearly every ship suffered some damage, but there were no injuries of which I was aware.

As we made our wide sweeping turn off the target, the fighters moved in again and pressed numerous attacks until we were fairly well out to sea. Several fighters were shot down, but they didn't succeed in shooting down any B-29s, although they did inflict some damage on several ships.

As we loosened up the formation and each ship independently set course for the Marianas, the pilot of one of those badly damaged by flak thought he might have to ditch, so I stayed with him all the way home. Among other things, he couldn't lower his gear. He crashed landed at North Field and did a beautiful job. There was no fire and his crew was no more than a little shaken up.

The post-mission recon photos showed the target over 75 percent destroyed, so like Tokyo, Japan's second largest city was fast becoming impotent and would probably no longer be a strategic target. This was our twenty-third mission—only twelve more to go. The happy day was getting closer.

In the last couple of months of our tour on Guam, and after the loss of the Heyke crew, we had the squadron "bad boy"— or, to put it more succinctly, the squadron "screw up"—in our hut. If my memory serves me correctly, at this point he had been reprimanded several times for a long string of juvenile antics both in the airplane and on the ground, had lost his crew, and was reduced to flying copilot for others. He was coarse, rough hewn, irascible, and irreverent, and had a constant scowl on his face—I don't think I ever saw him smile. He was a loose cannon with an untamed wild streak or perhaps just a knothead apparently without common sense. He pretty much kept to himself nurturing his huge ego and feeling sorry for himself. He didn't fraternize with the other pilots or "shoot the bull" with them about flying. He resisted authority both covertly and conspicuously—not an admirable or wise trait in wartime in a combat outfit. I remember on a couple of occasions he buzzed the field upon returning from a mission including once buzzing General LeMay's quarters, and then at the end of the runway pulling up into a half-assed climbing turn that he thought others would think was a chandelle. Like he was flying a peashooter instead of a B-29. I don't know what he thought he was celebrating. He'd been out for fourteen or fifteen hours, and may in fact have been over Japan, but that was about all that anyone knew regarding his journey. When he had left the States for the western Pacific, he had flown under the Golden Gate Bridge, and then one day in the Marianas, when test-hopping a B-29, he reportedly looped the airplane.

The whole group was up one day practicing formation flight around the Marianas both for the practice and to provide a photo opportunity to provide pictures to be used by the correspondents and reporters assigned to the wing. Our "bad boy" had been assigned the diamond position in a four-plane element. Another B-29 piloted by Colonel Storrie, our group commander, was flying above and around the formation directing the show. He was on the radio telling our boy to "move it up," to "close up your position," when the response came: "If you think you can fly this slot any better than I'm doing, then come on down here and do it." Whereupon the colonel told him to get the hell out of there, and the colonel did just that—dropped down and flew the position himself. I don't know what kind of a chewing out was administered later, but I would bet that there was a good one.

One night most of us were in the hut when we heard a jeep approaching, then racing its engine, and crashing into the hut. We all ran outside to see our "screw up" trying to knock the hut off its foundation. He would back up a few feet, put it in low gear, and ram the building. He was drunk. Four or five guys dragged him out of the jeep and threw him on his cot. Someone then took the jeep back where he had borrowed it (read: "stolen it"). He slept it off but showed no remorse the next day. He would probably do something like it again the next time he got plastered.

On another occasion, he came in and went to bed. I don't know whether he was loaded or sober, but shortly after lying down, he raised his head and issued an order in a loud voice: "Turn the goddamned lights off!"

Four of the guys from my crew and Hal Leffler's crew were quietly playing bridge, and one of them said, "Go to hell."

To which our delinquent responded, "I said, turn the god-damned lights off!"

"Fuck you!"

"Oh yeah? Well, fuck you, too! I'll turn the goddamned lights off!"

Out came his .45, and he started blasting away at the tran-som lights. Everybody hit the floor, and when the smoke cleared, the boys in that end of the hut jumped him and dis-armed him. I don't remember if there were any ramifications from this little episode, except that we had to patch the holes in the transom roof to prevent getting soaked in the next rain.

TWENTY-FOURTH AND TWENTY-FIFTH MISSIONS: NOBEOKA AND SHIMINOSEKI, JUNE 28 AND JULY 1, 1945

The next two missions—our twenty-fourth to Nobeoka on the eastern coast of Kyushu and our twenty-fifth to Shiminoseki—were easy missions as far as enemy opposition was concerned. There was some weather enroute on the Nobeoka flight, but we picked our way through most of it without logging any real instrument time. We were the first airplane over the target in clear weather, and we were in and out before there was any fireworks. It was a novelty to approach a target and not see a lot of flak ahead to fly through.

Shiminoseki, on the extreme southern tip of Honshu on a narrow strait separating it from Kyushu, was a target important for its steel and coal import and export activity as well as its rail lines and highways. Again, we had clear weather both en route and over the target—really unusual, particularly at this time of the year, but welcome. Night missions in bad weather were sometimes nerve wracking. You couldn't see, so you blundered into some very nasty stuff. The only clue you had at night when in the soup was observing lightning flashes and listening to the crashes of static in you headset. This racket was, however, a fairly accurate indicator of the distance to the turbulent disturbance by the volume in your ears. A really loud crash indicated you were almost in it.

TWENTY-SIXTH MISSION: TOKUSHIMA, JULY 3, 1945

Our twenty-sixth mission started out like the previous two but evolved into something quite different. It was scheduled on July 3 as a night incendiary strike against Tokushima on the island of Shikoku.

We completed our preparations in the afternoon and took off early in the evening. The flight was uneventful until we were about two hundred miles or so off the Japanese coast. Then the number one engine blew a cylinder, and the engine caught on fire. Flames were streaking back under the wing behind the nacelle. An in-flight fire is a pilot's worst nightmare. It rivets his attention right now. My first command was "Feather number one!" Pic went into action immediately and hit the feathering button. As the prop blades began to turn into the slipstream, my commands continued: "Cut fuel to number one!" He quickly pulled the mixture to the idle cut-off position and closed the fuel shut-off valve. "Cut ignition and close the cowl flaps on number one!" Pic complied. The prop was now fully feathered and had stopped turning. With fuel no longer going to the engine and with the cowl flaps closed, the fire should have been smothered. I could no longer see any flames and called for a report from the scanners (gunners). They reported back: "No flames visible." I waited a few seconds longer, watching the engine nacelle, and then, even though the fire appeared to be out, I instructed Pic to blow one CO_2 bottle just to be sure. He pulled the extinguisher handle, but it apparently was not necessary—the fire was out.

I had been flying on autopilot, so I shut it off and retrimmed the ship for straight and level flight and adjusted power on the other three engines to maintain my desired airspeed. We had burned one-half or somewhat more of our fuel at this point in the flight; however, we were heavy, still carrying our full load of bombs. As I settled the airplane into three-engine operation, I began to assess our situation and consider the options. If I salvoed the bombs and reversed course for the base, it would be considered an "abort," and we would not get credit for the mission. After this one we would only have nine to go, and I was determined to keep flying them—I wanted to go home.

We were within an hour of Japan, so I asked Freddie for the closest target right on the coast. He looked at his map and said, "The city of Temma." I hesitated only a few seconds and then said, "O.K., give me the course—we'll bomb it as a secondary target of opportunity." We proceeded to do so, and there was no opposition.

I turned to the course back to the Marianas, quietly analyzing and considering the effects and problems of facing a 1,500 or 1,600 mile overwater flight on three engines. The peril, of course, was the possibility, however remote, of losing another engine. If we did, and it was on the other side (number 3 or 4), leaving me with one good engine on each side, I could continue flight (the airplane was light) in a slow descent and perhaps make Iwo Jima or perhaps maybe even Saipan—but probably not Guam. It would depend on our position when the second loss occurred. I would have only one pass at a landing, there would be no possibility of a go-around. If I lost the other engine on the same side (number 2), then I would have a real problem; I would, in all likelihood, be unable to control the airplane except its descent to the water. I would have to ditch. But if I did not sustain another engine loss, I could make it home. We had enough fuel, and there was no severe weather ahead. This was what I elected to do.

I didn't want to go into Iwo on three engines. That would mean leaving the airplane there and catching a ride back to Guam with another crew. We would then be without an airplane and unable to fly missions until we got ours back. Engine change facilities on Iwo were not what they were on Guam, and it could be weeks before it might come back, if ever.

I was determined to fly missions as fast as I could. I was second high man in the squadron, and I wanted to finish up with the other crew, so I felt the calculated risk was worth it. I maintained course for Guam and, needless to say, had no further malfunctions, making it on three engines.

When my ground crew saw me coming in with one feathered, they all met us on the hardstand with questioning looks on their faces. They, of course, didn't know whether I had feathered it eight hours ago or eight minutes ago. I responded to them with a sort of smart-aleck remark: "I'm down to only seventeen cylinders on that engine, and for some reason it doesn't want to run right—plus it wants to burn!" We could afford some humor about it once we were on the ground.

Grand Slam was scheduled for an engine change, and the Engineering Section and "Little John" and his crew got to work on it immediately. They worked continuously until the job was done—some thirty hours without rest. I had a great deal of respect and admiration for the crew chiefs and the ground crews. They were among the most dedicated and devoted to their task and our overall mission objectives as any group of people on the field. Like the aircrews, they frequently worked twenty-four or thirty-six hours at a stretch—sometimes longer—with only a catnap under the wing of an airplane in stifling heat to rejuvenate themselves and maintain their pace. Their work was precise and exacting and they worked in less than ideal conditions. It ran the gamut from routine maintenance and replacement chores, including troubleshooting of all the systems of the airplane, to changing those giant 3350 engines. As the aircrew, we got the glory and the bombs painted on the side of the airplane for missions flown, but there was about as much unsung glory due the crew chief and the ground crew for what they did.

Recently, I have been privileged to make the acquaintance of Eugene M. Gillum, M.D., of Portland, Indiana. While we did not know each other at the time, he went through the "Battle of Kansas" and, in 1945, was an engine specialist on Guam supervising work on the B-29s—in particular, the Wright 3350s. In one of his letters to me, he described the behavior, the apprehension, and the concern displayed by the crew chiefs when a mission was launched:

> As ground men, we were subjected to a different stress than the aircrews. We lived in dread of having our plane not come home. First, we did not want an aborted flight—the whole world would know it if you launched a malfunction—either of plane, engine, radio or radar. Second was the takeoff—we all went down to the end of the runway and sweated it out. Many guys stayed until every plane was airborne—not just until theirs had left. I saw some guys break down and sob with tears when it was over; the sounds, the dirt, the smell, the heat, the tension—it was the worst I have ever experienced. Our bird usually launched at about five P.M.—due back at about eight or nine a.m. No one can know what that wait was like 'till the next morning: plane after plane on a long approach to the runway, and then finally ours would swing into line. I cannot describe what we felt when it touched down. The dread that you felt when it left for that long ride was like nothing else I have ever known.

So the flight crews were not the only ones whose emotions and sensory responses were highly charged and at times were worn on their sleeves.

TWENTY-SEVENTH MISSION: KOFU, JULY 6, 1945

As soon as the new engine installation was complete, we took off to test fly it and get a couple of hours time on it before we headed for Japan. We landed just about an hour before briefing for another mission. After the briefing, we grabbed a bite to eat and took off for a night incendiary attack against Kofu, an inland city west of Tokyo and just north of Mount Fujiyama.

Once again, the weather favored us, and it was very nearly clear over the target. We were the last ones to bomb on this trip so we observed the inferno below without the fear of the aerial fireworks that we usually encountered. There was no flak when we traversed the target, and we turned back out to sea for the long grind back to Guam. The city, with its railroad marshaling yards, was later reported to have been 64 percent destroyed. Major Evans accompanied us, and an extra pilot made a lot of difference. I was actually able to get a couple of hours of sleep stretched out in the tunnel over the bomb bays. Number twenty-seven was in the book—only eight to go.

I slept late that day upon our return and then test-hopped the ship again after some additional work and adjustments were performed on the new engine. We had been alerted to the possibility of another mission in twenty-four hours, so I wanted to be ready to go again.

TWENTY-EIGHTH MISSION: GIFU, JULY 9, 1945
July 9 saw completion of number twenty-eight for us—a night incendiary strike against Gifu. This was another medium-sized city important as the hub of mainline railroads, smaller war industries, and hydroelectric power plants. We were among the first few airplanes over the target and saw only meager flak— and none near us. We returned without damage or injury. These smaller Japanese cities were not well defended like the major ones so our missions were becoming easier. We couldn't understand why the Japs persisted in resisting. We had rendered their cities and their industries powerless and unproductive; we had mined the Inland Sea and all the significant straits around Honshu, Shikoku, and Kyushu, thereby destroying or interrupting their shipping; and their air force was no longer significantly effective. So why didn't they quit? The occidental mind simply could not comprehend the oriental mind.

There had been a more-or-less stationary front south of Guam for about a week, but as we returned from this mission, it began to move north and our weather turned bad as the group was landing. Everyone managed to get down safely, but it rained buckets all day. I was getting quite concerned about the weather. We were almost into the rainy season when we would be inundated like this everyday and just about all flying would be on instruments. I prayed for decent flying weather for just a few more weeks so we could finish our tour.

Uwajima was next on the list for a night incendiary raid. We launched the mission in the early evening in virtually clear skies, the sun still above the western horizon. This would have been number twenty-nine for us, but we had our first inflight abort in our career. Who knew what was really going on? Was fate intervening in our favor? Operations had not scheduled us for this mission, but I fought tooth and nail to fly it because we were so near finishing up, and I wanted to get all of the strikes behind us as rapidly as possible.

We took off on time as the mission was launched with no indication of mechanical problems until we were about thirty minutes into the flight when the number two engine began missing, backfiring, and running rough. I'd been expecting it, though: our engines were getting pretty old, and it was time things should be going wrong with them. There were no alternatives or circumstances to consider this time, and I didn't hesitate to feather the engine, salvo the bombs, and start my turn to the reciprocal course. I had barely completed the turn when number four started acting up in the same manner as number two. I was now faced with the loss of a second engine. At least it was on the other side—I had that new one in the number one nacelle. I had enough altitude to make it back on two engines if I had to, although it might be hairy. I had never flown a B-29 with two engines out. Thank goodness, we were close to home. I debated about feathering it, thinking that even though it was not producing full power, perhaps I could keep it going to landfall. I was contemplating this when number three started missing and backfiring, too. Now I had a real emergency situation, faced with the loss of three engines. Because three engines were missing and backfiring, I wondered if I could have a fuel contamination problem that would soon affect the new engine. If this happened, then there would be no more to it—I'd have to ditch, and do it without power. Not an encouraging prospect.

For the next twenty minutes or so, in a gradual controlled descent to Guam, I kept feathering and unfeathering number three and number four alternately to keep at least some power on the right side. Whenever I determined that the engine that I still had running had deteriorated to a condition worse than the one I had feathered, I restarted the feathered engine and shut down the one still running. Thus, over the time it took to get back to North Field, I started and stopped engines three and four several times. I still had no clue about the cause of the malfunctioning engines, or to put it differently, I was so busy dealing with the situation and trying to ensure that we made the field, that I was unable to do much analysis. That could come after we were on the ground. I do recall being fearful of fire because of the backfiring, so I had the scanners watching the engines for any sign of fire or a major oil leak flowing over or along a wing.

There would be no power to go around if I botched the approach or the landing. However, this didn't worry me because the mission had been launched and there was little or no traffic. I would have the approach pattern to myself. It was still twilight, for which I was grateful—I could see what I was doing. The airplane was heavy despite having dropped the bombs—we still had a nearly full load of fuel—but heavy landings had been done before. We had no way to jettison fuel, and even if we had had that ability, I no longer had the power to fly around while it was being pumped overboard. This then would have to be like my B-17 landing at Jackson, Mississippi—just grease her on and everything would be O.K. So I landed with two engines running, one on each side.

There was some consternation among the ground crews as I taxied in with two feathered and one backfiring and popping. They started working on them as soon as I shut down. The analysis was not a specific malfunction, but just completely worn out engines. They pulled a compression check on all three, and while I no longer remember any numbers, there was, in effect, almost no compression on any one of the three. The engines had about 325 hours on them, which at that time was considered very good service. The engines we had in the States sometimes gave up at only fifty or seventy-five hours. Obviously, we were scheduled for three new 3350s.

But what if this multiple failure had occurred on takeoff? Or, perhaps even worse, had occurred six or seven hours into the flight? This would have been catastrophic and we certainly would have been in the water—from which we might not have been rescued. We could have become a statistic. It was a godsend that it happened the way that it did: during daylight, close to home, and not on takeoff. Somebody was looking out for us. Thinking about it afterwards, I realized that half the mission would have been flown on Friday, the thirteenth, and operations had not wanted me to fly anyway. How would the story have played out if we had not started out on this mission and equivalent circumstances had occurred on the next attempt? What have I previously said about fate? We were blessed, I'm sure.

We had some time off while the ship was getting three new engines, and it was a welcome rest notwithstanding my desire to keep flying missions.

There were other things of note going on in our lives, or on the missions, that I have not mentioned—or have overlooked, and for which I have no real time frame. Some were things that became routine, and others were singular events.

One of the singular incidents is the story of the crew returning from a mission when they spotted the aircraft carrier *Ticonderoga* below. They dropped down to have a look at it. As they circled it at about 1,000 feet, someone (the pilot? of course!) decided to have some fun with the Navy. They set up a circular approach descending to about 400 or 500 feet following the course of the carrier, flying right up the wake. At about a half mile off the fantail, lined up with the flight deck of the carrier, they dropped their gear, deployed their flaps, turned on their landing lights and executed a standard approach with the touchdown spot anticipated to be at the arresting cable. Well, this started a wild display of blinking signal lamps and flag waving from the carrier flight deck people trying to wave them off, but the 29 persisted with its approach. At the very last moment they retracted the gear and opened the throttles as they banked away from the ship, laughing their heads off all the way. I think they were lucky not to get shot down. Apparently the captain, whether he liked it or not, realized that it was a prank and a bluff, but if he had thought otherwise, he would have been justified in shooting down the American "Kamikaze" to save his ship. I also imagine that there was plenty of blasphemy on the air from the carrier, but the boys in the 29 weren't listening or weren't on the right frequency for it to have had any effect. I'm not aware that the crew got chewed out about this, but they may have if their ship was identified by the Navy—and I don't see how it could not have been.

We were cruising back to Guam after a strike one day when Jim, monitoring an emergency frequency, told me that a B-29 in our vicinity was seeking help. I no longer remember how we found him, but we did, and I pulled up on his wing and began talking to the pilot. He said they had suffered considerable flak damage over the target and were fearful lest they might have to ditch. I assured him that if he did, I would stay with him throughout the ordeal as long as I had fuel to linger and still make Iwo or one of the Marianas Island bases. I also assured him that we would alert Air-Sea Rescue and direct them to his position before leaving him if he was in the water. As we flew along, I told him to hold it straight and level so I could slide under him and look for damage. I did that as well as over him but couldn't see any evidence of major flak damage. However, that did not mean that he had not suffered incapacitation of electrical, hydraulic, or control systems. I no longer remember what conversations I had with him about these subjects, but I continued flying abreast of him until we were nearing Saipan. I told him that I would stay with him right down to the runway if it would help and if he wanted me to. He thanked me, but said he would be O.K. He seemed to have his confidence back and was relieved to be near his home base. I wished him good luck as he altered course somewhat, and I continued on to Guam.

Three or four days later, I was stretched out on my sack trying to take a nap when a fellow showed up at my hut looking for Robertson. When I acknowledged that I was Robertson, he held his hand out and said he just wanted to thank me for "buddying" him home. I was flattered that he had taken the time and made the effort to catch a ride to Guam to see me in person. We sat on my bunk for a little while talking about the flight, and then he thanked me again and went looking for a ride back to Saipan. I didn't keep a record of who he was. I hope he made it through the war O.K.

I have mentioned numerous times the protective procedure, as we approached the Japanese coast or the rendezvous point, of donning our flak vests and helmets in preparation for flying the bomb run. Well, after the experiences of a few missions and the resultant observations, each man sort of worked out his own ideas about what to do with the flak vest. The predominant manner of deployment became putting it in the bucket seat and sitting on it. The rationality behind this was an assessment of the most logical way in which you might be injured or wounded. The most probable was from anti-aircraft fire. This came from the ground, and if sustained in the fuselage would be underneath you. The guys figured that if they lost an arm or a leg, they could live a pretty normal life afterwards although with some handicap. If they lost the family jewels, that would be the end—no normalcy, no children, no happy wife, so a lot of flak vests went on the seats. I no longer remember whether I wore my vest as intended or sat on it. I certainly had the same concerns for the jewels as anyone else, but I also was frequently looking down flaming gun barrels spitting lead at me so I may have chosen to protect my torso. Jerry Theisen told me once that the first time he observed heavy tracer fire coming up from the ground looking like a roman candle, he perceived his bottom to be exposed and vulnerable and thereafter sat on his vest.

This paid off for a blister gunner somewhere in the Marianas. His ship took a direct flak hit at his position and blew the seat completely off its mounting with him still strapped in it, rolling him around in the rear compartment. He may have been scared to death, but he was not seriously injured, and the jewels were intact, thanks to the flak vest upon which he had been sitting.

I flew several missions before Iwo Jima had been secured for an emergency refueling base. My recollection is that at that time we flew with full gas tanks (except bomb bay tanks), so we had some reserves beyond the mission requirements. I noticed, however, that after each mission, the maintenance section went around sticking the tanks on all the returned airplanes. If it turned out that within the fleet, there was a surplus in the tanks, then the gas load on the next mission would be cut by the average amount of the surplus. This then would allow the bomb load to be increased by about an equal weight amount. By monitoring the whole fleet this way, average fuel burn could be pretty well established and gas loads adjusted accordingly. Our typical load was ultimately worked out to be about 6,750 or 6,800 gallons or about 40,000 pounds. This would get us up there and back if the mission was flown as briefed, but if there were extenuating circumstances—having to climb to a higher altitude, unfavorable winds, poor cruise control procedures, or perhaps the increased fuel consumption of old engines—then return to base could be a problem. Landing at Iwo Jima was an alternative, and I did that on several occasions when it was clear that I wouldn't make Guam. I got a little surprise upon returning from one mission however. I landed normally, taxied to my hardstand and shut down all the engines. As we were departing the hardstand for the debriefing hut, Little John climbed into the cockpit to start the engines for his usual post-mission checkout and was unable to start any one of the four—they were out of gas. There is some fuel in the tanks that might be available in flight that is not available on the ground because of the way the airplane sits, but it struck home to me that if it had been necessary for me to go around, I might not have made it. Hal Leffler had a similar experience once. He ran out of gas on his landing roll-out and had to be towed to his hardstand by a tractor—very embarassing. In his case however, if he had landed on his first approach, he would have made it to his hardstand. He says he was squeezed out of the pattern twice, and flew two go-arounds before touching down.

Some crews ran out of gas and ditched on the way home. It's hard to say why. Sometimes their fuel management practices may have been sloppy, sometimes it may have been an honest belief that they had enough, but their calculations were inaccurate, and it just didn't work out. There was one incident in which a crew had lost an engine over Japan and were proceeding back to base on three engines. En route, they lost their electrical system—or at least the ability to transfer fuel from one tank to another. When they ditched, they still had enough fuel to get home, but it was isolated in the tank on the dead engine. Sometimes it may have been a pilot's reluctance to stop at Iwo because of the weather there or the delay of several hours or overnight before getting fuel—or, in one or two cases that we heard about, just the pilot's egotistical stubbornness and bullheadedness: "I can make it. There's nothin' I can't do."

In any case, continuous fuel management from takeoff to touchdown became one of the pilot's critical responsibilities on these missions. The only time I ignored these procedures was on the bomb run when typically I had the throttles to the firewall. However, this was only for a relatively short time, and the additional speed I achieved coming off the target enabled me to climb several thousand feet higher for the return flight, thus extending my cruise range back to the Marianas.

Fuel management, or "cruise control" as we called it, was a technique—indeed, almost a discipline—absolutely necessary on a constant basis during flight in order to realize the long-range potential and enormous load capacity of the B-29. It involved the infinitely esoteric and recondite flying techniques necessary to keep the airplane at its optimum performance relative to its passage through the air. It involved not only keeping the airplane "on the step," but keeping it in trim and, excepting when a particular altitude had to be maintained, taking advantage of atmospheric air movement to increase airspeed or altitude thereby extending range without additional fuel consumption. This, of course, was the primary responsibility of the pilot.

Important as well was the continual monitoring of fuel flow and fuel consumption, cylinder head temperature, fuel boost pump pressure, oil pressure, and oil temperature. Constant manipulation of cowl flaps and intercooler shutters was necessary to keep temperatures within the desired operating ranges. These functions were the responsibility of the flight engineer. We had operating data charts on board which gave us fuel consumption figures at various altitudes with various manifold pressure settings and RPMs. These charts also gave us the horsepower available within each of these engine operating parameters. The engineer kept a running log of all engine instrument readings so that he and the pilot could adjust power settings as fuel burned off and the airplane became lighter, and to enable them to efficiently and accurately predict airborne endurance. Doing this properly could, of course, mean the difference between getting home and ditching with the possibility of the loss of our lives.

There were also a few defensive tactics—besides the evasive maneuvers which we employed on the night raids—that I have not mentioned. On some flights, and I have no recollection of which ones or the criteria to designate which ones, we had a Radar Counter Measures (RCM) aircraft flying the mission with us. It would circle the target above us using its electronic equipment to jam the Japanese radar on the ground. The searchlights and antiaircraft batteries, at least around the principal cities and targets, were controlled or aided by radar. If it could be jammed successfully, then they would have to rely on visual sighting to aim at us. We flew without lights of any kind, so unless a B-29 was illuminated by searchlights or reflected in the glow of the conflagration, it was a somewhat difficult target.

On an individual aircraft basis, we also employed our own methods of confusion. On the bomb run we would drop large quantities of "chaff" and/or "window" out of the camera hatch in the back of the airplane. I no longer remember which was which, but the material was long, thin, metalized strips or squares like confetti. It was not unlike common tinfoil. The radar impulses from the ground would reflect off of the "chaff" as it floated down and thus, to some degree, camouflage the airplane or at least give multiple targets like snow on the scopes or receivers below.

I don't know how effective either the RCM aircraft or our aerial dispersal of reflective material was in confusing and cluttering the Japanese radar scopes, but we welcomed anything that would assist in getting us in and out of the target area without damage.

There was one other defensive procedure that we sometimes practiced. The gun-laying equipment in place around major targets used a harmonic detection device in addition to radar to pinpoint its target. So, to add to the confusion, we frequently desynchronized the props to change the component frequency of the sound wave emanating from our aircraft. Years later, Jerry Theisen told me that, on one of the missions to Tokyo that he flew with me, he reached for the prop controls to do this and found my hand already there manipulating the controls. Again, anything which might contribute to our safe passage was worth doing.

Back on July 13 at the briefing for the Uwajima mission, each phase of the mission was addressed by the individual briefer in a sequence that had become familiar to us. We entered the briefing hut and instinctively looked at the map wall as we took our places on long wooden benches. A yarn string was stretched from Guam to the target indicating our course—usually through Iwo Jima—and then direct to the city or military/industrial installation which would be our target. As the briefing got underway, Captain Yearly, our intelligence officer, explained the importance of the target, the best information known about gun emplacement, expected enemy opposition, geography of the area, and other general information that might be useful to us. The operations officer was next with a litany of enroute altitudes, target approach courses and altitudes, bomb and fuel loads, the location of air-sea rescue units, and other bits of information appropriate to this particular target. The weather officer was next with his maps. I always paid particular attention to him because weather was always a serious concern to me, often more than enemy activity. He sometimes tried to vary his forecast and prediction by pointing out something that he thought was "interesting" or "different," but the bottom line was nearly always the same: "weather will be bad." This was the case between Iwo Jima and our target on almost every mission, but he would at least try to predict whether the target would be obscured or clear. The chaplain was next with a prayer for Godspeed and a safe return.

Colonel Storrie was last with a pep talk usually designed to encourage us and give us confidence. He sometimes reviewed our accomplishments and emphasized our part and significant role in current operations and the defeat of Japan (following which we would be able to go home). Then, on this occasion, he got on the subject of morale—how important it was in everything that we did. He perceived that we had high morale. He then digressed with a statement to the effect that high morale was closely associated with sex. He said that he had it on good authority that high morale invariably produced boys and that low morale produced a high percentage of girls. He predicted that when we returned home, we would all father boys. I laughed at this along with the rest of the group. I thought his remarks a strange departure from the routine subject matter, and I wondered what he knew about X chromosomes and Y chromosomes that I didn't know? But he seemed convinced of the validity of his remarks.

The psychological warfare practiced by each side in the Pacific was really totally ineffective. Tokyo Rose's program was widely listened to each evening because she had the best selections of big band "swing" music on the air, but the propaganda that came with it fell on deaf ears. The attitude of our boys was, "You started this mess, but we are going to finish it and teach you a lesson you'll not forget." On the other side, generations of Bushido, Shinto, and Samurai codes had produced a devotion to their emperor, whom they considered divine, that made them ignore the defeat they were suffering and our propaganda urging them to surrender. Our broadcasts to the Japanese people were prohibited listening, so there was no way to tell how much of it was getting through anyway.

So in June and more intensely in July and the first part of August, we began dropping newspapers and leaflets on the home islands of Japan. They were dropped by our weather and photo-recon aircraft following our missions. By this time, a single B-29 overflying their cities went unmolested, the Japs not wanting to waste defensive resources on a lone U.S. aircraft. In some cases, the leaflets were mixed in with our own bomb loads. However, the 73rd Bomb Wing carried out most of the propaganda drops totaling well over 15 million leaflets in June alone.

The leaflets showed, on one side, a formation of B-Nijukus (B-29s) dropping bombs. The names of twelve Japanese cities bordered the picture. On the other side was a message in Japanese, which was revised from time to time, but essentially always said the same thing: that some or all of the twelve cities named would be bombed within the next seventy-two hours. Civilians were warned to evacuate immediately to save themselves. They were told that their government and military forces would not be able to protect them from our overwhelming power and determination. There was more: Americans were humanitarians and would bring Japan and its people a better life after peace was established and the military clique that had enslaved them was overthrown. Other messages encouraging rebellion by the civilian population were included.

As aircrews, we were concerned about telling them where and when we would be coming. Wouldn't they then move all their mobile rail-mounted anti-aircraft guns into the designated target areas? Were we sealing our own fate?

We then carried out the bombing raids exactly as the leaflets had warned we would. Later, reports from Japanese troops stated that leaflets dropped on front line soldiers were ignored and derided, and the Japanese civilians thought we were bluffing. However, after the first three cities on the list were hit, the others were practically depopulated in nothing flat. In 1999, I interviewed a woman who had lived in Japan during our 1945 offensive against its principal cities. She was thirteen years old and lived in both Nagoya and Kobe. She described to me their evacuation flight. With the cries in the neighborhood of "B-Nijuku! B-Nijuku!", all family members would quickly don two or three layers of clothing, grab a prized possession or two (in her case, a rag doll) , and run for the hills north of the city. They sometimes stayed there several days until the fires were all out.

So in one sense, the leaflets were effective, but the civilians still believed that, our raids notwithstanding, Japan was winning the war.

In June, the commanding general of the U.S. Army Air Force, Gen. "Hap" Arnold, visited the Marianas for the specific purpose of assessing the effect of 20th Air Force operations against Japan and estimating or predicting the date of the end of the war. He asked Gen. Curtis LeMay to tell him when the war would end, and after consulting his staff, LeMay responded to Arnold's inquiry stating that the war would be over by October 1. This prediction was made without any knowledge on anyone's part of the atomic bomb project and whether or not or when it might be used. In other words, General LeMay and his staff believed that the capitulation of Japan could and would be accomplished as a result of the continuing bombing activity in which we were engaged on a daily basis. The observations and experiences of the aircrews flying the missions tended to make them support the general's opinion. I have previously expressed such an opinion myself. The only thing that I could not understand was why it had not happened already.

General Arnold was the most zealous and ardent advocate of air power since Billy Mitchell and wanted desperately to prove that a major nation could be defeated by air power alone—without a land invasion. The land invasion of Japan was scheduled for November 1 against the island of Kyushu, to be followed one month later by a second-front invasion of the Tokyo plain. In light of his prediction, LeMay was sent back to Washington to convince the Joint Chiefs of Staff that air power would defeat the Japanese. LeMay later reported that the Joint Chiefs were not receptive to his opinion simply because air power alone had failed to defeat the Germans. An invasion was still necessary, and the same was expected in the Pacific. So our missions continued and, to some extent, increased in frequency.

DESCRIPTION OF GUAM

At about this same time, the prohibition against divulging our location was lifted, so descriptions of Guam and its peoples became common in our letters to wives and families. Canceling the ban was long overdue. The Japs knew we were there so from what enemy were we being concealed? The Guam location was rumored before we left the U.S., and beginning as early as the middle of February, all the newspaper reports of our missions were datelined Guam—in some cases "21st Bomber Command Headquarters, Guam." If people read the papers, they could, by simple deduction, figure out where we were. Of course, my family knew where I was because Jay Plank was visiting me on his Pacific runs.

Over the period of our tour on Guam, we had learned bits of history about the island and its inhabitants going back to Ferdinand Magellan's visit in 1521. He gave the native people the name "Chamorro" after observing their short hair. "Chamorro," in Spanish or Portuguese means, literally, "one who cuts his hair." In a letter to my wife, I described them thus: "They have light brown skin, black hair, round heads with broad faces, flat noses, and are generally short in stature. They have Western ways, speak English, dress much the same as we do, and have been Catholics for centuries. Their customs seem traditionally Spanish, although Spanish is not spoken—it's either Chamorro or English. The Chamorro language is a musical, sort of sing-songy sound. There does not seem to be a 'pidgin' language used—it's predominantly English."

My descriptive letter continued:

The people were peaceful, and subsisted on the natural produce of their jungle covered island, including breadfruit, bananas and coconuts, and fish. In more modern times, their main industry and export was copra, the kernel and dried meat of the coconut, from which coconut oil was extracted and used in the making of soap, among other things. In the days before the white man arrived, the Chamorros had quite liberal ideas about relations between the sexes. There was no prostitution (that came with the Europeans) but they thought that it was shameful for a girl to be a virgin by the time she was married. However, the promiscuity that was encouraged before marriage stopped with the wedding night. Any man who fooled with a married woman was always attacked by the villagers and sometimes killed. Again, in modern times, girls are pretty closely supervised under the Spanish chaperon system and there is little promiscuity.

With the white man's arrival with Magellan, as was the case later in North America and other places, the natives were exploited in many ways. Among the imports from the Europeans was venereal disease and many adults still suffer from yaws and gonorrhea. Perhaps our modern medicines such as penicillin can eradicate these diseases for them.

The Chamorros seem to be a proud people—proud of their heritage, customs and beliefs, but their race, or bloodlines, have been diluted over the years. During the 18th and 19th centuries, privateers, pirates and whalers used the island as a stopover, and between them and the rule of Spain, the natives were practically wiped out. There are probably few pure-blood Chamorros left.

In June, 1898, the American Cruiser *Charleston* entered Apra Harbor and opened fire. The Governor asked about the noise and was told that the Americans were probably paying their respects to him by firing a salute. So, the Captain of the Port rowed out to apologize for not returning the salute because there was no ammunition. That was when Guam learned of the Spanish-American war. The next day they surrendered and the Island has belonged to the U.S. ever since except for thirty-one months of Japanese occupation during the current war.

After World War I, the League of Nations gave the other islands of the Marianas to the Japanese as Class "C" mandates—not to be fortified. The same prohibition applied to us, and we kept our promise, but as everyone now knows, Japan didn't—she fortified Saipan and Tinian and that was why Japan captured Guam so easily three days after starting the war.

Geographically, Guam comprises 225 square miles—being the largest of the chain with Saipan second in size with 71 square miles. It is of volcanic origin, and is the southernmost of the Marianas. Its location is 1,590 miles east of Manila, 1,565 miles south of Tokyo, and 3,338 miles west of the Hawaiian Islands. Or, for another perspective, about 5,600 miles west of Los Angeles. It is the largest island in 5,000 square miles of ocean from Hawaii to the Philippines, and in 2,000 square miles from New Guinea to Japan.

Before the war, Guam's capital, Agana, was a thriving city comparable to a town of the same size in the States. It had a population of about 12,000 people and was an attractive place with streets, stores, and comfortable homes—not just a mud village like those in the jungle. It had rather an old-world atmosphere about it although the architecture was a mixture of Spanish and American. There was a good sewage system, an electric plant and other modern infrastructure. Retaking the island however, destroyed much of the city, and it now looks to a great extent like some of the pictures of bombed out European cities.

Biologically, the Island is considered the garden spot of the group, as it was jungle covered. I say "was"

because a tremendous amount of it has been cleared
for military installations. There are practically no ver-
min, although rats are on the increase (courtesy of the
white man and his commerce). There are no snakes,
but a couple of kinds of lizards and big brown toads.
The toads are the biggest I have ever seen, and, when
disturbed or captured, blow themselves up to about
two or three times their normal size. One of the
lizards is large too—called a Monitor, it grows to two
or three feet. The other fellow is a gecko—a small
lizard only a few inches long with a blue tail—much
like those we have in the Southwestern U.S. Birds
inhabit the jungle, but I don't see many around the
airfield—and that includes seagulls. That pleases me
because the last thing I want is a collision with a flock
of seagulls on takeoff. Many of the jungle birds resem-
ble those that we have at home—there is one that
looks just like our mourning dove except that it is
bright blue. There are many blue and orange birds,
and also one that is almost identical to our grackle or
blackbird. Small fruit bats are plentiful also. They are
very smelly, but the natives eat them and consider
them a delicacy.

Well, I've probably told you more than you wanted to hear
about Guam by quoting from my letter, but at the time, our
families were very interested.

One day while our ship was getting three new engines, I
arranged for passes to prohibited areas of the island and a six-
by-six truck to transport us, and took the crew on an all day tour.
The decent roads ended about where the military installations
ended, and we proceeded into the hills on what were little more
than jungle trails. The villages, however, proved so interesting
that the jouncing around in the truck was worth it. One village,
Talafofu, was back up in the hills and was the place where the
Japs held out the longest. Even so, the village itself seemed to
show very little sign of war. Others we visited were quite battered
up, but this one was clean, neat, and seemingly well organized.

It was located on a small, high plateau amid banana, breadfruit and coconut trees. There were little vegetable patches, a goat tethered here or there, a few chickens, and the local beast of burden and mode of transportation—water buffalo. The huts were made of palm leaves and looked as if you could blow them over with one breath, but they apparently were dry. The people's clothing reflected both the traditional and modern, usually depending on the age of the wearer. The men wore dungarees and odds and ends of shirts; the younger women wore simple calico dresses, but the older women, without exception, wore long, ankle length skirts and starched blouses of a material that resembled organdie. They were reminiscent of Spanish peasant costumes, and I assumed that their origin dated back to the days of Spanish rule. Everyone was barefooted—there was just no need for any kind of footwear.

There was no industry beyond caring for their truck gardens and animals—the demands of their climate and simple agrarian life provided tranquility for them except for the occasional typhoon. They didn't even require furniture; their huts were bare except for the occasional table or chair. They slept on mats on the dirt floor or on a platform just a few inches above the floor. They carried everything on their heads; for example, we saw a young girl carry a huge earthen jug easily on her head. It was not unusual to see three or four people, one behind the other, on the back of an ambling buffalo, or several of them in a primitive cart drawn by a big buffalo with a ring through his nose.

We talked to some of them, and while they seemed to be rather shy and modest by nature, they were amiable. I wondered, though, how much of what they said could be believed. One would say that the Japanese occupation was terrible, that the Japs enslaved them and raped their women; another would say that the Japanese occupation wasn't so bad, not much different from our own. We had been there about a year and a half and I wondered if they had not just forgotten about the Japanese and gotten used to us. Some Marines, however, had told us that when we reoccupied the island, the native women in particular were afraid of them; they didn't act like they were being repatriated.

The second village we visited was quite different from the one located in the jungle. It was very pretty, located on a small bay on the south side of the island. It was called Inarajan. When we were there, the women were doing the laundry—a simple process of beating the clothes on the rocks in the surf until they were clean. Their dress was about the same as the natives in Talofofu, but their village was quite different. Here they had access to stone and concrete, and all the structures were of masonry materials. They had a beautiful little chapel or cathedral and the architecture was "old world." We could have seen a similar structure in Spain or Italy or France. We were impressed with the number of little kids running around— there seemed to be a zillion of them. We decided that, as soon as a girl reached puberty, she became pregnant and that was all there was to it—I might be wrong there, but that's the way it looked. We noticed the scarcity of men in both villages, but then one of the women told us that they were all employed by the U.S military on construction projects. That made sense.

On the way back across the island, we scoured the jungle for orchids that we understood grew wild, but we found none. We proceeded over to Apra Harbor and secured permission to board an aircraft carrier at anchor. It was an interesting tour and wound up our day's trip.

About the first week or so in July, I received the outfit identification and location of a boy from my class in Omaha whose parents were friends of my parents. He was a Navy lieutenant based at Apra Harbor at the other end of the island. We visited back and forth a number of times, and those visits are not important to this story—I only mention them because of my amazement at the luxury in which he lived as compared to the Spartan existence that I endured.

He had a jeep assigned to him for his exclusive use and drove to work everyday, just as he would have done at home. He had regular daytime hours, quitting at about 4:30 in the afternoon, so he had time for recreation or elbow bending—whatever he wanted to do. He had a private room with a bed (springs and mattress, pillow, and bedspread), a highboy dresser, a table with a couple of chairs, and an armoire for his clothes. The head in his quarters had real flushing toilets and hot and cold running water. As I have previously recounted, I slept on a cot with an air mattress in an open hut with fourteen or fifteen other guys—and if I wanted hot water, I heated it on a survival stove in my canteen cup. On one of my visits, I took a razor with me just for the luxury of shaving in front of a big mirror with running hot water.

We went to dinner at the officers' mess, and I felt like I was back in the States. Lo and behold, there were white linen tablecloths and napkins, silver tableware, and real china. Colored waiters in starched white coats looked after our every need or want. We had a five-course meal with T-bone steak, fresh asparagus, fruit salad, and pie and ice cream for dessert. The Army was never like this—what a difference there was from one end of the island to the other. At my end I was eating beans and slumgullion and powdered eggs and pancakes that laid in your belly like so much lead.

TWENTY-NINTH MISSION: OKAZAKI, JULY 19, 1945

Back at North Field, our ground crew and the maintenance section had been working tirelessly to get our three new engines installed. The next day, we test-hopped the ship and everything checked out beautifully. We had our airplane back and were ready to fly missions again. We were scheduled for a mission to Hiratsuka, but Freddie was sick, so we stood down. I was getting anxious again—we were no longer at the top of the list; several crews having passed us up while our ship was out of commission. It seemed as though we had had seven to go for a long time.

July 19 got us back in the groove with a night mission to Okazaki. We had some tough weather to fly through on the way between Iwo and Japan, but like one of the other recent missions, the turbulence wasn't so bad. However, the lightening flashes were the brightest I'd ever seen—really blinding. I had not felt particularly good on this flight—nothing I could blame or pin down, but I was tired when we returned. A couple days' rest saw me with some of my energy back again, and I was eager to fly—only six to go!

With only six missions to go, my thoughts were increasingly focused on the completion of my tour and going home. At the rate we were flying raids, I could see number thirty-five being completed in the first weeks of August and being home by about the first of September. This was without consideration for the possibility of the war ending, just the progression of events for us. My letters to my wife were filled with speculation about all this, and plans for our reunion and future. Also, at about this time, my crew and I had been offered what was considered to be a highly important and desirable assignment to Muroc, California, immediately upon completion of our tour. We had volunteered for it and were looking forward to our involvement. One of the appealing things was that within a day or two of completion of our thirty-fifth mission, we would be provided with priority transportation to Muroc where, as a crew, we would be advisors, consultants, and instructors in the training of lead crews and other aspects of B-29 crew operations and bombing techniques. The assignment was to last at least 140 days, after which the Army would decide whether to extend the program or reassign us, as a crew or separately, to other posts or duty. It sounded as though we were getting some recognition for our experience and competence, and Muroc could be a cushy assignment. Muroc's location was ideal for me. It was about seventy-five miles northeast of Los Angeles, just west of my old station at Victorville, where I had spent about one and a half years. It was close to my wife's family's home, too, so the prospect pleased her. At least such an assignment would get us out of the western Pacific in a hurry.

Other rumors about the war were beginning to circulate again. While there was no indication yet that they would declare war, Russia had canceled their neutrality pact with

Japan as they were about to attack Japanese held territory in Manchuria. We thought this might be a precursor to a declaration of war, thus helping us end hostilities sooner.

There were other rumors that Japan might be moving toward peace. We heard that food shortages in Japan were so acute that people were encouraged to gather acorns and anything else that was edible to sustain themselves. We also noted that the missions we were flying in July met with much less opposition than earlier in the campaign, so our supposition was that they no longer had the munitions to fight effectively. We were aware that the edict of the Allies at the Potsdam Conference demanded unconditional surrender by the Japanese, but apparently they were not yet convinced that they could do that. So the missions continued with medium- to smaller-sized cities as the targets. And the propaganda leaflet campaign continued as we made good on our warnings.

THE FINAL MISSIONS

On July 24 we flew our thirtieth to Handa and then, on July 26, our thirty-first to Omuta, a city of about 177,000 on the Ariaki Sea on the west side of Kyushu. These were both night incendiary missions, and we met virtually no opposition, observing only sparse flak, and that not near us. The weather enroute was not too bad, and it was clear over the targets. I had a cold and felt lousy, so after landing from the Omuta mission, I brewed a pot (canteen cup) of tea, laced it liberally with whiskey, drank it, and went to bed. I was not about to see the doc and take a chance on his grounding me—I wanted to fly. We were so close to going home.

On July 28 we pulled off number thirty-two to Ogaki just north of Nagoya on the island of Honshu—another milk run with little or no opposition. However, the fatigue from three missions in six days was taking its toll on me—I was tired, and on the Ogaki mission, I did little but takeoff, fly the bomb run, and land. The rest of the flight was principally on autopilot with Bud monitoring things while I dozed in my seat. I no longer seriously worried about the ship since we had four new engines. All sorts of mechanical malfunctions were possible, of course, but our new engines were the ones with the latest modifications and "combat" improvements, so they were much better than the old ones. For some reason, weather on these last few missions had not been severe either, so we were winding up our tour on the easy side.

After landing from the Ogaki mission, I found a pile of mail waiting for me, and among other things from my father was a copy of the *Kiplinger Newsletter* outlining some of the negotiations for the Japanese surrender. It confirmed many of the rumors we had been hearing in the Pacific but also pointed out the obstacles to surrender. It seemed the Japanese were willing to withdraw from China, Formosa, Manchuria, Korea, and all the Pacific islands, surrender their shipping, destroy their war industries, and surrender their military forces, but they would not countenance an American occupation force in their country. They also wanted to preserve the divine status of the emperor. Our terms were specific and not negotiable—unconditional surrender—so on with the war. My crew and I would soon be out of it, however—only three more missions to fly.

After a couple of days rest, we flew another "show of force" mission on August 1 to celebrate the thirty-eighth anniversary of the U.S. Army Air Forces. Over 800 B-29s were launched against four Japanese cities, all of which had been warned of our intention to bomb them. Our target in this offensive was the city of Mito on the island of Honshu about fifty or sixty miles northeast of Tokyo. One B-29 was lost on this mission, but it was not from our group or over our target. We had an RCM aircraft accompany us, and we dropped a lot of chaff. The RCM crew reported that the Japanese radar operators changed frequency and seemed confused—all to our advantage. The radar jamming and chaff had paid off. We suffered no damage and returned safely.

Air Force records later reported that the improvement in fuel management by B-29 crews was dramatically demonstrated on this mission. Carrying an average of 6,600 gallons, the average consumption was 5,850 gallons where the flight plan called for 5,828 gallons.

With only two missions to go, we were getting apprehensive. In my letter to my wife following the mission, I said that I was as nervous as "a pregnant nun in church"—we might be able to fly those two missions in the next week! All I could think about was going home. I had promised all my stuff to other people in the hut—my desk, chair, a lamp, a couple of cabinets, and a footlocker. I planned to ship the rest of my stuff in a big duffel bag and a converted ammunition box that I had. I would then carry only my B-4 bag with clothing, toiletries, papers, orders, etc. We would turn in all our flying equipment and be able to "travel light." We had to clear all the departments on the field, including the medical boys, from whom we got a final physical exam and to whom we certified that we had not been injured, and who took our temperature a couple times a day for two or three days to be sure that we didn't have a communicable disease that we could transmit back to the States.

I hoped that I was not jumping the gun. There were still two missions to fly, and I could buy the farm on the last one as easily as the first. Well, maybe not quite as easily—there had been a lot more opposition and fireworks on the first ones.

Replacement crews were showing up in substantial numbers now, and two arrivals were pilots whom I knew. One was from Victorville, and the other was from my class at Roswell. Soon all my old cronies would be in the western Pacific. Our squadron roster was changing so rapidly that I hardly knew anyone anymore. These two had more rank than I had, notwithstanding the fact that they had been in the Training Command all that time. It used to be the other way around— the combat guys had the rank and the Stateside guys didn't. There must have been something about military politics that I didn't comprehend.

We had a little dry spell for a few days, during which we got some much needed rest and my ground crew worked on our prop governors to correct a problem I'd been having with them. On the fourth I flew two test hops to check them out and, after the second one, told "Little John" that everything appeared to be normal, so we were ready to go again.

At this time, Tom, Bud, Freddie, and Al decided that they didn't want to be included in the Muroc assignment, so Major Evans got substitutes for me from other crews. Maybe my officers thought a southern California assignment was too far from their homes, I don't know. Anyway, all my enlisted men were still gung-ho about it. The others would be sent to reclassification centers for reassignment after our return to the States.

On August 4, we were awarded the DFC (Distinguished Flying Cross) for the Tachiari mission in May. The citation read:

AWARD OF THE DISTINGUISHED FLYING CROSS.
By direction of the President, under the provisions of the Act of Congress approved 2 July 1926 (Bull 8, WD, 1926), and pursuant to authority delegated by Headquarters, United States Army Strategic Air Forces in classified letter, File 323, subject: "Delineation of Administrative Responsibilities", dated 16 July 1945, announcement is made of the award of the Distinguished Flying Cross to the following named officers and enlisted men, 43rd Bombardment Squadron, 29th Bombardment Group.

For extraordinary achievement while participating in aerial flight on 3rd May 1945. These individuals were combat crew members of a B-29 type aircraft based in the Marianas Islands on a daring daylight assault on Tachiari Airfield, Kyushu, Japan. As their airplane approached the assembly point, several fighters attacked it in an effort to make a kill before the plane could get into formation. Superb gunnery and crew teamwork warded off the enemy fighters and accounted for two probably destroyed. As they started on the bomb run, a larger group of hostile interceptors savagely attacked the B-29's to prevent destruction of the vital enemy installation. Although their aircraft was badly hit, this crew stayed on the bomb run, accurately attacked the target, and definitely destroyed one of the fighters. After the formation broke up, the badly damaged plane was flown safely to its home base. The outstanding airmanship and heroic devotion to duty displayed by these veterans of more than twenty-one bombing missions, reflect the highest credit on themselves and the Army Air Forces.

The citation then went on to name each member of the crew. The language is somewhat flowery, and somewhat inaccurate—we were not that badly damaged, as compared to Hayes for example, and we made it to Iwo before proceeding to our home base. However, they wanted us to have the award for our part in the defeat of Japan.

August 5 saw us off again on a night incendiary mission to Fukae/Nishinomya on the bay between Osaka and Kobe. Weather was clear over the target, so we bombed visually. We were pathfinders again, and about the third ship over the target. There was, at the time we bombed, only meager flak, and we sustained no damage. We returned without injuries.

On the morning of August 6, we learned of the dropping of the atomic bomb on Hiroshima by Col. Paul Tibbets flying the *Enola Gay* from Tinian. We listened to the radio most of the day, hearing descriptions of the awesome power of the device and the total devastation it had wrought on Hiroshima. We didn't know much about atomic energy or atomic bombs, but anything that could help us end the war was welcomed. I had somewhat mixed feelings as I listened to the reports. On one hand I regretted and feared the news that man had at last discovered how to end civilization and obliterate himself from the face of the earth. On the other I felt that the Japs would have to give it up now—even their fanaticism couldn't survive this holocaust. We would see.

For the next nine days we stood down, presumably while the Japs were deciding what to do, or negotiating or whatever—we didn't know. Then the second atomic bomb was dropped on Nagasaki on August 9 at 11:02 A.M. Russia declared war on Japan the same day, although there was no military activity initiated at that time. It was later determined that the two atomic bombs and Russia's declaration of war enabled the Japanese to break the deadlock in their cabinet over acceptance of the Potsdam terms, and they capitulated.

So we waited. Four days went by, and as far as we knew, nothing happened. Therefore another mission was scheduled for the night of August 14.

Our target was the city of Kumagaya, an industrial center north of Tokyo. We prepared for it with both dread and joy. What a tragedy it would be if we didn't return from this one, but if we did, it would complete our tour, and we could go home. No more combat missions. No more people shooting at us.

There was a general on the field whose name I no longer remember and who came to our group operations facility looking for a ride on this mission. He wanted to tell his grandchildren he'd flown a mission in the big war, I guess. The boys in operations said, "Hey, go with Robbie—this is his last one, so he'll be back in the morning for sure!" I don't know what kind of sense that made, but anyway, I had a passenger, and I couldn't refuse him—he outranked me by some. Unfortunately, he was never able to tell his grandchildren anything: he was killed in a P-51 accident on the field a couple of weeks after our last mission.

We departed Guam and proceeded on the long flight to Japan. We had been instructed to monitor certain radio frequencies enroute, and if the war did end, we were to abort the mission and return to base. Now that we were flying our last mission, my thoughts were somewhat different. I didn't want the war to end— just yet. Completing my tour changed a lot of things for me, and I even thought of telling Jim to shut the damn radios off so we wouldn't hear it if we were called back. I didn't do this, however, but just flew on hoping to complete the mission.

There had been all sorts of rumors flying around the last six or seven days—if Japan did surrender, what would happen to us? We heard that when the war ended, the whole XXI Bomber Command would be transferred back to the U.S.; or that when the war ended, we would stop flying missions and be transferred to Australia (why?); or that when the war ended, we would be transferred to Japan as part of an occupation force; or that when the war ended, we would remain in the Pacific as a sort of trouble shooting and peace keeping force (why? if the Japs surrendered, what peace would we be keeping?). Colonel Storrie had said that immediately upon capitulation by the Japanese, he wanted to lead a contingent of our group's ships up there to see if we could find any of our boys in P.O.W. camps. He wanted to be first to repatriate them.

However, if I completed this mission, none of these speculative events would be of any concern to me—I could go home. We were scheduled to hit our target around 1:00 A.M., and I wanted the war to last just that long—and then terminate.

We flew on through the night with a seven and a half ton load of incendiaries in our bomb bays—only one aircraft in an armada carrying 593 tons to deposit on the city. With us on the raid was an RCM aircraft and a superdumbo—the former to aid us in confusing the enemy searchlight and anti-aircraft batteries, the latter to assist anyone who went in the drink on the way home. Another fleet of B-29s was attacking Iaesaki at the same time we were obliterating Kumagaya. We really wanted to convince the Japs of the futility of continued resistance.

As we approached the Japanese coast, the general, who had been dozing in the tunnel over the bomb bays, came up on the flight deck and sat down beside me on the aisle stand. I could see the glow of fires on the clouds up ahead. I advised Tom that we would have to bomb by radar as there was nine-tenths to ten-tenths cloud cover over the target. I turned from the IP (initial point) to the bomb run heading, and as I approached the target, I became worried about the same thing that had worried me on my first mission and many others afterward: the potential for midair collision. Not only was the target nearly obscured, but at our bombing altitude, we were busting through the tops of the build-ups of that same cloud layer. I felt uncomfortable and kept scanning the atmosphere for other ships when suddenly, emerging from a build-up, I hit something that felt like a brick wall. The airplane shuddered and rocked, then quickly resumed smooth flight. I knew instantly what it was. I had slammed through somebody's prop-wash, and although I never saw it, I could not have missed the other plane by more than mere yards. That was much too close for comfort—Jesus, I didn't want our last mission to be our *last* mission. I stayed on the bomb run until bombs away, and then banked sharply away from the target and started a climb to get out of the tops of the clouds. At that point I also may have turned on my running lights. I did this at various times over Japan when I thought it judicious to do so, and this was one of those times. There were no fighters up because of the cloud cover and we were out of the flak area. I wanted other B-29s to be able to see me; that encounter on number thirty-five made me shudder. I wondered if the general was a jinx? He hadn't said much during the flight, and after we headed back out to sea, he disappeared back to the tunnel. I had previously routinely refused to take passengers on missions, except for one of my ground crew on one trip, and I wondered if I should have refused the general, notwithstanding his rank?

Anyway, we were now headed back to the Marianas in one piece. I was not sleepy—I was energized, happily anticipating landfall at North Field. We had pulled it off. Thirty-five missions. I only had to think about how to get home.

CHAPTER 8

It's Over!

In the last hour or two of our flight, or maybe on the approach to Guam, we heard that the Japs had finally agreed to an unconditional surrender—the war was over. The emperor made his concession speech to the Japanese people about noon that day—August 15—and the western world rejoiced. I touched down and acknowledged a smiling chaplain at the side of the runway checking us back in for the last time. My ground crew were all smiles as I turned into my hardstand, the euphoria of its being over permeating the human attitude everywhere.

We deplaned and General Power's jeep was waiting to take me to his quarters. It was the general's tradition to host each pilot in the wing immediately upon the successful completion of his tour, so I was whisked down to the other end of the field where we shook hands and sat down to a breakfast of real eggs and bacon. Our only previous face-to-face meeting had been the night when he was going to shoot my bombardier, but there was no discussion of that on this occasion. The whiskey flowed like buttermilk. The general's batman stood by my elbow with the bottle, and each time I took a sip and set my glass down, he poured more. When I left there an hour later, I couldn't have been feeling much pain.

The sequence of events and the timing escape me after all these years, but Jay Plank and Ted Cochran had arrived on Guam either the night before while I was flying my last sortie, or the morning of the fifteenth, and they found me not long after I left the general's quarters. They had a jeep and a bottle, and we drove to their tent and celebrated. I really don't remember much about the rest of the day, but I have evidence that I did cable my wife advising her that I had completed thirty-five missions and would be home as soon as I could find a ride. The cable was delivered to her at 9:30 A.M. August 16.

The war's sudden end had canceled our Muroc assignment—there would no longer be a need for B-29 lead crews—and with that retraction, our priority transportation back to the States had also evaporated. An air of uncertainty prevailed over our operations and destiny. Some B-29 sorties were being flown to drop food and supplies to survivors in P.O.W. camps, but everything else was at a standstill pending a move of our forces to Japan. Gen. Douglas MacArthur had been appointed Supreme Allied Commander of the Occupation Forces in Japan, and plans, of course, were being made for the formal surrender ceremonies. Our outfits didn't know how this would affect them or what part might be played by them. Everyone was on standby.

The effect of all this on me and my crew was one of some anxiety and frustration. I couldn't find transportation: nothing was going east. After two or three days of searching for a ride, including with the Navy, I went down to operations to see if I could get an airplane to fly home. They told me that I couldn't fly mine because it had four new engines and might be needed in future group operations. But my friends there—principally Harry Evans and Bill Marchesi—came up with a war-weary one for me. It had four run-out engines on it, so I asked for one new engine on each side, theorizing that I wouldn't lose two on the same side, and they accommodated my request.

We checked out all of our flying equipment again, orders were cut for our flight, and we prepared to leave for the good old U.S.A. There was another crew in our group that had also finished their tour, and I proposed to take them with me. But operations or Bomber Command decreed that flying a war-weary plane nearly 6,000 miles over water was too hazardous to risk losing two crews, so I was prohibited from carrying anyone other than my own crew members when I left Guam. I was not aware of any war-weary B-29 losses enroute back to the States, but perhaps there had been some. With one new engine on each side, I was fairly confident that I could make it. I wouldn't have a bomb or equipment load, and the bomb bays would be empty. I would be light and could cruise at a conservative airspeed and altitude, thus not straining the engines. Anyway, this was my ticket home, and you couldn't have talked me out of it.

Accordingly, on August 20, I took off from North Field and hopped down to Harmon Field in the middle of the island. I landed there, filed my flight plan with ATC and took off for a night flight to Kwajalein. I don't know why this procedure could not have been accomplished by radio from the air, but regulations were regulations. The weather in those latitudes was clear for the first two legs of our journey. Freddie navigated by the stars, and we hit Kwaj on the money 7:05 hours after leaving Guam.

We got a few hours rest, ground personnel gassed the ship and filled the oil tanks, and we prepared for our second leg to John Rodgers Field in Hawaii. There were a bunch of Marines, veterans of Pacific Island wars, trying, like I had been, to find a way home. I took six or seven of them on board—what the hell. Again, we had a pleasant, uneventful flight of 10:30 hours from Kwajalein to Hawaii, landing about two hours after daylight.

I was buoyed, of course, by the prospect of going home, and I was completely lacking the anxiety and dread of a mission flight where the people at the other end would be shooting at me. The legs of this flight were only one-half or three-quarters as long as the missions I was accustomed to flying, and the weather was not fighting me, so it was a comfortable, satisfying trip with the best of all rewards at its termination.

As we parked on the flight line, we were boarded by customs agents to check for contraband (yes, they even checked returning flyboys). We were only minutes before the shift change—which meant the agents were tired and ready to quit for the day—so they delayed us only momentarily. An airplane landing behind us got the new shift and spent all morning being searched and questioned. We had no desire to become tourists again; we just wanted to get some sleep and be off. Again, the line crews gassed and serviced the ship, and that evening we departed on the last leg of our return. At John Rodgers, like Kwajalein, there were more Air Corps and Marine enlisted personnel hitch-hiking back to the States. I boarded seven or eight more. My recollection is that when I landed in California I had twenty-six on board, including my crew.

There was an extensive cloud layer at about 12,000 feet, so I climbed above it to be able to navigate celestially and find favorable winds. The night passed fairly quickly, and with the first evidence of light, all eyes searched for a glimpse of the coast at our landfall ETA. The marine layer below had it hidden, but the Eastbay and Solano County hills poked up through it and part of the San Joaquin Valley and the Sierra Nevada slowly became visible and told us we were home. I let down for my landing at Fairfield-Suisun Army Airbase. The old B-29 had not missed a beat in nearly 6,000 miles and twenty-six hours in the air. It had truly brought us home.

CHAPTER 9

Home at Last

The day was consumed with the process, for me, of turning in equipment and getting orders issued for a leave of absence, as I was leaving the airplane. It was my understanding that others would take it east, and some of my crew members would go with it. This was the parting of the way for my crew after a nearly a year together. There was no emotion involved, it was just "so long" or "see ya." Each one was now simply concentrating on getting to his individual home or family.

I received orders for a thirty-day leave (later extended to forty-five days) and caught a ride into the Eastbay area and found that the most practical way to get down to southern California was on the "Nite Owl"—a train that ran regularly between the San Francisco/Oakland area and Los Angeles. I wired my wife that I would arrive in Glendale at eight o'clock the next morning and boarded the train. I was too wound up to really sleep, but I managed to doze off and on until morning.

When the train arrived and I walked from the railroad car toward the station, there was this wisp of a girl whose very being had been the object of my longings and had dominated, except for flying, all my thoughts and dreams for the past six and a half months. She wore a small derby and was dressed in a black tailored skirt and jacket that her mother had made for her out of her father's old tuxedo. It sounds corny, but it wasn't—it was pure class, and she looked like a million bucks. I dropped my bag; took her in my arms for a long kiss; then, looking in her eyes, said something stupid, like, "Where did you park the car?" As if that mattered.

She sat very close to me with her hand on my leg as I drove to her father and mother's house. Her family was there to greet me—lots of hugs and "welcome home" greetings. Then her mother said, "I'll bet you haven't had breakfast," which was true, so she proceeded to make a big one for everybody. I ate with one hand, the other being entwined in my wife's—I couldn't let go. The conversation was mostly about my trip home, no one feeling it appropriate to talk about my experiences yet. Anyway, they already knew a lot about that from my letters to them.

After breakfast, lingering over coffee gazing into each other's eyes, we excused ourselves. I picked up my bag, and we walked out through the patio and across the back yard to the guest house. Upon entering, we immediately embraced in a long passionate kiss, and then, seemingly without even abandoning the embrace, the floodgates of passion burst; six and a half months of loneliness and celibacy exploded like spring following winter. In a sudden microburst of frenzied and desperate activity, trousers and shorts hit the floor, step-ins were discarded, skirts rose to armpits, and we fell onto the bed behind her. Her still stocking clad legs rose above me as my arms pressed the backs of her knees and my hands slid under her bare bottom. Oh boy! Shades of the horny sergeant!

Other friends stopped by to welcome me home as the day progressed, and I called my father in Omaha to talk with him. After the enthusiastic and sincere welcoming greetings had pretty well run the gamut, we decided that we really wanted to be alone. We packed another bag, used some hoarded gas ration coupons to fill the tank on the Ford, and left for a trip up the California coast.

Santa Barbara was about a two-hour drive, and a motel on the beach suited our mood. We ended the day with dinner in a restaurant at the end of the pier, and as I watched the sun sinking into the western Pacific, whence I had just returned, I thought, "If I ever fly those skies again, they will be peaceful—not filled with lead and steel and shrapnel and fire and hate and fear, but as gentle and civilized as the skies above me at the moment." What we had accomplished out there since Pearl Harbor would guarantee that.

We slept late the next morning and, after a leisurely brunch, explored old Santa Barbara and the Mission. Next day, it was on to Carmel to roam among the artists' shops and gorge ourselves on shellfish and other marine delicacies at Cannery Row in Monterey. San Francisco was next, where we sipped twenty-year-old Scotch whiskey while the fog rolled in and enveloped the "Top of the Mark," and we continued our bacchanalian feasting at Fisherman's Wharf.

Interesting and vibrant as "The City" was, a big city wasn't what we wanted, so we left, crossing the San Joaquin Valley to the Sierra Nevada. I rented a little cabin without utilities in Sequoia Park, where we spent a week all by ourselves. Time meant nothing. We ignored the clock and just did whatever we liked—or maybe nothing. We acknowledged no responsibilities. We didn't go hiking as such; we just meandered, hand in hand, arm in arm, among the Sequoia Giants, benign smiles on our faces, not talking much, but just knowing, once more, the warmth, comfort, contentedness, and happiness that our perfect companionship gave us. We were awash in the glow of the joy of just being together again. I was savoring and relishing being home and being in love.

This was a time also when I felt at peace with myself. The war was over, and I would not have to take off into combat again. I had been challenged and had met the challenge. Indeed, all America had been challenged and passed with flying colors. The war had united the people of the country like nothing else ever before in history. It had been a moral war— right against wrong, good against bad, good guys against bad guys, white hats against black hats—and we had been the good guys in the white hats. I could not help but feel that, in a sense, we had preserved a moral civilization from repression and enslavement by immoral forces.

We didn't talk about the war, but we did, to some extent, contemplate the future. Should I apply for a regular commission in the Air Force? Should I get out and try for a pilot's job with the airlines? Or should I get out and go back to school to get my degree? But no decision had to be made at the moment; there would be plenty of time for that later. We simply enjoyed the beautiful Indian summer in the mountains.

On our whole trip, everywhere we went, in each of our retreats and sanctuaries, we made love until we were satiated—like there was no tomorrow. It was ardent, it was intense, it was impassioned, it was fervent, and it was deeply affectionate and loving. As the spasmodic flurry of orgasmic impulses subsided and our bodies ultimately parted, she would relax into a semi-fetal position on her side, and I would curl around her, my leg jammed between her thighs, one arm draped protectively over her body, my hand gently grasping her pudenda, my other arm around her neck and over her shoulder, my hand cupping her breast. My lips caressed her hair and the back of her neck as we luxuriated, adrift in the pleasant post-coital ecstasy and afterglow. Morpheus then slowly wafted us off to dreamland.

Our son was born the following June, almost exactly fulfilling the prescribed gestation period for humans from my homecoming. There is no question but that he was conceived in love. Maybe the colonel knew something after all.

In due time my leave came to an end, and I reported to Fort MacArthur, California for reassignment. After processing there, I was sent to—guess where—Pratt, Kansas, where the whole B-29 adventure had started a little more than a year before.

We drove to Pratt and found a place to live, following which I got involved in the programs there. For some reason, I have little recollection of this second assignment to Pratt. What I do recall is triggered by reviewing various orders in my officer's 201 file and my logbooks. I was no longer keeping a diary, and my wife being with me, I wasn't writing letters. I do remember that I was able to do some duck hunting, and I recall scouting the Kansas potholes and waterways and cornfields flying either a Taylorcraft L-2, a small 65-horsepower, two-place airplane, or a Stinson L-5, a similar small aircraft principally used by the Army for spotting, low-altitude reconnaissance, and courier service. It was a little rocket compared to the L-2. It had a 185-horsepower engine, and I zoomed all

over the local countryside at only a few hundred feet (or less).
I was back to flying by the seat of my pants when it was considered a skill and not recklessness. We had an inactivated auxiliary field at Jet, Oklahoma, and I flew down there every few
weeks to let the lone occupant/resident/pilot/commanding
officer/caretaker fly the L-5 to keep his hand in. I would certify
his flying time so he could collect his flight pay.

The training program at Pratt, indeed in the whole Air
Force, was rapidly being downsized and discontinued, and our
activity was similarly affected. I made only one cross-country
flight to Chicago in a B-29 while I was there - all the rest were
local, and those were not all that frequent. That's why I had
time to duck hunt and flit around in the lightplanes.

In December, I received a week's leave for Christmas, and
we spent it visiting my father in Omaha—the first time we had
been able to spend together since my return from the Pacific.

Sometime, either before or after my leave, I cannot recall
which, was the occasion of my last claim to fame flying a B-29.
We put on local airshows from time to time, and one of the
demonstrations was to bomb a wooden pyramid in the center
of the field. However, we couldn't hit it. We came across the
field at low altitude—probably 500 feet so that the people
could see the airplane, see the bomb fall, and see the target
explode. Unfortunately, we were back to the problem we had
encountered in our early training when the light 100-pound
exhibition bombs wouldn't fall properly. It was embarrassing;
the guy on the public address system was talking up the
demonstration and heaping accolades on the pilot at the controls—a veteran of thirty-five missions over Japan and thousands of hours as an airplane commander—and then the
bomb would miss the target. So we decided to deactivate the
bomb, place an explosive charge in the wood pyramid, and
have someone detonate it by remote control at the proper
moment. This didn't work either. The people watching would
see us approach, see the bomb fall, see the target blow up, and
then see the bomb bouncing out across the field somewhere.
What a disappointment!

So we were reduced to low-altitude fly-bys. That wasn't much of a thrill, though, because the local people saw B-29s all the time at low altitude either taking off or landing. We had to figure out something else.

Robertson to the rescue! I thought that if I could make a glider out of a B-29, it might attract some attention. After trying it a couple of times at altitude, I came across the field boundary at about 500 feet—maybe less, I can't remember—and feathered all four engines. For a second or two, I floated by the spectators in near silence with the props turned into the slipstream. The procedure was to dive on the approach to achieve an airspeed of 300 miles per hour (redline) or perhaps slightly more, then at the appropriate spot: "feather one," "feather two," "feather three," "feather four." Then as number four prop was coasting to a stop: "start one," "start two," "start three," "start four." I don't recall how much airspeed I lost in the maneuver, but it was nowhere near down to stalling or requiring flaps to provide more lift. I only remember doing this once. I don't know whether the brass thought it was hazardous or whether we just didn't have any more "open house" airshows.

By January 1946 the demobilization was on in earnest. Factories were being closed, airplanes were being declared surplus and parked at various places around the country, airbases were being closed, and personnel were being discharged in ever increasing numbers. My turn came toward the end of the month, and I was transferred to the Separation Center at Santa Ana, California for return to status as a reserve officer. A terminal leave running into April was granted, and I was turned loose.

The journey was over.

Epilogue

I must acknowledge that we were blessed with an inordinate amount of luck. There were so many times, as I have related in the story, when we were in the right place at the right time—or had just left the wrong place. We had skill, knowledge, discipline, and devotion to the necessity of doing what we were doing, but still, all of that wouldn't have saved us if we had had a catastrophic mechanical failure of the aircraft at a critical moment or if the enemy had succeeded in destroying our ship in the air. In the hundreds of hours of flying B-29s, I never experienced on takeoff an engine failure, a runaway prop, or a fire, and the Japs never damaged us enough to prevent our getting back to base. "Little John" and the ground crew kept us flying and deserved every bit of the confidence I had in him and in them.

Looking back, there was perhaps more luck involved than just the B-29 experience and the combat tour. What if, in the spring of 1943, I had gone to the European Theater to fly P-38s? The majority of my classmates never made it back home. My one and a half years in the Training Command delayed my entry into combat and provided me with the most formidable airplane we had for my combat tour. I could go on with the "what ifs," but the point is that I recognize and acknowledge that I was extremely fortunate during all of the slightly more than four years I spent flying airplanes for Uncle Sam.

My father told me once that my mother, who had passed away in 1938, was looking after me. The chaplain had a different idea of who was looking after me, but I had some questions about his candidate—not that he might not be right, but I couldn't figure out how He made His selections. What was there about me that was worth saving? We lost 485 B-29s in total in the Pacific and almost half of the 29th Bomb Group— weren't all those guys just like me? All I can say is that I shall always be grateful—what else is there that I can say?

After the war, many returned servicemen—maybe most—didn't discuss their wartime experiences very much. Some of them just wanted to forget. I knew a couple of pilots who never wanted to see an airplane again. For many, it was just that they were starting out in business careers, marrying and having children, and their thoughts and activities were involved in those pursuits— delayed about five years because of the war. They were home again, back to the normalcy of life; the war had just been an aberration in their lives. But I have long thought—in the many years since the war and at times during the writing of my own story—that the overwhelming reason was that the people to whom we were talking simply did not understand—they just didn't understand. At first you were talking to your own generation who, for one reason or another, didn't go to war; then you were talking to the generation just behind you who were slightly too young to be in World War II; then you were talking to everybody else—all the generations that came along later.

How could you convey to them what it was really like to be pinned down for days at a time in freezing cold in a foxhole in northern Italy under withering German artillery fire, your buddies being blown to bits all around you; or what it was really like to be aboard a ship off Okinawa taking kamikaze attacks against which it was almost impossible to defend yourself, and where your fellow sailors were killed by the hundreds; or what it was really like to fly through flak thick enough to walk on while tracers were coming up from the ground like rain in reverse and where enemy fighters shot down airplanes and then shot your fellow airmen while they were suspended in their parachutes?

So most just didn't talk about it anymore. And there were some who were like a person in shock or in denial—they were successful in putting the whole experience out of their minds forever.

There was another aspect of not understanding, and that was the lack of an appreciation for the thinking, the beliefs, the presumptions, the convictions, the principles, and the attitudes, the *zeitgeist*, the general intellectual, moral, and cultural climate of our era and our generation. Much of what we might have said would fall on deaf ears because the *zeitgeist* of those following was quite different from that of our World War II generation. Over the years, many of us had become very disappointed in the behavior, the demeanor, the manners, and the morals of our young people. They had, in our opinion, deteriorated far below our standards and had lost the strength of our convictions. So many just shut up about who we had been and what we had done. Not only did the listeners fail to understand, but most were not interested.

There was a further aspect of not understanding—a failure to comprehend who and what our foes were. First, there was the sneak attack on Pearl Harbor on December 7, 1941, characterized by Roosevelt as "a date that will live in infamy." If it had been us, we would have made a public declaration of war—"We're coming after you; you'd better prepare to defend yourselves"—not launched a surprise attack. Then there was the violation of the mandate not to fortify the Marianas. Obviously, Japan was not a nation that could be trusted.

Then there were the people. We fought an enemy who was completely and absolutely uncivilized, unprincipled, cruel, inhuman, and sadistic. They brazenly, contemptuously, and boldly demonstrated all these attributes during their fourteen-year-long attempt to conquer East Asia and the Pacific Rim. The atrocities against the Chinese and other East Asian peoples were reported in the U.S. news media in the late '30s, but the young men of my generation, approaching college age, while noting the reports and the events, really pretty much ignored them. The barbarism had occurred, or was occurring, on the other side of the world—Asians doing things to other Asians. These types of incidents had also been engaged in historically at other times over several centuries involving the

Mongols, the Chinese, and the Japanese, none of which had
affected or influenced the Western world's peoples, cultures,
or economies to any significant degree. It was natural then that
we paid relatively little attention to it as it was being reported.
We had been much more concerned since about 1936 with the
emergence of the German Third Reich and the rise of fascism
in Italy, both or either of which presented the possibility of
another war in Europe in which we might become involved. So
we didn't think seriously about atrocities in a Sino-Japanese
war. We didn't see how such a conflict could affect us. However, after Pearl Harbor was attacked, we suddenly became concerned about the Japanese, and, as I have previously indicated,
felt it was our burden to defeat them. The Pacific War was to
be ours alone. As our campaign moved closer to their home
islands, they continued and accelerated their depravity against
those of our forces who became their victims or prisoners.

It started in 1931 when they occupied Manchuria, then
intensified in 1937 when they conquered Peking, Shanghai,
and Nanking. In these occupied cities, and particularly in
Nanking, they engaged in the most heinous behavior imaginable. They killed people—almost all civilians—indiscriminately:
men, women, children, old, young, and the unborn. It has been
estimated that as many as 350,000 non-combatants were slaughtered just for amusement by the Japanese soldiers in Nanking.

They rounded up tens of thousands of Chinese and then,
herding them into fields, mowed them down with machine-
gun fire. They soaked them—alive—in gasoline and immo-
lated them. They threw babies into the air, impaling them on
bayonets as they fell, or threw them—alive—into pots of boiling water. They rounded up pregnant Chinese women,
stripped them, and used their bulging bellies as targets for bayonet practice, or they placed bets on the sex of the fetus about
to tumble from its mother's womb cut out with a Japanese
sword or bayonet. They tied others to stakes and repeatedly
thrust bayonets into them until they collapsed, disemboweled
and dying. They would round up groups of men, strip them,
and then castrate them, tossing severed testicles into the street
to be devoured by packs of hungry dogs. They killed hundreds

by tying their hands behind them, forcing them to kneel, and then decapitating them with their sabers. The Jap officer who lopped a Chinese head off with one fell swoop got cheers and applause from his troops and fellow officers.

There have been postwar writers who have characterized these atrocities as being the exclusive acts of a rogue army, but all high Japanese officials, both military and civilian, knew about it and condoned it, including the emperor. The populace also knew about it. In 1937, an incident of two Japanese officers having a decapitating contest between themselves was widely publicized in the Japanese newspapers with the score being recorded for them as 105 and 106. They couldn't decide which had passed the 100 mark first, so they extended the contest to another 50. They were characterized in the newspapers as "heroes" and "brave warriors." Brave warriors? For decapitating defenseless, unarmed human beings? POWs, women, and the elderly? Don't tell me the Japanese people didn't know about all these atrocities. They supported the Japanese Imperial Army wholeheartedly even while devouring this kind of publicity.

Much has been made in post-World War II history about German atrocities, particularly involving the Jews in the Holocaust. The difference, however, between the Germans and the Japanese was that the Germans' venom and mistreatment were directed primarily against the Jews, whereas the Japanese torture, enslavement, and murder was committed against all those whose countries they invaded in their attempt to control the Pacific and the Far East—the Russians, the Chinese, the Koreans, the Filipinos, and the Americans taken prisoner in these places. Prisoner deaths in the German P.O.W. camps averaged 1.1 percent, but deaths in the Japanese P.O.W. camps averaged 37 percent.

They raped women by the thousands, indiscriminately, sometimes cutting off their breasts, disemboweling, or otherwise killing their victims after they had raped them. A couple of Japanese soldiers, after raping a Chinese woman were quoted as saying, "When we were raping her we thought of her as a woman, but after we were through with her, we just thought of her as a pig so we killed her." The Japanese conducted germ

warfare against the Chinese in the northern provinces, accounting for millions of lives, and they used Chinese individuals as
"guinea pigs" in hideous live medical experiments. Then, as
they invaded and conquered the Philippine Islands, Filipinos
were tortured and enslaved, and the Japanese conducted the
infamous Bataan Death March, during which it is estimated that
as many as 10,000 died, 2,330 of whom were Americans. Later,
as we recaptured the Philippines, as a final act of barbarism,
they destroyed the churches, convents, schools, and universities
and slaughtered 100,000 Filipinos. In the process of building
the railroad between Thailand and Burma, 12,000 Allied
P.O.W.s and 30,000 Asians died working as slaves. Another
50,000 Chinese were massacred in Malaya and Singapore. In
the battle for Tinian in the Marianas, as they realized they
would be defeated, the Japanese systematically machine-gunned
about 5,000 Korean slaves to death to prevent their repatriation
by U.S. forces.

In regard to our airmen: in December 1944, crewmen, after
being shot down and taken prisoner, were forced to run a
gauntlet through the streets, during which they were beaten
and tortured and then saturated with gasoline and burned
alive. In Singapore, downed B-29 crewmen were paraded
through the city naked, then had their heads chopped off in
public. In May 1945, doctors at Kyushu University subjected
eight B-29 crewmen who were shot down over Tachiari on May
5 to vivisection. They removed the airmen's organs while they
were still alive. These men were from the Marvin S. Watkins and
Ralph E. Miller crews of the 6th Squadron in the 29th Bomb
Group. The doctors cut out lungs, livers, and stomachs; they
stopped blood flow in an artery to see how long death took;
with one crewman, they drained the blood out of one side of
him and pumped sea water in the other side of him—just to see
what would happen. They dug holes in one airman's skull and
then stuck knives into the living brain—again just to see what
would happen. All of this while the men were still alive.

On June 5, 1945, the Carl T. Hull crew of the 462nd
Group, 58th Wing, was shot down as they approached Kobe.

Eight of the crew bailed out. They landed near a military compound where they were captured and taken before the commanding officer. He convened a court martial on the spot and sentenced all eight to death. They were taken outside and summarily beheaded.

The accounts of their treatment by the Kempei Tai at Ofuna, Omori, Tokyo Military Prison, and other compounds by the few survivors of these prison camps revealed endless and continuous torture, mistreatment, and beheadings by the guards. One of their favorite tortures was to force-feed a prisoner large amounts of rice, then shove a hose down his throat until his belly swelled, and then mercilessly jump on him until his intestines exploded. Most B-29 crewmen taken prisoner were murdered—either by the mobs who captured them or by the depraved guards who imprisoned them. Even after the emperor's surrender speech, the killing of American prisoners continued. The Osaka Kempei Tai commander ordered over fifty B-29 crewmen beheaded following the speech. The same day, Japanese guards at Fukuoka chopped sixteen airmen to death with their swords. Though all of the atrocities mentioned here have been well documented, Japan still, to this day, denies that any of it ever happened. The Koreans and the Chinese in particular have petitioned the Japanese government numerous times for an admission of their behavior and an apology, but to no avail. The Japanese are still denying it.

This, then, was the character of the people who attacked Pearl Harbor and sought to conquer the United States. I don't suppose it could ever have been in the cards that Japan could defeat a major industrial nation like the U.S., but she exacted a dreadful toll in her attempt. It was important for us to understand their temperament, attitude, and reputation to fully assess and appreciate not only whom we were fighting, but the shocking and terrifying tragedy it would be for us if we lost. We were fighting an enemy who was not only depraved, but who recognized no rules whatsoever.

I speak only for myself, although my feelings were shared by many, if not most, but I was convinced that we had to scourge from the earth this monstrous anomaly we had been fighting for nearly four years. What we had learned about them and what we had witnessed of their behavior left no room for any other conclusion. We either had to eliminate them or destroy their ability to make war so that we could control them and prevent any future aggression by them. With what we knew about them, even before the surrender, made it obvious, in my opinion, that they did not deserve membership in the world society of mankind. There are certain principles that are inviolate, universal, and eternal. Breaches of fundamental internationally recognized individual rights are crimes against humanity. Anyone, or any group, who deliberately and intentionally abuses other human beings brings upon himself or the group an intense loathing. I had virtually no compassion for them. Just considering the campaigns in which I was involved—Iwo Jima, where approximately 6,000 Marines died, and the Japanese home islands, in which approximately 5,000 B-29 crewmen lost their lives—was enough to influence my feelings. This was war, and I knew that Japan had never ratified the Geneva Accords and we were killing a lot of them, too, but they could have quit anytime, and then I would have stopped killing them. It was up to them—not me.

We had to win, and we were there to win. That's what the B-29 was all about. Can you imagine the magnitude of the slaughter if we had to invade Japan? If our bombing campaign could prevent the necessity of that invasion, we would save hundreds of thousands of lives on both sides.

Our offensive campaign included traditional strategic targets such as the tetraethyl lead plant at Koriyama and the oil cracking and storage plant at Otake as well as various airfields. All of these could be classified as customary military targets. However, their cities were also our targets, the objective being to destroy them as completely as possible. There were several reasons for this. Within these cities were located all sorts of war industries, including aircraft plants, engine plants, munitions factories, arsenals, and other enterprises supporting the war effort. These then were also strategic targets. But there was another purpose besides destroying their infrastructure: to deprive their war industry of a labor force and to so demoralize their people that they would lose the will to resist.

I have been the object of remarks on infrequent occasions implying that I should be ashamed for participating in raids like the March 10 strike against Tokyo during which we killed 83,000 people and inflicted nearly 200,000 total casualties. To those people who were critical, I say you are misinformed, and you were not there; you were not a part of our generation and you have no understanding of what was involved. I have no guilty conscience whatsoever. We were trying to end a war we did not start, and we did what had to be done to do just that.

I have the same feelings about dropping the atomic bombs. I believe, without question, without any doubts whatsoever that Harry Truman made the correct decision. It's simply a hard, incontrovertible fact that detonating those bombs saved hundreds of thousands of lives—more by far than they extinguished.

The Americans, in the end, brought the Japanese out of the nineteenth century and gave them a new start in the world order. We did not eliminate them, and we did not enslave them as the vanquished. We met the challenge of changing a centuries-old culture, which could not have been more unlike ours, and, notwithstanding the immediate postwar feelings of those who had fought the battles on a daily basis, gave them the foundation upon which to establish a moral, humane society, patterned after ours, in which they could be a credit to themselves and take a productive, civilized position in the world. The constitution which we imposed upon them contained certain restrictions to prevent them from making war, but beyond that, generally, it enabled them to rebuild their cities and their industries and to participate in foreign trade.

The terms of surrender included the occupation of Japan by Allied military forces, restriction of Japanese sovereignty to the four main islands, and surrender of Japan's colonial holdings. Under the direction of Gen. Douglas MacArthur, the Supreme Commander for the Allied Powers, Japan's Army and

Navy ministries were abolished, munitions and military equipment were destroyed, and war industries were converted to civilian uses. War crimes trials found 4,200 Japanese officials guilty, 700 were executed, and 186,000 other public figures were purged. State Shinto was disestablished, and on January 1, 1946, Emperor Hirohito repudiated his divinity.

Constitutional reforms were accompanied by economic reforms including agricultural land redistribution, the establishment of trade unions, and severe proscriptions on zaibatsu and state Shinto. The new constitution included numerous guarantees for civil rights and liberties including separating the Japanese judiciary from the rest of government and giving it the power to strike down laws that violated the constitution.

Ultimately, fifty-one nations met in San Francisco in September 1951 to reach a peace accord with Japan. In this agreement, Japan renounced its claims to Korea, Taiwan, the Kuril Islands, Southern Sakhalin, islands it gained by League of Nations mandate, South China Sea islands, and Antarctic territory, while agreeing to settle disputes peacefully according to the United Nations charter. In 1952 the Japan/United States Mutual Security Assistance Pact was ratified, ensuring a strong defense for Japan and a large postwar role in Asia for the United States. So, the American people and their nation became benevolent providers and overseers to the Japanese people and not despotic victors. We did not treat them as they had treated us.

Today Japan is a staunch ally of the U.S. and one of its principal trading partners.

Finally, I think my generation's concern with today's attitudes is in part the lack of recognition, regard, veneration, and gratefulness for the freedom all of us enjoy today. If we had not done what we did in World War II, and if we had lost the war, most of those under the age of about fifty would not even be here today. If this sounds like self-pity and a plea for recognition, be assured that it is not. It is just that I think an appreciation of freedom is a basic requirement for citizenship and residence in this country. It goes all the way back to the American Revolution, our forefathers, the framers of our Constitution, Abraham Lincoln, the doughboys of World War I and the GIs of World War II. Present generations may not have any comparative basis to evaluate freedom, so I remind them here—freedom feels awfully good.

Chiseled on a gravesite marker on Iwo Jima is this epitaph:

> When you go home,
> Tell them for us, and say
> For your tomorrow
> We gave our today.

Please . . . don't let the enormity of those few lines escape you.

Appendix: 29th Bomb Group Crew Losses

Squadron	Crew	Mission	Date
6th	BEDFORD, Frederick J., & Crew	Nagoya	05-14-45
6th	BUTTFIELD, William S., & Crew	Nagoya	04-07-45
43rd	CANNON, Earl F., & Crew (Training)	Dallas	10-08-44
6th	CROWCROFT, Frank A., & Crew	Nagoya	04-07-45
52nd	EVERDON, Waldo C., & Crew	Shizuoka	06-20-45
52nd	FRANKLIN, Joseph W., & Crew	Kobe	06-05-45
43rd	FRITSCHEL, Robert L. & Crew	Tokyo	04-14-45
52nd	HALTEMAN, Clarence W., & Crew	Kawasaki	05-11-45
43rd	HEYKE, Adolph Henry, & Crew	Osaka	06-15-45
43rd	JOHNSON, W. F., & Crew	Tokyo	03-10-45
6th	LICHTE, Gilbert M., & Crew	Tokyo	03-10-45
52nd	MANSFIELD, Richard M., & Crew	Tokyo	05-25-45
6th	MILLER, Ralph E., & Crew	Tachiari	05-05-45
43rd	MUSSER, John J., & Crew	Tokyo	03-10-45
52nd	NEAS, Lucas M., & Crew	Tokyo	03-10-45
52nd	RUSSELL, Earl A., & Crew	Kawasaki	04-15-45
6th	SHUMATE, James L, & Crew	Tachikawa	08-08-45
6th	WARD, Irving H., & Crew (Training)	Puerto Rico	01-08-45
6th	WATSON, William W., & Crew	Kawasaki	04-15-45
6th	WATKINS, Marvin S., & Crew	Tachiari	05-05-45
52nd	WYATT, Firman E., & Crew	Tokyo	03-10-45

NOTES

BEDFORD: Crashed at North Field on return. Right gunner and Tail gunner survived.

CROWCROFT: The left gunner, right gunner, and engineer, bailed out, were captured and were repatriated after the war.

HALTEMAN: Crashed on take-off.

HEYKE: Crashed immediately after take-off.

LICHTE: The crew ditched, were picked up by the Navy and returned to base. All survived.

MANSFIELD: Eight crew members were captured after bailing out and were repatriated after the war.

WARD: Went down with four passengers in addition to the crew and all squadron records without a trace enroute to Puerto Rico.

WATKINS: Watkins was a P.O.W. and was repatriated after the war. All the rest of the crew was lost.

Acknowledgments

In my declining years, I have had a typical old man's problem—insomnia. So my manuscript was written in bed, in longhand, during the sleepless hours of the night. After I had written twenty pages or so, I'd type it on my old IBM typewriter and send it to my son, Bruce, who would scan the typewritten pages into his computer, do some editing, proofreading, spelling correction, and formatting, and handle all the computer details. I wish to thank him for his persistence and patience and for his encouragement during the writing of my wartime memoirs.

I am also indebted to my surviving crew members—Tom Henry, Jim Kingston, and Rich Ranker—for their help in confirming or correcting my memory about numerous incidents during the year that we spent together. A few years ago, Tom Henry wrote a limerick about one of the incidents in the book:

> An Airplane Commander named Ben
> The leader of ten gallant men
> Through an unexplained glitch
> Hit the bomb salvo switch.
> He promised not to do it again

Thanks, Tom!

I am deeply indebted to the late Loomis Dean, who took many of the photographs of the 29th Bomb Group that appear in this book. Mr. Dean was a photographer of considerable note with credit for numerous outstanding wartime pictures as well as fifty cover photographs for *Life* magazine in the postwar period. Mr. Dean was most considerate of my requests for pictures and courteously provided me with excellent original prints together with his consent for their use. Some of these have not been published previously.

I wish to thank Eugene M. Gillum, M.D., author of *The Beast*, the story of the development of the Wright 3350 engine and its mating to the B-29. Dr. Gillum's experience predated his tour in the Marianas in the 315th Wing as he was, prior to that, an employee of the Wright Aeronautical Corporation during the development of the engine. While on Guam, he recorded many examples of B-29 nose art, which are pictured today in the 20th Air Force Album. His contribution to my efforts is much appreciated.

I must thank Frederick D. "Dusty" Worthen, author of *Against All Odds*, his own wartime story as a bombardier flying on B-24s against Germany. Dusty kindly volunteered to draw the map that appears here and identify the targets we bombed in Japan. He also was a cadet at Victorville, California during my assignment there and may have flown with me at that time.

I also wish to thank Debbie Marshall and Diane Adams of my office staff, each of whom helped with copying and collating the manuscript through several rewrites. They also assisted with research on the Internet and with library reference desks to confirm exact dates of certain events reported in my story.

To contact the author, please write to
    G. B. Robertson
    22647 Ventura Blvd.
    Woodland Hills, CA 91364

Index

Page numbers in italics indicate illustrations

STACKPOLE
MILITARY HISTORY SERIES

REAL BATTLES.
REAL SOLDIERS. REAL STORIES.

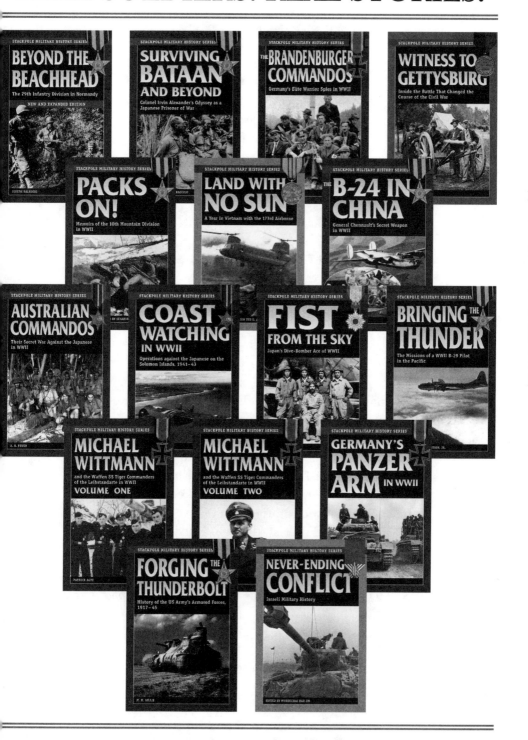

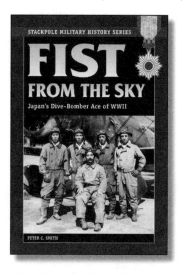